THE UNIFICATION CHURCH IN AMERICA

SECTS AND CULTS IN AMERICA
BIBLIOGRAPHICAL GUIDES
(General Editor: J. Gordon Melton)
(VOL. 9)

GARLAND REFERENCE LIBRARY
OF SOCIAL SCIENCE
(VOL. 211)

BIBLIOGRAPHIES ON SECTS AND CULTS IN AMERICA
(General Editor: J. Gordon Melton)

THE UNIFICATION CHURCH IN AMERICA
A Bibliography and Research Guide

Michael L. Mickler

With an Introductory Essay by
J. Stillson Judah

GARLAND PUBLISHING, INC. · NEW YORK & LONDON
1987

Library of Congress Cataloging-in-Publication Data

Mickler, Michael L., 1949–
    The Unification Church in America.

    (Sects and Cults in America. Bibliographical guides;
vol. 9) (Garland Reference Library of Social Science;
vol. 211)
    Includes index.
    1. Unification Church—United States—Bibliography.
2. United States—Church history—20th century—
Bibliography. I. Title. II. Series: Sects and Cults
in America. Bibliographical guides; v. 9. III. Series:
Garland Reference Library of Social Science; v. 211.

Z7845.U45M53 1987 [BX9750.S435U6] 016.289.9 83-48225
ISBN 0-8240-9040-3 (alk. paper)

Printed on acid-free, 250-year-life paper
Manufactured in the United States of America

To

Dr. George Detlefsen

CONTENTS

PREFACE

This bibliography and research guide surveys literature produced by and about the Unification Church (UC) in America. In general, this material can be organized into three major categories. The first consists of material generated by the Church. This includes publications issued by the Holy Spirit Association for the Unification of World Christianity (HSA-UWC), as the UC is formally known, and publications of the Church's numerous organizational affiliates. A second category consists of responses to the Church in popular literature, both religious and secular. A third category, more detached in orientation, consists of scholarly treatments and government documents.

Within this basic scheme, I have made a number of decisions regarding the inclusion and placement of items. The most important are as follows:

1. The bibliography includes a complete listing of speeches delivered in America by Unification Church founder, the Reverend Sun Myung Moon. Inclusion of these speeches is somewhat problematic since those delivered prior to 1977 are out of print and are said to contain faulty translations. I have elected to include them here, however, based on several considerations. First, they are a matter of public record. That is, the speeches have circulated widely not only within the Church but also outside and have been cited in numerous published documents. Second, despite inadequate or faulty translations, the speeches were issued by the Church. In fact, those included in this volume were compiled from HSA publication lists. A final reason for including these speeches is their obvious importance for anyone seriously interested in understanding the Church or Rev. Moon. The speeches, themselves, are arranged alphabetically by title. In addition, each entry lists the translator, where the speech was delivered, and, on earlier speeches, order numbers for identification purposes. A major Church effort is currently underway in Korea, Japan and the U.S. to issue an authorized series of Rev. Moon's collected speeches. On completion of that project, speeches included in this bibliography should be available to a wider audience.

2. The bibliography includes a comprehensive listing of material published by UC organizational affiliates. While some of these organizations are closely related, even interchangeable with the UC and entirely staffed by Church members, others, though funded by the Church, are relatively independent and directed by outside professionals. In the case of more autonomous affiliates, some authors may be surprised to see their work cited in a bibliography on the Unification Church. Further, it may be that certain affiliates will eventually gain independent funding and the Church's role will

have been primarily a liberal supply of initial seed money and inspiration. Nonetheless, I have included their publications to date as at this stage they are integral to the UC's broader social vision and identity.

3. The bibliography includes an exhaustive listing of responses to the Church in popular literature, both religious and secular, compiled from standard bibliographical indexes. This has provided balanced coverage for the most part, although certain Protestant denominations, such as the Southern Baptists and United Methodists, and sectarian bodies, such as the Seventh Day Adventists, are overrepresented because they have produced their own indexes. Rather than eliminate these entries, the majority of which elaborate fairly restricted in-house concerns, I chose in this case to err on the side of inclusiveness.

4. Along with scholarly treatments that focus exclusively on the UC, the bibliography includes many that treat the UC within the context of issues raised by new religious movements (NRMs) generally. For example, some psychological studies listed include UC members in tests administered to adherents of several NRMs. Similarly, a number of law journal articles cite litigation involving the UC or its members in addressing emergent constitutional and legal issues. Interdisciplinary approaches have posed some problems of placement. A few sociological studies, for instance, also refer to psychological and legal issues raised by the UC and other groups. In these cases, I have cross-referenced entries under appropriate sections. Finally, the bibliography includes a number of mostly theological studies resulting from conferences sponsored by the Church.

5. The bibliography is limited in several respects. It, for example, excludes a bulk of ephemera -- flyers, meeting notices, festival programs, minor brochures and the like. It also excludes newspaper articles. In addition, the bibliography is mainly limited to material published in the United States. It does, however, include some items published elsewhere if they have circulated in the U.S., help explain the UC's American development or are based on research conducted in the U.S. Finally, the bibliography is limited to items published from 1960 through 1985. That is, it essentially covers material produced during the UC's first twenty-five years in America.

Consistent with other volumes in this series, individual entries are not annotated. Instead, I have prefaced each section with a bibliographical essay highlighting the background, interrelationships and central themes of material included. This approach has seemed useful for providing comprehensive coverage while at the same time directing the reader's attention to the most prominent and significant items. Entries are numbered consecutively throughout the volume. When referring to a particular entry in any of the introductions to various sections, I have utilized brackets with the particular reference entry number. When quoting from a source I have used parentheses with page numbers. In addition, periodicals when they appear are separated from monographs within each section.

In compiling this volume, I made use of several collections and reference materials. The resources of HSA Publications, 4 West 43rd St., New York, N.Y. 10036; Unification Theological Seminary Library, 10 Dock Rd., Barrytown, N.Y. 12507; the New Religious Movement Collection at the Graduate Theological Union Library, Berkeley, California; and the files of the Institute for the Study of American Religion now housed in the library of the University of California at Santa Barbara were most useful for collecting Church-published material. Publications of UC organizational affiliates were obtained through direct contacts. A number of these organizations operate out of the UC's World Mission Center, 481 Eighth Ave., New York, N.Y. 10001. For non-UC published material, I utilized public, university, theological and law libraries as well as all standard bibliographical indexes. I also examined several private collections.

This bibliography, obviously, could not have been undertaken or completed without the help of numerous persons. First, I'd like to thank J. Gordon Melton for inviting me to compile this volume and for his advice throughout; David S.C. Kim, President of Unification Theological Seminary, whose initial support helped further this project; and J. Stillson Judah for his excellent introduction. I'd also like to thank Julia Johnson and Pamela Chergotis, my editors at Garland. For supplying references, helpful comments and, in some cases, needed encouragement, I am grateful to Gordon Anderson, Eileen Barker, James Baughman, John Biermans, Paul Bullen, David Carlson, Joseph P. Chinnici, Dianne Choquette, B.J. Darr, Eldon G. Ernst, Adri de Groot, A. Durwood Foster, Jonathan Gullery, Brock Kilbourne, John Lofland, Pat Minichello, Richard Quebedeaux, Dale Roberts, Walter Ruf, Alan Seher and Anson Shupe. For word processing and final layout, I am grateful to Paul Weigand of Word Association, Berkeley, California. Finally, I'd like to thank my wife, Reiko, for her love and support during the extended length of time it took to bring this project to completion.

Michael L. Mickler
Berkeley, California
January, 1987

The Unification Church
in America

INTRODUCTION TO THE HISTORY AND BELIEFS
OF THE UNIFICATION CHURCH

BY J. STILLSON JUDAH

The Unification Church, more formally known as the Holy Spirit Association for the Unification of World Christianity, has been one of the most controversial new religious movements in the United States and in other countries. It has received much critical attention not only from the media and various branches of the United States government, but also from articles and books written by some sociologists, psychiatrists, deprogrammed apostates, their parents, and others. Although the public is acquainted almost entirely with these unfavorable sources, the Church's willingness to sponsor conferences of all kinds and to dialogue particularly with Christian theologians ranging from liberals to fundamentalists has made Unificationism the most thoroughly examined among the new religious movements. Unfortunately, however, many publications resulting from such encounters, although offered to the public, have been little read. Therefore, it is important that a definitive bibliography which includes material on both sides of the controversies, and a much fuller picture of the Unification Church and Rev. Moon, should be published. This introduction will outline the cultural background, philosophy, theology, and history of the Unification Church in the context of rapid cultural and social change.

KOREAN BACKGROUND OF THE UNIFICATION CHURCH

Sociologically, the Unification Church must be viewed as the product of the religious and cultural ferment following Korean independence from Japan after World War II. From the second century B.C. until 1895 Korea had paid tribute to China most of the time, and frequently to Japan from the third century A.D. to 1873. After its declaration of independence from China in 1876 there was war between Japan and China during the Korean Tong-hak insurrection in 1894. Then followed a brief period of independence until Japan annexed Korea in 1910 (Vos 1977: 5, 21, 26; Gowen 1927: 329-37, 356-431).

Due to such contact with both China and Japan for so many years it is not surprising that the culture and religions of Korea show their influence. While still retaining an indigenous shamanism, Korea's religious history was largely that of Buddhism, Confucianism, and Taoism until Christianity and Western culture began to make an impact in the nineteenth century (Vos 1977: 5, 156, 175-77). In that period of cultural ferment there was very great insecurity and new religions appeared. Additionally, there was a need among Koreans to rediscover their roots and national identity. Likewise, after World War II and the liberation from Japan, Spencer Palmer noted that new religions "sprang up like mushrooms after the rain," and concluded that these religions with their popular following are a powerful force in Korea today. In their efforts to meet the needs of Koreans in their rapidly changing scene they are challenging the conventional faiths (Palmer 1967: 1). The anthropologist Felix Moos credited their prominence after World War II to "accelerated change, uncertainty, discontent, and the need for a belief that provides answers to physical, mental and spiritual aspirations" (Moos 1967: 12).

The new Korean religions, including the Unification Church, have similar characteristics:

1) Having emerged during a period of national restoration, they all have a strong spirit of nationalism. Thus, just as Israel has unique significance for both Jewish people and Christians, Korea likewise receives veneration as the birthplace of their religion by both Korean and foreign members of the Unification Church.

2) A second feature of these new movements is their messianism, the belief in the return of one who will redeem them from suffering. In this respect, the office of the Second Advent of Christ for which other religious leaders vie with one another is not a unique claim of the Unification Church.

3) These Korean new religions offer plans for a physical utopia and the transformation of the present world into an ideal one. Further, efforts are made to achieve economic security.

4) A fourth common trait is that the followers consider their particular teachings to have been divinely revealed to the founder. In some cases a god or spirit has spoken through him or her; in others, a dream or a vision revealed the divine will. Or sometimes the mind of the founder was simply divinely inspired to understand and to proclaim the truth (Moos 1967: 12-13).

5) The Korean new religions make organized and conscious efforts to integrate traditional patterns with the plethora of foreign influences unleashed by sudden socio-economic changes (Moos 1967: 27). They are syncretistic (Palmer 1967: 1). They combine, reconcile, and often transform differing beliefs into new systems as did Christianity which formed a synthesis of conflicting Jewish, Greek, and popular religious doctrines. Thus the Unification Church, while reinterpreting Christianity as its foundation, unites with it elements of Oriental philosophy such as are found in Confucianism, Korean Buddhism, other new religions, and a native shamanism.

THE INFLUENCE OF ORIENTAL PHILOSOPHY AND NATIVE RELIGIONS

Philosophically, the Unification concept of God with dual characteristics of positivity and negativity, male and female represents the Confucian principles of Yang and Yin, respectively. These dual characteristics of God, Rev. Moon relates to Genesis 1:27 wherein it is written that God created male and female in His own image. Rev. Moon then adds another reciprocal relationship between two dualities: external form and invisible character. These correspond respectively to body and mind, effect and cause, object and subject. Such correspondences apply also to God and the entire universe in which God is the cause and its internal character. God as the masculine subject and cause created the earth, the effect, as His feminine external form (*Divine Principle [DP]* 1973: 20-25). Thus, God corresponds analogically to the Confucian Heaven (masculine) and Earth (feminine), a transfer and transformation of symbols.

Unification teaching refers to the Chinese classic, the *Book of Changes (I Ching)* in presenting its philosophy of creation. According to the text, the foundation of the universe is Taeguk (ultimacy) in Korean, corresponding to the Chinese Tai Chi. From this comes Yang and Yin (positivity and negativity) and all things. Positivity and negativity together are called the "Tao," defined as the "Way" or "Word." Thus, Taeguk produced the Word (creative principle), and the Word produced all things (*DP* 1973: 26-27). When God's dual essentialities enter into reciprocal relationship, this action causes the dual essentialities to separate into two substantial objects centered upon God. Then, the substantial subject and object pair enter into give-and-take action, forming one unit as an object to God. Professor Tai Soo Han views this "origin-division-union" process as representing the movement of the Tai Chi in the process of creation according to the *I Ching* (Han, T. 1981: 262-63).

Other Confucian characteristics have similarities with Unification thought and help explain some of its ideas and emphases. Confucianism is both a political and moral philosophy like that of the Unification Church. To become a Sage-King is Confucianism's highest ideal, according to the eminent Chinese philosopher, Feng Yu-leng, and this represents the Oriental aspect of Rev. Moon's messianism. "It is not necessary that the sage should be the actual head of government in society ... it only means that he who has the noblest spirit should theoretically be king. As to whether he had or had not the opportunity to be king, that is immaterial" (Feng 1962: 2-4). This suggests an explanation for some of Rev. Moon's seemingly antithetical statements concerning his role. Confucian also is the Unification belief that the ideal state on earth, i.e., the Kingdom of Heaven can only come to pass through humanity's cooperation with God as co-creators (Chang 1981: 74-75). Confucianism has contributed even more to Unification thought in its emphasis upon the family, and rules of filial piety both in reference to the present and spirit worlds. Moreover, the priority of the family as a whole above the individual member in Unification soteriology requires that individual salvation depend upon the salvation of one's entire family. This emphasis upon the family unit rather than the individual may help explain Rev. Moon's distaste for American individualism, concerning which more will be said.

Some Korean scholars have cited the importance of the Haedong School of Buddhism as a predecessor to Rev. Moon's revelation. This indigenous movement of Won Hyo (617-686 A.D.) has been so enduring that even Korean school children know about him. He, like Rev. Moon, tried to reconcile divergent views and form a synthesis that would break down the barriers of race and religion, and unify the ideals of a divided society and existing sects. This would be accomplished by each person's sacrificial living for others, e.g., for the family, the family for society,

society for the nation, for humanity, and for God--a theocracy with one world under God (Choi, M. 1981: 97-108; and discussion, 109-11).

Unification also has patterns similar to Ch'ondogyo. Che-u Ch'oe, who founded the school in 1860, combined elements of Confucianism, Buddhism, and Taoism with features of Korean shamanism and Christianity (Weems 1964: 157). Ch'oe, who originally called his movement Tong-hak or Eastern Learning to distinguish it from Western Learning, protested against the growing power of Western culture and Roman Catholicism. Ch'oe believed that God had called him to instruct men in the way or the "Principle." His commission was to serve God, causing his own heart to become identical with the creating power of God, thereby attaining perfect holiness. To teach this principle to others and to urge them to self-sacrificial action for humanity would harmonize their actions with God's, resulting in the Kingdom of God on earth (Vos 1977: 189-97). These concepts of Ch'oe and his sucessor, Sihyong Ch'oe, are also part of Rev. Moon's Principle. Also, similar to the intensive training Rev. Moon gives to his disciples were the religious Training Institutes for actual and prospective Ch'ondogyo leaders. Benjamin Weems remarks how this intensified review of Ch'ondogyo philosophy helped create a disciplined, well-indoctrinated, patriotic movement which by 1919 had built up a large nation-wide membership (Weems 1964: 12, 68, 75-76).

One, however, cannot fully understand the resonance of Rev. Moon's thought, particularly in Korea and Japan, without understanding the importance of an indigenous shamanism in these countries. Shamanism is Korea's oldest and one of the most important indigenous religions. In its expression the shaman, a priest, communicates with spirits or deities while entranced. Koreans under foreign subservience have always felt a special security in their indigenous guardians against evil spirits and misfortune, and Dr. Young Oon Kim asserts that Koreans of all classes have turned to the Mudangs (shamans) for guidance in periods of stress (Kim, Y.O. 1976, vol. 3: 175). I have also observed that many Americans have turned to Spiritualistic mediums in times of similar need. Spiritualism, akin to shamanism, and also an indigenous American religion, has as its protectors the native American Indian guides who speak through the medium. Rev. Moon's asserted ability to communicate with the spirit world makes the Unification Church related to both shamanism and spiritualism.

In concluding this section on the influence of Oriental philosophy and native religions upon Rev. Moon's thought, it would be dangerous to conclude that he consciously borrowed from any one particular religious movement or tradition. The similarities are more likely due to the huge reservoir of common thought present in Korea, partly of foreign origin, partly indigenous and often contradictory, but usually remolded and reinterpreted by religious figures from early times to Rev. Moon's. Such is the case with most religions, if their histories are examined in the context of ideas prevalent at the time of their origins. The popularity, influence and growth of most such movements have been dependent upon their abilities to use the beliefs in such a way as to transfer and reinterpret religious symbols so as to give meaning at particular periods of national and/or personal crises.

At such times of insecurity during Korea's long history, charismatic saviors have given new patterns that have provided hope and relief from suffering and alienation, even as they have in the case of Christianity and other world religions.

REV. MOON'S THEOLOGICAL INTERPRETATION

Probably the most important aspect of Rev. Moon's thought has been his interpretation of Christian theology, over which theologians have debated as to the extent that it can even be called Christian. Whereas the Oriental influence has presented us with a generally impersonal concept of God, Rev. Moon's interpretation of Christian theology shows us a personal deity with whom he has conversed as he has with Jesus. This is a loving God who experiences both joy and sorrow: joy through the perfection of men and women when they reflect the Divine nature; sorrow and grief over the sinfulness of the world which began with the fall of mankind (DP 1973: 43, 103; Kim, Y. 1975: 35-39).

According to *Divine Principle*, God planned three stages of development for Adam and Eve: formation, growth, and perfection. These were to be completed before marriage and the production of progeny, and perfection was to be attained by uniting their minds and bodies through give and take action centered on God. Had Adam and Eve completed these three stages, it would have been the first blessing of God. The second was to have been their marriage, the production of children, and the formation of a four position foundation, i.e., the two parents and the children were to form a God-centered family. This accomplishment would have qualified them and their ancestors to dominate the whole of creation without sin, as the third blessing, and would have resulted in God's Kingdom of Heaven on earth. Such oneness with God's heart in love and perfect goodness would have prevented any fall.

Unfortunately, God's Kingdom on earth was lost to Satan when he seduced Eve resulting in the spiritual fall. Her premature union with Adam in the same growth period was the physical fall. Thereafter they and all their descendents have been subject to the pollution of the Satanic lineage (DP 1973: 41-46, 53, 74-80, 101, 241-42; *Principle of Creation* 1979: 18-19).

THE PATH TO RESTORATION

Human history which entails the transformation of the world from Satanic dominion occasioned by the fall is represented as having a series of dispensations during which the restoration could have been accomplished, e.g., at the time of Noah, Abraham, Moses, and Jesus, but in each case the restoration was incomplete because of failure of human responsibility. Jesus as the messiah was to accomplish the restoration and fulfill salvation of both spirit and body. Because of disbelief in Jesus, however, he was crucified, and his body invaded by Satan. As a consequence, even though all may have spiritual salvation by redemption through the blood of Jesus, our bodies are still within Satan's power, and it is necessary for the Christ to come again to fulfill the purpose of the providence of physical salvation and redeem us from original sin.

Divine Principle teaches further that Jesus was born as the only begotten Son of God without original sin, who as perfected man was both God and second Adam (*DP* 1973: 196, 209). He came to fulfill the position of True Parent of mankind as was God's intention for Adam and Eve. Although Jesus did not marry, however, and the Kingdom of Heaven on earth was not fulfilled as intended, he established the spiritual foundation of faith, and his disciples, the spiritual foundation of substance. This meant that only spiritual salvation could be attained through the Holy Spirit, as True Mother, necessitating a return of Christ in the flesh to become the True Parent. So the True Parent is to give both spiritual and physical salvation by establishing a physical foundation centered on God (*DP* 1973: 210, 214-18, 368, 511-21).

The Unification Church interprets the doctrine of the Providence of resurrection to mean the restoration of fallen humanity's original nature. It further interprets the history of the Western Christian world since Jesus' time in terms of attempts and failures to set up the proper foundations for the Second Advent and the providential Restoration. Each attempt is treated symbolically and numerologically as recapitulating the paradigm of Adam and Eve, the fallen archangel Satan, and the positions of Cain and Abel and their necessary reconciliation. Each time a central figure fails to carry out his portion of responsibility, it is believed that God sets up another "to restore the foundation to receive the messiah." This entails the repetition of the same course of history.

Now, it is believed the time is right for the Second Advent. It is taught that in the last days although Satan still dominates the world, fallen humanity may set up good conditions that will put it on the side of God. This is restoration through indemnity, which means restoration by setting up conditions that will help return mankind to its original status before the fall (*DP* 1973: 223-24). National catastrophes such as world wars and suffering of various kinds are sometimes interpreted as indemnifying conditions induced by sin. The Church, itself, may also set indemnifying conditions such as prayer conditions to reach specific goals; individuals too may set them to accomplish personal objectives in furthering the cause. Fasting and even cold showers may be used as forms of indemnity, as well as prayer and other forms.

While individual perfection is necessary, the family centered on God in a heartistic reciprocal relationship is also an absolute requirement for attaining heaven. The Church teaches that this love is always an expression of give and take: of God, the subject and cause, acting upon us as object and effect and then our response. It is like husband and wife reciprocating with each other in a give and take arrangement, and uniting with God to create a God-centered family. This pattern which begins with the family centered on God is meant to be duplicated over and over again, for the nation and for the world. The Kingdom on earth according to the Principle will be attained when the people in the world are one family centered on God.

THE KINGDOM OF GOD

The *Divine Principle* offers a utopian picture of the Kingdom of God on earth and what it will include, but less about its attainment except through conversion and indemnity. First, at the consummation of human history, it asserts the two worlds of communism and democracy, representing respectfully the Satanic and Heavenly sides, must be united after a Third World War. This war may be fought ideologically, however, to unite all the world under a "new ideology," or "new truth."

Second, the the *Divine Principle* provides a clue to the political order when the messiah "will be able to set up God's sovereignty on the earth by the will of the people, thus restoring the Kingdom of Heaven on earth" (*DP* 1973: 442). As it is believed, "the world of creation was made with the structure of a perfect man as the model," in the ideal world all organizations of the ideal world operate only under the commands of God. These should be transmitted directly to society through "the saints" centered on Christ. His purpose "is to make the present political system ... display perfectly its original function centering on God's will ..." (*DP* 1973: 469-71). During his lifetime, however, the Lord of the Second Advent would be the final interpreter of God's will, and democracy would really be a stepping stone to a "heavenly monarchy."

A third characteristic of the latter days poses a world in which there would be no competition over markets because of excessive production and consumption. The goal would be to distribute the world's goods fairly to all in proper quantities according to God's original ideal for which we were created, and one for which we are striving in this final period of the consummation of human history. This will be a world of coexistence, coprosperity and common cause. The imperialistic system of economy monopolized by an individual or a certain class will be broken in favor of an equal sharing by all (*DP* 1973: 441-46).

In the fourth place, the unity of religion and science will enable humankind to assert Godly dominion over the things of creation as ordained before the fall. All will live in an extremely comfortable living environment due to the economic development accompanying scientific achievement (*DP* 1973: 107-8, 128-29).

Finally, it is argued that a worldwide cultural sphere is forming centered on Christianity. This points toward a unity of cultures, religions and languages with all people living together as one family having the Lord of the Second Advent as the True Parent of mankind (*DP* 1973: 107-8, 128-29). As an agent of unity, the Unification Church pictures its ideology fulfilling the purpose and expectations of all religions. The messiah, which all the great religions have been expecting is to be the Christ. "Therefore, the Lord of the

Second Advent ... represents the second coming of the founder of every religion" (*DP* 1973: 132, 528-29).

THE EARLY LIFE OF REV. MOON

In the milieu of religious and cultural ferment and insecurity, Sun Myung Moon was born on January 6, 1920 in the hamlet of Cheong-ju, Pyeong-an Buk-Do in Northwestern Korea. His family had become Presbyterian converts when he was ten years old, and the young boy, the fifth of eight children, was said to have become quite religious early in life (Sontag 1977: 78; Sun Myung Moon n.d.: 25; Kwang 1974a: 4-7). His life's work was ordained on Easter morning in 1936. He had a vision of Jesus who explained God's desire to establish His Kingdom on earth and requested that he take this responsibility. Having consented to this mandate, he began receiving the revelation which has been presented as the *Divine Principle*. It is said that he received this progressively over a period of nine years not only through prayer and study of different religious scriptures (Sontag 1977:78), but also through direct spiritual communication with Jesus, Moses, and the Buddha, as well as with God, the Father (Sun Myung Moon n.d.: 25). Rev. Chung Hwan Kwak, one of the leading authorities in the Unification Church, said that the term "inspired interpretation" to describe the Principle is partly true, but the "fundamental essence" came by "direct revelation" (Kwak 1980: 320-22). Mr. Hyo Won Eu published the first Korean edition as *Wol-li Hae-sul* (Explanation of the Principle) in 1957. In 1966 he published *Wol-li Kang-ron* (Discourse on the Principle). Rev. Kwak cautions us that these works are only lectures on the Principle, since only Rev. Moon is able to "speak Principle" (Kwak 1980: 320-21; Kang 1980: 1).

While keeping his mission secret at first, Rev. Moon studied electrical engineering first in Korea and then for two years in Japan at Waseda University. While there he became a political activist, promoting an underground Korean independence movement among students that led to his arrest. He later returned to Korea in 1943 (Kwang 1974a: 4-7; Lee 1981: 68).

In November 1945, he became affiliated for about six months with Paik Moon Kim who had founded a community north of Seoul known as the Israel Monastery. It was said that some there, believing Rev. Moon had received a revelation that this group was to prepare forces to receive the Lord of the Second Advent, began to follow him. When Kim was unable to agree, however, Moon then left the movement (Sudo 1971; Kwang 1974a: 4-7). Because of their association, however, rumors were started that Rev. Moon had borrowed from Kim to formulate the Principle. Rev. Moon as well as some of his first Korean members countered the accusation by replying that in Northern Korea especially there were several movements known to him whose leaders independently had revelations from God, Jesus Christ and/or the spirit world. These collectively declared: 1) the Lord of the Second Advent now comes again, born of a woman as a male Korean; 2) those receiving him would fulfill things Jesus had been unable to complete; 3) the fall of man was due to misused sex; 4) the Lord of the Second Advent would establish a new blood lineage so that all receiving him must have purified bodies and minds; 5) that the Garden of Eden would be re-established on earth (Sudo 1971; Kim, W. 1979: 5; Moon 1971: 2-3). Such movements and ideas the Unification Church has interpreted as preparatory in the way that John the Baptist prepared the way for Jesus (Sudo 1971).

On June 6, 1946, Rev. Moon was said to have had a sudden revelation from Heaven to go immediately to North Korea, and though on an errand at the time, he obeyed without even returning home to say good-bye. He began anew in Pyongyang (Kim, W. 1979: 6) by establishing the Kwang-ya Church (Lee 1981: 69). There he tried also to communicate with the leader of the Inside Belly Church, so-named because it was waiting for the Lord of the Second Advent, whom it believed had been born from his mother's womb as Korean (Sudo 1971: 21). Although the leader refused to receive him as the chosen one, it is alleged that when the Communists at the request of the Christian churches accused the leaders of deception and sent them to jail, Rev. Moon was included, although unconnected with them. After almost dying from severe torture, he was released on October 31, 1947. A new beginning brought further accusations from Christian ministers, and once more he was arrested on February 22, 1948 (Moon 1971: 5-8). Sentenced to five years imprisonment, he remained in Hung-nam prison camp until the United Nations, forces liberated him on October 14, 1950 during the Korean War (Lee 1981: 69).

Because there were but few followers remaining in Pyongyang, he fled on foot with two disciples via Seoul to Pusan, where he worked on the docks at night, and began writing the Principle manuscript and lectured on it by day (Kwang 1974b: 11-12; Sontag 1977: 79).

After moving again to Seoul in 1953, in 1954 he officially established the Unification Church as the Holy Spirit Association for the Unification of World Christianity (Sontag 1977: 81), known as the Tong-il Kyo (Unification Church) in Korea.

There were only a few members until the conversion of Dr. Young Oon Kim, a professor from Ewha University. This opened the door to students and professors from both Ewha and neighboring Yonsei University (Kwang 1974c: 23), but also increased the criticism of the movement. Whereas in America, where the Church has been most influential among young adults of the youth culture, the greatest criticism has come from parents who accuse the Church of breaking up families by "brainwashing" their children, not so in Korea. There the early Church was more influential on married people and particularly women, so that opposition was more likely to come from their husbands. Because of the length of services which frequently ran past the state-imposed curfew, many members were obliged to stay overnight. Unless both husbands and wives were involved, however, accusations of adulterous activites often were made. Moreover, since women often became celibate before they were officially blessed in marriage by Rev. Moon, their husbands made the same charges. Early members agree that these accusations were false (Kim, W. 1979: 8-9; Han, J. 1976; Kwang

1975: 15). Because newspapers had given publicity to this criticism before, Rev. Moon, four leaders, and several senior members were arrested after new accusations were made (Choi, S.D. 1967: 169). Most of the accounts in printed stories in the United States, however, do not mention that he and the others were entirely cleared of such charges. Dr. Young Oon Kim reported, however, that to placate the opposition, he was again arrested for draft evasion, but after three months in jail he was completely exonerated (Kim, Y.O. 1984: 14).

BEGINNINGS OF MISSIONARY EXPANSION

The established churches of Christianity have carried on missionary work throughout the world offering needed services at the same time, such as education in their Church schools and colleges, health care in their hospitals associated with their medical missions, or just the important feeding of starving people. The Unification Church started expanding, however, even more simply. It began by setting aside two periods of forty days each year in the summer and winter when most of the members in Seoul who had some education would go to various places in Korea to teach children mathematics and the Korean alphabet in addition to the Principle. Others without special education offered their services freely to farmers and villagers, however needed (Choi, S.D. 1967: 172). Out of their effort, in 1957 thirty new churches were established (Stewart 1975: 35). This pattern of offering themselves to people in various sacrificial ways has been characteristic of Unification Church members. If, however, it would seem impossible to separate such actions from efforts to win more converts, the same is also true of missionary educational and medical programs of established churches. Thus, if its primary purpose is to make converts, its capability to do so as well as it has, owes much to its ability to relate its philosophy to world problems we all recognize in our changing times and to the belief that the solutions are divinely ordained but require sacrificial efforts to fulfill.

MISSION TO AMERICA

The beginnings of the Unification Church on the West coast of America are associated with three missionaries: Dr. Young Oon Kim, known more familiarly to her converts as Miss Kim, Mr. David (Sang Chul) Kim, and Mr. Sang Ik Choi, all three of whom had quite different backgrounds. Dr. Young Oon Kim, former Professor of New Testament and Comparative Religion at Ewha Women's University in Seoul, translator-editor of the first English edition of The Principle, and author of several books interpreting Unification philosophy and comparative religions, is currently Professor at the Unification Theological Seminary at Barrytown, New York. Mr. David Kim, the current President of the Seminary had been a Korean government official before his conversion. Although a deacon and choir director in the Presbyterian Church, he had dreamed of uniting the Christian and Buddhist religions. Mr. Choi was a non-believer but converted to Christianity during a week-long Christian revival meeting in Korea. After graduating from a Holiness theological seminary, and serving as Chaplain during the Korean

War, he started his own church in Korea. Disturbed, however, by the distressing state of the nation and the Church, he attended a three-day period of lectures and was converted to the Unification Church (Mickler 1980: 94-96). Dr. Young Oon Kim, who had been converted to Christianity at a prayer meeting in a Japanese Christian church in Korea, went to Japan to study theology at a liberal Methodist seminary associated with Kwansei Gakuin University. Even though later she taught at Ewha Women's University, she was unable to reconcile her liberal theological education with her religious experience. While suffering from a psycho-somatic illness because of her spiritual conflict, she was persuaded to attend lectures at the Unification Church, and after three days and the testimonies of members with similar spiritual experiences, she was converted and healed (Kim, Y. 1963).

In January 1959, Dr. Kim came to Eugene, Oregon, as a student at the University of Oregon and started her missionary work. With little success in interesting clergy of the mainline churches in *Divine Principle*, she did better with laymen and others who belonged to either Pentecostal or "new age" spiritual groups. Then in September 1959, Mr. David Kim arrived in Portland to attend Western Conservative Baptist Seminary and began his own missionary work. When two of Dr. Kim's most loyal members, whose husbands had become disaffected with their wives' involvement, fled to California and criticism also spread, she relocated in San Francisco and turned her own groups over to Mr. Kim (Mickler 1980: 8-14).

With a nucleus of six Oregon transplants the Unificationists established a communal center in a seven-room flat and supported themselves by outside jobs. The demographics of those most attracted at this early stage included also a cross-section of predominently young people below the age of thirty-five, primarily Protestant, mostly of lower middle class and small town backgrounds, but in addition a few older women from the occult subculture. For various reasons, according to sociologist John Lofland, who studied the movement during this period, none had felt sufficient fulfillment in life, and each was looking for a way to solve his or her particular problem. Although these factors were probably not qualitatively different from those affecting an unknown proportion of the general population, it appears that they were experienced more acutely with higher levels of tension over long periods of time. Lofland argues again that though there were other ways they could have attacked their problems, e.g., through psychiatric help, or radical politics which the secular world offered, these pre-converts to the Unification Church chose religion. This community gained but few new members and associates in the next eighteen months, and the established Christian churches were still relatively unresponsive to the new message (Lofland 1977: 5-6, 32-48; Mickler 1980: 15-17, 27-32).

In 1961 Mr. Bo Hi Pak, a Korean convert of Dr. Kim's and later Rev. Moon's public translator, visited the San Francisco group on his way to Washington, D.C. As Military Attache at the Korean Embassy he began a new sphere of missionary activity by establishing a bible study group, spoke widely in churches, but disturbingly to the Bay Area members incorporated a separate organization (Mickler 1980: 35-36). This marked a new element in the factionalism which first began with David Kim's arrival and was to continue until Rev. Moon later consolidated the movement.

During the years 1960-1963 Dr. Kim's group tried numerous strategies to gain converts, such as public lectures, articles, handbills, personals in newspapers, and even letters, not to mention operating a sound truck with a bullhorn--all to little avail. Nor was the door-to-door canvassing more effective and was soon discontinued (Mickler 1980: 43-50; Lofland 1977: 8, 72-73, 78-79, 84-86, 89). From 1961 to 1963, the little group provided tape recorded lectures on the Principle for those who had showed some interest but still had little success. With the dispersal of missionaries into nearby cities in the spring of 1962, the results were still relatively poor. Out of more than 700 who had attended briefings less than half had gone to a follow-up study session even once, and only a very few of the remainder became converts. It was evident that conversion required more than merely accepting a teaching and that a close fellowship (affective bonds) and a more dynamic approach were necessary. There were even those who knew the Principle and yet were uncommitted (Lofland 1977: 177-86; Mickler 1980: 53).

By the fall of 1963, lectures took the place of taped introductions or oral readings of the text, and these were popularized. Also, after Kennedy's assassination, the Moonies were stimulated enough to abandon their covert presentation and publicly assert, "Christ is on earth" (Lofland 1977: 263-64).

After trying to visit regularly the nearby centers, Dr. Kim began having guests brought to the "headquarters" in December, 1963. Thus began the weekend training session as a viable method of recruiting. By covering the material in lectures on one weekend, together with the close fellowship and testimonies, the training session became the standard recruiting device (Mickler 1980: 58-60). Through this close fellowship (affective bonds) and testimonies the group had discovered two important ingredients to effect conversions. These are standard procedures even today in many mainline established Christian churches, especially among those that are conservative or fundamentalist.

TRANSITION PERIOD

If the weekend training session did not produce as many converts weekly as it did later, there were several reasons. First, in 1963, the core group was weakened when five foreign members were sent back from the center to their native countries as missionaries, and others to cities farther removed. Second, there was a loss of authority and an accelerated decline when Dr. Kim took a trip to Korea after stepping down from the presidency of her group. The new president, whose assumption of spiritual leadership weakened that of Dr. Kim's, then moved to Dallas, leaving the group with no local authority (Mickler 1980: 61-69). Its in-house periodical, the *New Age Frontiers,* that period records its turning frequently to local mediums to compensate for this loss and to receive support. In the third place, Lofland observed that at that time the recruitment efforts were only part-time, and the movement lacked the tight organization to work as sacrificially as it did after Rev. Moon moved to the United States (Lofland 1977: 279, 282, 287; Mickler 1980: 150). Fourth, and most important, this transition period occurred just before the real surge of the counterculture that united young people in their search for a new way of life to replace or reform the institutions of the Establishment.

THE ONSET OF THE COUNTERCULTURE

The latter part of the 1960s was a period of beginnings of some new religious movements, as well as the accelerated growth of others, particularly in the San Francisco Bay Area. This had become an important center for countercultural youth emanating from demonstrations at the University of California. As sociologists Bromley and Shupe note, demonstrations for civil rights involving youth had taken place in the fifties; Kennedy had spoken of a "worldwide scale for human rights and dignity ... implicit in the values of the American civil religion," while Johnson had promised a "Great Society." When the social realities did not match the ideal, the protests began. Protests over testing of nuclear weapons began in the early sixties among a few college youth, and in 1964, after the Gulf of Tonkin incident was followed by bombing of North Vietnam, the anti-war demonstrations increased (Bromley 1979: 60-63). Then, combining with elements of the new left, students expressed grievances against the government with the cry of "power to the people" and against control of the police with "off pigs!" scribbled on public buildings.

Originating earlier with the civil rights demonstrations in the South, the egalitarian spirit spread among youth and found symbolic expression in long hair and jeans for males and females alike that blurred their distinctions. The same egalitarianism partly explained the disappearance of many sororities and fraternities from the campuses. This protesting spirit led to demands for participatory democracy on campuses, which affected the administrations of many institutions of higher learning, and demonstrations against meritocracy and purposelessness of many courses taught led respectively to discontinuance of examinations in some schools, and new experimental courses often given by students themselves. If Berkeley was one chief initiator of demonstrations, similar repercussions were also felt on other university campuses, particularly in the larger cities of America. The media's daily coverage, which graphically portrayed the demonstrations, the tear gas and violence, was carried around the world. Riots on the Berkeley campus were often repeated the next day by sympathetic students in Paris and Tokyo.

Many dissatisfied students everywhere were dropping out of school to fill the hippie ghettoes throughout the world. The Haight-Ashbury district of San Francisco attracted such youth from all over the United States and from other parts of the world. There they gathered together for free sex in love-ins and to experience ecstasies through psychedelic drugs. As the center for dissatisfied youth gradually moved from San Francisco to Telegraph Avenue in Berkeley near the University campus, Berkeley became and has remained a Mecca for disenchanted youth, who still appear with bed-rolls on their backs.

Students of countercultural movements have observed two stages in their development: first, the charismatic stage, which hippiedom exemplified in the sixties; second, the organized stage, the separation by 1970 into communes all those who wanted to continue their alternate way of life from others who seemed too "freaky." By 1972, as many as 5,000 communes were estimated to be in the United States and Canada (Constas 1972: 191-94). The seventies marked the development of numerous new countercultural communal religions as well.

THE UNIFICATION CHURCH AND YOUTH CULTURE

During the latter years of the sixties, it should not be surprising that in the Unification Church membership among youth increased at a great rate, since so many were searching for meaningful answers. My own research supports Bromley and Shupe's contention that the amount of support a movement receives is a function of the nature, location and amount of discontent, the ability to channel it, and the amount of social control the Establishment employs. They maintain further that youth were a major source of members because of the "disproportionate impact of cultural change on individuals undergoing socialization" and their relative freedom from commitment to family and careers (Bromley 1979: 78-79).

When Dr. Kim was invited to take leadership of the movement in Washington, D.C., most of her group went with her, leaving the field in the Bay Area to Mr. Choi to develop from 1964 to 1970. In Berkeley, however, her center expanded in one year from a single bedroom apartment with two members to a three room flat and eight members in 1968 and then to forty in three centers at the end of 1970 (Mickler 1980: 155-56).

Of course change in methods helped also. Following the pattern of Washington, D.C., they sought out likely members among the protesters on college campuses. They gave "New Age" courses, and new clubs were formed like Koinonia, an educational outlet for those in "search for deeper understanding." They also had weekly programs of a religious nature with outside guest speakers, even though studies and work left only evenings and weekends for recruiting new members (Mickler 1980: 159-60). This rapid growth coincides with the similar increases in Mr. Choi's group during the same period.

The growth of new religious movements among countercultural youth was similar but less intense in other countries in the late sixties. For example, Reiner Vincenz, converted to the Unification Church in Germany by one of Dr. Kim's converts, was sent to France as a missionary. Without knowledge of French, he told me his first convert did not join until two years later, but from three members in 1969, the movement there grew to one hundred and forty members in 1973.

THE ADVENT OF REV. MOON

The years from the latter part of 1971 were even more significant ones for the Unification Church in the United States due to the arrival of Rev. Moon. In this period he unified the Church's organization as well as its theological interpretations and emphases, its methods of mass recruitment, and he provided a better financial base. By 1974, all the missionary groups had united, and membership in the United States had increased ten-fold. First, in order to get needed solidarity of the separate movements, he broke down old sources of authority by transferring members from one group to another and by enforcing a system of rotation, while having all members go through his special training sessions.

Next, he began a three-year period of heavy evangelization. Members drafted from their centers not only arranged, publicized and solicited people to attend his lectures in cities throughout the United States but also carried on week-long revival meetings which attracted many young adults. The first of these "Day of Hope" tours visited seven cities. During the stopover in Los Angeles a new evangelical organization, the One World Crusade (OWC), was formed (Mickler 1980: 160, 173-79, 193-94, 204-5). Subsequently, mobile teams of twenty-five members each, moving in separate directions from Washington, D.C., covered forty-two states and forty-three cities from March to August, 1973. By July 1973 there were units in all fifty states. The seven-day workshops of the bus teams and lists of contacts they made for local representatives to follow up resulted in an increase of members. To augment the American Church still further, seventy Dutch and Japanese members were imported to join one hundred and nine European members already added in 1973. Vans in the New York area carried guests to the Belvedere estate which had been purchased in Tarrytown, New York as a training center in 1972. As a result of these methods and the use of so much manpower the *Director's Newsletter* of July, 1973 reported the number of new members who had joined that year to have been four times that for the same period the previous year. The gains were not without losses. Long-time members said that changes in leaders in the centers resulted in drop outs.

If during the first eighteen months from 1971 to mid-1973 the concern was for solidarity and increasing membership, during the next three years (to September 1976) these goals were augmented by an emphasis on public visibility. Whereas the seven-city tour had been low in publicity and attendance, this was now to change. During this period four tours of twenty-one, thirty-two, ten, and eight cities, in addition to rallies in New York and Washington, D.C., were conducted with greater sophistication. The first two tours from October 1, 1973 to March 18, 1974 were covered well by the media, and during the inaugural banquet at the Waldorf-Astoria Hotel congratulations from Mayor John V. Lindsay and several congressmen were read. Cardinal Sheehan sent his blessing when the tour reached Baltimore; Governor of Georgia Jimmy Carter proclaimed November 7, 1973 as a "Day of Hope and Unification," and Rev. Moon was given the "key to the city" when the tour reached San Francisco and Berkeley, respectively. By the end of the second tour, the topics of which were "Christianity in Crisis: New Hope" and "The New Future of Christianity," Rev. Moon had set up a foundation for the movement in every state, and the country was divided into ten regions for evangelization, each with its own commander and team (Mickler 1980: 198-208, 221-34). Nevertheless, although crowds thronged to hear him because of the publicity, as I have noticed and members have admitted, because the lectures were given in Korean in a style unfamiliar to Americans, and then translated, much of the appeal was lost. People left in throngs before the lectures were finished.

Rev. Moon's final tour, the "Day of Hope" Eight City Tour, which began at New York's Madison Square Garden September 18, 1974, revisited some of the cities on earlier rounds. Seven hundred team members plus representative missionaries from forty countries, augmented by members of local churches, made several months advance preparation. In New York, over 380,000 tickets were distributed and 500 buses were used to transport more distant recipients to the event which was publicized by full page ads in the *New York Times* and eighty thousand posters plastered all over Manhattan. Not unexpectedly, the event proved to be a great success in terms of gaining public visibility. Nearly two hundred reporters were present and an estimated ten to thirty-five thousand people were turned away (Mickler 1980: 246-47; Schmidt 1974b: 104-111). Yet a statistical analysis of the Eight City Tour showed that although a total of 47,499 people attended, because of the number leaving during the talks, only 46% stayed through the lectures (*Way of the World* 1975: 134).

Only two other general public appearances were made by Rev. Moon: a Yankee Stadium Rally followed soon after in 1976 by a rally at the Washington Monument in Washington, D.C. In preparing for the first, the Bicentennial God Bless America Committee made America more conscious of its two hundredth birthday. Bombarded with thousands of broadsides, brochures, and a monthly periodical, the public was well informed of the coming event. During the performance, however, huge gusts of wind, the precursor of heavy rain, snapped the cord of a seventy-five foot hot-air balloon. Its escaping air jet-propelled it erratically across the field, destroying many carefully prepared decorations. As the rain subsided, the band raised spirits while members were cleaning up the mess, and it concluded by leading the crowd in singing "You Are My Sunshine" (*New Hope News* 1976: 6-7).

Rev. Moon's message began by celebrating panoramically again what Robert Bellah and others have called our civil religion, the belief in the God-endowed mission of America as a land where all races and nationalities could find righteousness and freedom centered on God--a leader among nations toward a better world. Rev. Moon repeated the message he had given so many times, and concluded with the vision of America building the Kingdom of God on earth as a God-centered nation (Moon 1976a: 2-3).

What had seemed an apparent disaster due to the inclement weather Rev. Moon called a spiritual victory, and indeed it was for his disciples. The next day he compared what happened to the Unification Church to the crucifixion of Jesus, but stated their renewed spirit and unity symbolized the resurrection (Moon 1976a: 1, 11). Indeed, my own observations of their preparations for the next rally in Washington, D.C. indicated that the victory was apparent in the spirit and hope the members showed during preparations. Some new members, however, being more reserved, confided that they would stay through the rally before making up their minds finally about the Church.

The plans for the Washington Monument Rally to be held on September 18, 1976 were begun as early as June 15, and included a number of projects of community aid, such as a clean-up program, an arts and crafts contest, and whatever a community might suggest (*Way of the World* 1976: 98-99). I, myself, witnessed the effect at a party given by a resident for the workers and the whole neighborhood. He expressed to me his gratefulness for the work the group had done in changing the attitudes for the better in a racially mixed area.

When an estimated 300,000 gathered at the rally, a still greater victory was proclaimed, viz., the physical foundation for restoration on the world-wide level (Dijk 1977: 27). In fact, Moon himself declared it to be "the most significant event in human history and God's history." Because of it, he said, all the barriers in the spirit world which had separated those of differing religions were broken and the spirits were liberated. From then on spirits could descend fully to our world to participate in the physical crusades on earth. October 4, 1976 was designated later as the Day of Victory of Heaven, a holy day commemorated each year. Further, Rev. Moon declared his own earthly mission consummated. All the dispensational history of resurrection was ended; all conditions of indemnity fulfilled. For the Unification Church this was the beginning of the first year of the Kingdom of God on earth--a Kingdom which must be completely attained by the year 2000 (Moon 1977: 15-17; see also 1979d: 15-16).

Although these extensive, expensive, but well-organized campaigns climaxed by the two final rallies, greatly increased the size of the movement, the goal of 30,000 of strong faith was not nearly attained. In 1972 Rev. Moon considered that number as the minimum they should have in America to influence the whole country. The request for 30,000 members by 1978 was again repeated in July prior to the Washington Monument Rally with the promise that all members in the United States would be one of 3,000 center directors (Moon 1976b: 1-8).

The great amount of work and the high spirits that produced the success at the Washington Monument Rally, however, were difficult to sustain after the climax had passed. Already by October, only two weeks after the rally, Rev. Moon was instructing his disciples to indemnify themselves for not gaining two converts each in the past two weeks. He cautioned that unless they achieved the goal by 1978 there would be problems, and that they should keep up the intensity of the Washington Monument Rally (Moon 1976c: 2). In December he repeated his warning that they could not continue to do so poorly. Each would have to bring in at least three people before receiving the blessing in marriage, and spend an additional three years working before family life could be started (Moon 1976d: 7-8).

THE HOME CHURCH--A NEW DIRECTION

Rev. Moon, noting the members who were leaving the movement, the low spirits of the members, and still the necessity of recovering their former zeal, introduced a new approach. He suggested that each member in the New York area be responsible for lending *Divine Principle* books to 120 households, answering their questions, and having workshops. With 500 members in the area who would contact 60,000 homes, the goal of 30,000 members could be reached in two years (Moon 1976d: 1-8). This appears to be the forerunner of the home church movement in the United States. In March 1978 he was much more serious about it. He reasoned that despite heavy witnessing on the streets, the new converts soon leave and have to be replaced (Moon 1978a: 5-10). He justified further the change four months later, citing the inefficiency of street witnessing because of the difficulty of relocating people after initial contact, and he suggested that each member perform some chore for the household (Moon 1978b: 4). Each member was to find a home with someone and to identify himself or herself with the area. Then he made an even more significant change. He said that in the future one's mate would be found in the home church, and the blessing (marriage) would be made on the recommendation of the home church to the "True Parents." He then warned that in the future there would be no blessing until the home church program had been completed. "This," he said, "is a statement of the Principle" (Moon 1979a: 14).

In this utopian vision, the home church in each household would replace ultimately all churches, even the Unification Church. When completed, he promised, one would not need to go to church or even to pray, but only to "live by the law of the heavenly country ... If this doesn't happen," he said, "then the *Divine Principle* is just another ideology that doesn't work" (Moon 1980c: 9; see also 1980b: 11).

The ethical philosophy of the home church movement is that rather than worrying whether people love them or not, all members should give more love and service to their people in the realization that God first gave love before asking to be loved. This, he concluded, was the goal of the restored family, because the Kingdom of Heaven would be built on such units of families (Moon 1979b: 12-14). All members are to become parents to their people, as an extended family, which will become the model for the larger extended foundation. When the home church was completed and perfected there would be no sovereign nationhood needed, he promised (Moon 1979c: 12). He warned, however, that without consummating the home church, none could be accepted in heaven (Moon 1980a: 10-11).

If the home church movement were to become a success and the actual expression of the Unification Church, many of the movement's present problems could be solved. In the first place the home church would replace the street approach of youths, thereby reducing the charge of "heavenly deception" followed by the accusation of "brainwashing." Second, there would be no separation of families and mysterious conversions. Third, if successful, it would embrace people of all ages instead of remaining almost entirely a youth movement in the United States. This accomplishment would be necessary for it to become an important religion.

Although the home church has become the ultimate goal, Rev. Moon has not relied on it alone in this period of transition. Even after its beginning, because of the further stagnation of the movement in 1978 while he was away in Europe, Japan and Korea, he initiated another 40-day campaign in 1979. For this he inaugurated three International One World Crusade teams to go from state to state to evangelize, with a goal of each member to win four "spiritual children" in 120 days (Moon 1979a: 18).

From all indications derived from interviews with those who have been involved, the home church movement has not yet succeeded very well in America, but membership was increased by a new mobilization for missionary work in the United States. Beginning on April 1, 1983 ten mobile teams, which had expanded to 52 by May 1984, moved from city to city in each state every 21 days. These teams of the International One World Crusade were augmented by more than 30 other smaller mobile units within each state. In June 1984 the IOWC teams settled in each state in order to "pioneer," i.e., establish new centers there (*Unification News* 1984: 6).

THE TASK OF LEGITIMATION

Although criticism of the Unification Church had begun locally almost from the beginning in Korea, Japan, and the United States, it grew nationally in the United States with Rev. Moon's increased visibility during the seventies. Legitimation by the Establishment was further impaired by his much publicized defense of Richard Nixon in November, 1973. Similar was the effect of adverse publicity associated with the U.S. government investigation (1977-78) of the Church's relationship to the Korean government, even though nothing substantial was established. Later, what would seem to present the biggest problem for legitimation turned to his advantage when Rev. Moon was sentenced to eighteen months in prison on the charge of tax evasion in that 16 *amicus curiae* briefs were filed by 40 major religious and civil rights organizations in defense of his innocence. The Rev. Donald Sills, a Southern Baptist minister and president of the Coalition for Religious Freedom, reported that more than "13,000 ministers representing several hundred thousand people have gone on record in support of Reverend Moon's right to be free and practice his religious beliefs...." Dr. Franklin Littell, a Methodist minister, said that "Rev. Moon held the funds in trust for his church in the same way 'every Roman Catholic bishop in this country does.' " On the day of his liberation from prison, Rev. Jerry Falwell, head of the Moral Majority, and Rev. Joseph Lowery, president of the Southern Christian Leadership Conference, representing usually opposite sides of religious-political issues, united at a press conference in urging President Reagan to pardon Rev. Moon (Anthonis 1985a: 1; 1985b: 1-2).

Rev. Moon also has made a growing number of friends through

scientific, educational, and social programs financed by the Church. He has received some favor from scientists, for example, through his sponsorship of the International Conferences on the Unity of the Sciences (ICUS) which, meeting annually since 1972, have attracted many scholars and scientists, including a number of Nobel prize winners. Rev. Moon further broadened his legitimization among the intellectual community through the New Ecumenical Research Association (New ERA), organized in 1980. This interreligious organization of more than eight hundred scholars from a wide range of disciplines and religious traditions was an outgrowth of meetings in which Unification theological students discussed their various teachings and practices with scholars from a very wide range of Christian traditions. The organization expanded its horizons to include dialogue in conferences among scholars of non-Christian religions as well, and then again to include some for sociologists. Many of these have resulted in published monographs.

Concern about communism and the desire to develop strategies for peace have attracted an increasing number of people to two other organizations the Unification Church has sponsored and funded. The first, an anti-communist organization which has sought to influence the American religious community, is CAUSA International and its teaching subsidiary, the CAUSA Institute, which took the place of the Freedom Leadership Foundation in 1980. While CAUSA, though controversial, has attracted numerous ministers, the Professors World Peace Academy (PWPA), which was founded in Korea in 1973, has appealed to professors interested in study and amelioration of problems facing the world. Here, as in other countries, there are both local and regional chapters which have seminars relating to problems of peace, generally germane to their respective areas. PWPA also sponsors research and publications on issues relevant to formation of public policy. In America, it was instrumental in establishing the Washington Institute for Values in Public Policy in 1982, which has now been incorporated, and is a sister organization to PWPA-USA.

If these organizations are designed to appeal to intellectuals, e.g., the clergy and professors, whose favor by virtue of their positions are important for influencing others, of greater immediate influence on politicians and the masses of people is the Church's incipient media empire. Besides sponsoring an annual "World Media Conference" and fact-finding junkets which had feted some 2,500 journalists by the end of 1984, the Unification Church is establishing newspapers in various places all over the world. Beginning with the *Sekai Nippon* in Japan in 1976, in the same year *The News World*, which became the *The New York City Tribune* in 1980, began publication. If this newspaper and the *The Washington Times* are the Church's most important and influential newspapers, its others are also reaching many people. *Ultimas Noticias* began publishing in Uruguay in 1981; *The Middle East Times*, in Cyprus in 1983; *Noticias del Mundo*, a Spanish-language newspaper, in New York in 1980; the *Harlem Weekly* in 1979; finally the *Saegae Shinbo*, a Korean-language newspaper was first issued in New York in 1982. While all of these are financed by the Unification Church and are still losing money due to insufficient advertising, some are entirely independent of the Church, e.g., the *Saegae Shinbo* and the *Ultimas Noticias*. Although they all have a conservative viewpoint, further limiting their circulation, their reporting compares favorably with other dailies, and Mayor Edward Koch's 1984 weekly column in *The New York City Tribune* should aid its credibility. Stephen Hess of the Brookings Institute, in surveying Washington media, allegedly said he saw *The Washington Times* everywhere, even in the White House, and concluded it was influential (Rothmyer 1984: 23-31).

In the area of social services Project Volunteer, which was established in Oakland, California in 1975, by 1980 had not only distributed three million pounds of free food to the needy at home and abroad but had also engaged the local community in a variety of projects to alleviate social ills. Moreover, the California Department of Agriculture in 1980 made Project Volunteer its cold storage facility for the government's free surplus commodity program for Oakland, Berkeley and 12 other towns (Castille 1983: 20). Its counterpart, which began in the East, is the National Council for Church and Social Action, an interdenominational, interracial, and ecumenical organization founded in 1977 to provide social services to the needy. Although funded in part by the Unification Church, it is an independent organization with 49 autonomous chapters in 34 states. Both of these organizations now also supply food to the World Relief Friendship Foundation, which in 1980 began operating in 27 different countries (Johnson 1982: 82).

Although there are still a number of other organizations and projects sponsored and funded by the Unification Church, we will conclude with the Church's efforts to hold an Assembly of the World's Religions in 1993. This will commemorate the 100th anniversary of the 1893 World's Parliament of Religions, which was held in Chicago. This Assembly is the outgrowth of four international annual conferences on "God, the Contemporary Discussion," initiated by New ERA, and three "Youth Seminars on World Religions." Among its objectives it is hoped that the Assembly can give opportunity for the religions to provide an environment "to take the lead in initiating projects for world peace," and to bring "the world's religious traditions in a more fruitful relationship" (International Religious Foundation, n.d.: 5-6).

CONCLUSIONS

Many scholars would agree that as a new religious movement the Unification Church owes its origin to the cultural ferment in Korea, even as did major world religions, including Christianity, in their respective countries. One may view its development in both Korea and Japan in part as a result of the ameliorating synthesis it has made of conflicting ideologies and cultural patterns during their periods of change, just as again the world religions did in their countries of origin (Judah 1984, *passim*).

In America, before the counterculture took effect in the later sixties and seventies, the movement attracted only a few who for various reasons had not found an identity, socialization, and religious fulfillment in the mainline churches of the Establishment. When I made a national survey of the movement in the seventies, the results indicated that those surveyed were largely idealistic youth, whose dissatisfaction with our society reflected many of the important countercultural protests of the sixties. They, however, had responded favorably to the goals of the Unification Church in working sacrificially toward creating a utopian world in their time, a concept which was expressed theologically as the realization of the Kingdom of God on earth.

The continued survival, development and establishment of any religion must in some measure be in proportion to its degree of accommodation to the particular culture (Judah 1984: 16-28). Therefore the apparently greater achievement of the home church movement among older adults in Japan and Korea may owe more to its re-enforcement of declining social patterns and to its greater ease of socialization there than in the much different American culture. Further, anyone who has studied the Unification Church for a number of years will have noticed the very high dropout rate of members and the repeated mobilizations of the Church to reach Rev. Moon's goal of 30,000 core members in the United States, which is far from being attained. One can point to a number of problems which have prevented stability in membership and its planned increase. Among these have been certain problems in organization:

1) In order to centralize the authority of the movement in himself rather than in leaders of smaller groups with close fellowships, Rev. Moon adopted a policy of constant rotation of leaders. This caused identity problems for some followers, who left the movement.

2) The continual change of leaders, often to inferior positions has also contributed to some of them dropping out.

3) The disruption and separation of families with children to perform special missions, when the members had worked sacrificially for years and were expecting a more settled life, has been a contributing factor for leaving the Church.

4) The "Koreanization" of leadership in America, with Korean members placed in all the highest positions of authority except for that of the President, has affected the morale of many members.

There are also theological problems affecting stability of membership and inhibiting the increase. The charismatic stage of the counterculture of the late sixties changed to the communal stage which began disintegrating in the late seventies. The hippies gave way to yippies and then to yuppies, the young urban professionals. As a consequence:

1) Among young adults there is a renewed emphasis upon American individualism: education to make money for themselves, to achieve the "good life" and enjoy the fruits of their labor. This militates against Rev. Moon's severe criticism of individualism where the self is given a priority he would not condone.

2) Messianic movements like the Unification Church often suffer losses when their prophecies do not materialize according to the timetable. Lofland noticed that many in the early Unification Church in America believed the fully restored world would be realized in 1967 (Lofland 1977: 25). In the ensuing years many prophesies were made concerning the restoration, but always dependent upon the sacrificial work in gaining members for its completion. The tardiness of the arrival has caused the departure of some from the movement.

3) The belief in Rev. Moon, who is to be the real or symbolic head of a "heavenly monarchy" and the interpreter of God's will, is a stumbling block for Christians in mainline churches in our culture. This belief will create further difficulties for Americans who adhere to the separation of church and state, and to all those among the free Western nations who believe in the democratic way of life.

4) Finally, the authoritarianism of the movement over its core members will continually cause problems for many in our time of change when even the Roman Catholic Church is having similar troubles with rebellion and dropouts from its orders.

Thus, on the one hand, the failure to accommodate its teachings and practices more closely to important elements of American culture have been in part reasons for failure to achieve its expected goals. On the other hand, the Church's measure of continued success will depend to a great extent on the annual replenishment of millions of dollars from Korea and Japan to support its programs, which are playing an important role in furthering ecumenism, greater understanding of significant problems, social improvement, and world unity.

REFERENCES

Anthonis, Dirk
1985a   Other Pastors Are Alarmed at Imprisonment "Travesty." *Unification News* 4(July): 1-2.

1985b   Religious Leaders Urge a Pardon for Rev. Moon. *Unification News* 4(September): 1-2.

Bromley, David G., and Anson D. Shupe, Jr.
1979   *"Moonies" in America; Cult, Church, and Crusade.* Beverly Hills, Calif.: Sage.

Castille, Joseph
1983   Project Volunteer Holds Annual Awards Banquet. *Unification News* 2,11.

Chang, Ki Kun
1981   Unification Principle and Oriental Thought. In *Research on*

the Unification Principle. Seoul, Korea: Sung Hwa.

Choi, Min Hong
1981   The Unification Principle and Korean Thought. In *Research
               on the Unification Principle.* Seoul, Korea: Sung Hwa.

Choi, Sang Ik
1979   Interview at Alamo, California, with J. Stillson Judah.

Choi, Syn-duk
1967   Korea's Tong-il Movement. In *The New Religions in Korea.*
               Edited by Spencer Palmer. Seoul, Korea: Royal Asiatic
               Society, Korea Branch.

Constas, Helen, and Kenneth Westhues
1972   Communes; the Routinization of Hippiedom. In *Society's
               Shadow; Studies in the Sociology of Countercultures.*
               Toronto, Canada: McGraw-Hill Ryerson.

Dijk, Henk
1977   Father's Life. Photocopy of typed manuscript in archives of
               the Unification Theological Seminary Library. Barrytown,
               N.Y.

Director's Newsletter
1973   Washington, D.C.: HSA-UWC.

Divine Principle
1973   Washington, D.C.: HSA-UWC.

Feng, Yu-leng
1962   *The Spirit of Chinese Philosophy.* Translated by E.R.
               Hughes. Boston: Beacon.

Gowen, Herbert Henry
1927   *An Outline History of Japan.* New York: D. Appleton and
               Company.

Han, Joo Cha
1976   Interview at Baltimore with J. Stillson Judah.

Han, Tai Soo
1981   "The Unity of Eastern and Western Civilization through the
               Unification Principle." In *Reserach on the Unification
               Principle.* Seoul, Korea: Sung Hwa

International Religious Foundation
n.d.   *Assembly of the World's Religions; Spiritual Unity and
               Future of the Earth.* Brochure.

Johnson, Kurt
1982   Social Action and Politics. In *Lifestyle; Conversations with
               Members of the Unification Church.* Edited by Richard
               Quebedeaux. Barrytown, N.Y.: Unification Theological
               Seminary.

Judah, J. Stillson
1982   Belief and Behavior amid Cultural Change; Some Thoughts
               on the Dynamics of New Religious Movements like the
               Unification Church and Others. In *Lifestyle; Conversations
               with Members of the Unification Church.* Edited by Richard
               Quebedeaux. Barrytown, N.Y.: Unification Theological
               Seminary.

1983   Caveats in Considering a Unity of Religions. Paper presented
               at the New ERA Conference on the Unity of Religions,
               Madeira, Portugal. Revised, 1984.

Kang, Hyun-sil
n.d.   Testimony of Mrs. Kang, First Korean Member.
               Typewritten copy in the Unification Theological Seminary
               Library.

Kim, Won Pil
1979   Testimony of Father's Life.

Kim, Yong-Choon
1975   Ch'ondogyo Thought and Its Significance in Korean
               Tradition. *Korea Journal* 15(May): 47-52.

Kim, Young Oon
1975   *Unification Theology and Christian Thought.* Rev. ed. New
               York: Golden Gate.

1976   *World Religions.* 3 vols. New York: Golden Gate.

1984   Three Histories of the Movement. *Unification News* 3(May):
               12, 14.

Kwak, Chung Hwan
1980   Closing Remarks. In *Virgin Island Seminar on Unification
               Theology.* Edited by Darrol Bryant. Barrytown, N.Y.:
               Unification Theological Seminary.

Kwang, Yol Yoo
1974a   Unification Church History from the Early Days. *New Hope
               News* 1(October 7): 4-8.

1974b   On the Road from Pyongyang. *New Hope News* 1
               (November 25): 11-12.

1974c   The Church's Birth in Pusan. *New Hope News* 1 (December 23).

1975   Success and Persecution in Seoul. *New Hope News* 2 (January 6): 15-16.

Lee, Hang Nyong
1981   Sun Myung Moon - His Faith and Thought. In *Sun Myung Moon: The Man and His Ideal*. Seoul, Korea: Future Civilization Press.

Lofland, John
1977   *Doomsday Cult: A Study of Conversion, Proselytization, and Maintenance of Faith*. Enlarged ed. Irvington, N.Y.: John Wiley & Sons.

Manke, Annemarie
1975   Getting to Know Japan. *Way of the World* 7(March): 37-48.

Mickler, Michael L.
1980   *A History of the Unification Church in the Bay Area: 1960--74*. M.A.thesis, Graduate Theological Union, Berkeley, Calif.

Moon, Sun Myung
1971   History of the Unification Church. *Master Speaks*. Washington, D.C.: HSA-UWC, Dec. 27.

1976a   God's Hope for America. In *New Hope News* 3(June 18).

1976b   Father's Talk to State Leaders. New York: HSA- UWC, July 10.

1976c   Perfection and Gratitude. *Reverend Moon Speaks*. New York: HSA-UWC, October 3.

1976d   Self-Reflection. *Reverend Moon Speaks*. New York: HSA-UWC, December 1.

1977   The Will of God and Individual Perfection. *Reverend Moon Speaks*. New York: HSA-UWC, February 27.

1978a   Where God Resides and His Course. *Reverend Moon Speaks*. New York: HSA-UWC, March 19.

1978b   The Start of the 40-Day Witnessing Condition. *Reverend Moon Speaks*. New York: HSA-UWC, July 4.

1979a   Home Church and the Completion of the Kingdom of Heaven. *Reverend Moon Speaks*. New York: HSA- UWC, January 1.

1979b   Restored Family. *Reverend Moon Speaks.* New York: HSA-
             UWC, January 21.

1979c   Historical View of the Dispensation. *Reverend Moon Speaks.*
             New York: HSA-UWC, September 18.

1979d   Abel's Path from the Providential Point of View. *Reverend
             Moon Speaks.* New York: HSA-UWC, December 30.

1980a   True Parents Mission. *Reverend Moon Speaks.* New York:
             HSA-UWC, April 20.

1980b   The Way of Tuna. *Reverend Moon Speaks.* New York: HSA-
             UWC, July 13.

1980c   Our Duty, Our Mission. *Reverend Moon Speaks.* New York:
             HSA-UWC, October 5.

Moos, Felix
1967   Leadership and Organization in the Olive Tree Movement. In
             The New Religions in Korea. Edited by Spencer Palmer.
             Seoul, Korea: Royal Asiatic Society, Korea Branch.

New Hope News
1976   New York: HSA-UWC, June 18.

Palmer, Spencer, ed.
1967   *The New Religions of Korea.* Seoul, Korea: Royal Asiatic
             Society, Korea Branch.

Principle of Creation; the Nature of God and Man, and the Purpose of Life.
1979   *Divine Principle Home Study Course.* Vol.1. New York:
             HSA-UWC.

Richardson, Herbert, ed.
n.d.   *Documents Concerning the Theology of the Unification
             Church.* Typewritten manuscript.

Rothmeyer, Karen
1984   Mapping Out Moon's Media Empire. *Columbia Journalism
             Review* 23(November-December): 23-31.

Schmidt, Joy
1974a   32-City Tour Begins. *Way of the World* 6(February): 134-43.

1974b   IOWCs Spearhead All-Out Campaign. *Way of the World*
             7(September-October): 104-11.

Sontag, Frederick
1977   *Sun Myung Moon and the Unification Church.* Nashville,
            Tenn.: Abingdon.

Stewart, Therese
1975   The History of the Seminary. *Way of the World* 7(October):
            34-37.

Sudo, Ken
1971   *Father's Life, from Father's Word.* Dec. 27,1971 (Typed
            copy in the Library of Unification Theological Seminary).

Sun Myung Moon.
n.d.   brochure

Unification News; Newspaper of the Unification Church.
1983   Our Church on the Move, April, 3.

1984   IOWC Report, March-June.

Vos, Fritz
1977   *Die Religionem Koreas.* Verlag W. Kohlhammer, 1977 (Die
            Religionen der Menschheit, hrsg. von Christel Matthias
            Schroder, 1977, hft. 1).

Way of the World.
1975   Capsule Day of Hope, January, 130-34..

1976   News&Reports: Washington Monument Campaign Kicks
            Off, July.

Weems, Benjamin
1964   *Reform, Rebellion and the Heavenly Way.* Tempe, Ariz:
            University of Arizona Press.

I.

CHURCH PUBLICATIONS

A. SPEECHES AND STATEMENTS OF REV. MOON

As yet, there exists no single authoritative edition of the speeches and statements of Unification Church founder, the Reverend Sun Myung Moon. For this reason, items in this section come from a variety of sources. In general, published materials include in-house speeches delivered to members and public speeches and statements delivered to outsiders. In addition, a large quantity of unpublished or untranslated speeches of Rev. Moon exist as do a number of Church publications written under his direction or influence.

Rev. Moon's in-house speeches are voluminous and mostly unsystematized. For this reason, generalizations are hazardous. Nonetheless, they have four characteristics in common. First, they are all occasional. That is, they consist entirely of sermons, speeches on Church holidays or special occasions, instructions at director's conferences, lectures to trainees, and addresses to membership during visits to local centers. Second, they are all spontaneous, that is, delivered without a prepared text and subject to simultaneous translation from Korean. Third, in terms of content, they all interpret core theological concepts in light of new circumstances and ongoing UC development. Fourth, the in-house speeches have been underutilized. That is, their impact beyond the immediate occasion of their delivery has been subject to distortion and neglect. Church critics, for example, have combed pirated copies of these speeches for passages that discredit the Church. Sympathetic outsiders, on the other hand, either have not have access to in-house speeches or have relied on more systematic formulations of UC doctrine and their own observations. The UC, due to the negative use made of them and to inadequate or faulty translations, has allowed Rev. Moon's pre-1977 speeches to go out of print.

While it is useful to point out what Rev. Moon's in-house speeches have in common, it is also important to differentiate among them and, where indicated, note patterns of development. In terms of content, the major development has been in issues addressed and overall expectations. For example, Rev. Moon's earliest U.S. speeches, given during an initial visit in 1965, were delivered to small, somewhat older audiences and were tilted toward explanations of mystical experiences. In 1969 and especially after Rev. Moon's more-or-less permanent return to the U.S. in late 1971 through 1976 when the UC boomed with young, activist converts, in-house speeches included strongly millennial pronouncements. In the post-1976 milieu, earlier emphases and expectations have not disappeared, but new issues of negative societal reaction and the complexities of institutionalization have emerged. In short, the content of Rev. Moon's in-house speeches reflect ongoing phases of UC development.

These same phases are reflected in the formats used to serialize in-house speeches. *Leader Speaks* (1965, 69) consists of speeches from Rev. Moon's initial visits. *Master Speaks* (1965-76) contains 1965 and 1969 material reworked into a question-and-answer format as well as 150 speeches from 1971-76 which reflect UC developments referred to above. That is, while *Leader Speaks* and the earlier *Master Speaks* series were published at a leisurely pace with substantial editing, the 1971-76 speeches were published almost immediately and went virtually unedited from translation to printing. With societal reaction and institutionalization, a copyrighted *Reverend Moon Speaks* series displaced *Master Speaks* in 1977 and continues to the present time. The current format is edited more carefully with translators consulted and legal advice sought on difficult passages. As a result, *Reverend Moon Speaks* is available to a wider audience.

Additional sources for Rev. Moon's in-house speeches (frequently in abridged form) include Church periodicals, especially *Blessed Family* [471], *The Blessing Quarterly* [472], *New Hope News* [479], *Today's World* [486], *Unification News* [489], and *The Way of the World* [490]. These are helpful in that they occasionally incorporate material not in speech series and set Rev. Moon's remarks within the context of ongoing Church developments. The UC also has published selected speeches and excerpts from speeches in book form. Some of these, such as *God's Warning to the World* [4, 5], *New Hope: Twelve Talks by Sun Myung Moon* [9, 10], and *A Prophet Speaks Today* [11] are intended for outside audiences. Others, such as *Home Church: The Words of Reverend Sun Myung Moon* [7] and *The Way of Tradition* [15] are for internal use. During his confinement in Danbury Federal Penitentiary, Rev. Moon selected thirty-eight in-house discourses for outside distribution. Entitled *God's Will and the World* [6], this volume includes several newly-translated speeches from Japanese and Korean.

Rev. Moon's public speeches and statements differ from in-house speeches. In terms of style, whereas in-house speeches are informal with numerous digressions and delivered spontaneously in Korean, public speeches are usually formal and delivered from a prepared text, sometimes in English. In terms of content, whereas in-house speeches are, at times, critical of mainline churches and Western culture, public speeches and statements are ecumenical and respectful of democratic traditions. Still, Rev. Moon's public remarks have provoked reaction on two counts. First, though affirming religious liberty, alleged blendings of civil and religious themes have led to accusations of theocratic intent. Second, perceived amalgams of religion and science or, more specifically, the subordination of science to "absolute values" in some talks have led to charges of medievalism, fundamentalism and the buying-off of intellectuals.

The chief occasions for Rev. Moon's public speeches have been evangelistic crusades and Church-sponsored conferences. Speeches delivered during evangelistic tours are published in several volumes, booklets and reprints. *Christianity in Crisis: New Hope* [2], *The New Future of Christianity* [8] and *Reverend Sun Myung Moon: Public Talks* [12] contain representative speeches delivered during 1972-74 speaking tours. *God's Hope for America* [3] and *America and God's Will* [25] contain texts of speeches delivered at Yankee Stadium and the Washington Monument in 1976. The most important of Rev. Moon's speeches at Church-sponsored conferences are his founder's addresses delivered annually to participants at the International Conference on the Unity of the Sciences (ICUS). The first ten of these are collected in *Science and Absolute Values* [13], as well as in annual conference proceedings.

Additional public documents include official statements written or signed by Rev. Moon on matters of Church interest or policy, published interviews and sworn testimony. The most important of the official statements are "America in Crisis; Answer to Watergate: Forgive, Love Unite" [24], which appeared as a full-page ad in fifty-three major U.S. newspapers, and "Statement on Jews and Israel" [359], in response to charges that the Church was anti-semitic. Rev. Moon's thought on a variety of subjects is expressed in published interviews conducted by *Newsweek* [1156] and by Fredrick Sontag in *Sun Myung Moon and the Unification Church* [985]. In addition, sworn testimony was subpoenaed from Rev. Moon before the Federal District Court in Manhattan on details of his personal beliefs. This testimony, however, was halted by the U.S. Court of Appeals of the Second Circuit [1778].

Besides published and available material, other sources remain unpublished, untranslated or inaccessible. These include a large number of recorded speeches never transcribed as well as speeches delivered in Korea or Japan but not translated into English. Finally, there are numerous Church publications, none of which Rev. Moon has authored directly but which have been undertaken at his suggestion, written under his supervision or published with his authorization. The most important of these are formulations of theological doctrine.

Monographs

1. *America in God's Providence*. New York: Bicentennial God Bless America Committee, 1976. 26 pp.

2. *Christianity in Crisis: New Hope*. Washington, D.C.: HSA-UWC, 1974. 123 pp.

3. *God's Hope for America*. New York: Bicentennial God Bless America Committee, 1976. 15 pp.

4. *God's Warning to the World: Reverend Moon's Message from Prison.*
   Edited by Tyler Hendricks. New York: HSA-UWC, 1985. 163 pp.

5. *God's Warning to the World.* Vol. 2. Edited by Andrew M. Wilson.
   New York: HSA-UWC, 1985. 164 pp.

6. *God's Will and the World.* New York: HSA-UWC, 1985. 677 pp.

7. *Home Church: The Words of Reverend Sun Myung Moon.* Edited by
   Leslie Holliday. New York: HSA-UWC, 1983. 471 pp.

8. *The New Future of Christianity.* Washington, D.C.: Unification Church
   International, 1974. 144 pp.

9. *New Hope: Twelve Talks by Sun Myung Moon.* Edited by Rebecca
   Salonen. Washington, D.C.: HSA-UWC, 1973, 82. 103 pp.

10. *New Hope: Twelve Talks by Sun Myung Moon.* Vol. 2. New York:
    HSA-UWC, 1984. 96 pp.

11. *A Prophet Speaks Today: The Words of Sun Myung Moon.* Edited by
    Farley Jones. New York: HSA-UWC, 1975. 159 pp.

12. *Reverend Sun Myung Moon: Public Talks.* London, England: U.F.E.
    Publications, 1972, 82.

13. *Science and Absolute Values.* New York: International Cultural
    Foundation, 1982. 115 pp.

14. *The Way of God's Will.* New York: HSA-UWC, 1980. 418 pp.

15. *The Way of Tradition.* 4 vols. New York: HSA-UWC, 1980.

Speeches and Statements

16. "The Abel's Right Path from the Providential Point of View." *Reverend
    Moon Speaks.* Translated by Sang Kil Han. Belvedere, N.Y.,
    December 30, 1979, 39 pp.

17. "About Myself." *Reverend Moon Speaks.* Translated by Sang Kil Han.
    Belvedere, N.Y., February 27, 1983, 10 pp.

18. "Address to Prayer and Fast Participants I." *Master Speaks.* MS-432.
    Translated by David Kim. Barrytown, N.Y., July 29, 1974, 16 pp.

19. "Address to Prayer and Fast Participants II." *Master Speaks.* MS-433.
    Translated by David Kim. Barrytown, N.Y., July 31, 1974, 13 pp.

20. "The Age of Judgement and Ourselves." *Reverend Moon Speaks.* Translated by Bo Hi Pak. Belvedere, N.Y., November 21, 1976, 11 pp.

21. "The Age of New Dispensation." *Reverend Moon Speaks.* Translated by Sang Kil Han. London, England, May 14, 1978, 20 pp.

22. "The Age of Repentance." *Reverend Moon Speaks.* Translated by Sang Kil Han. London, England, September 1, 1978, 14 pp.

23. "All Things Depend on Us." *Reverend Moon Speaks.* Translated by Bo Hi Pak. Belvedere, N.Y., January 8, 1978, 11 pp.

24. "America in Crisis: Answer to Watergate: Forgive, Love, Unite." *A Statement by the Reverend Sun Myung Moon.* Washington, D.C.: HSA-UWC, 1973. 1 p.

25. "America and God's Will." Text of Speech Delivered at Washington Monument. New York: HSA-UWC, 1977. 4 pp.

26. "Am I Really Needed?" *Master Speaks.* MS-439. Translated by Won Pok Choi. N.p., November 10, 1974, 12 pp.

27. "The Attitude of the Evangelist." *Master Speaks.* MS-325. Translated by Won Pok Choi. Belvedere, N.Y., January 26, 1973, 9 pp.

28. "The Basic Formula for the Realization of the Kingdom of God on Earth." *Reverend Moon Speaks.* Translated by Bo Hi Pak. World Mission Center, N.Y., January 1, 1978 (midnight), 13 pp.

29. "The Basis of Good and Evil." *Master Speaks.* MS-336. Translated by Won Pok Choi. Tarrytown, N.Y., February 19, 1973, 10 pp.

30. "Becoming a Responsible Person." *Master Speaks.* MS-426. Translated by Won Pok Choi. Tarrytown, N.Y., July 14, 1974, 12 pp.

31. "Before Our Father." *Master Speaks.* MS-341. Translated by Won Pok Choi. Belvedere, N.Y., March 2, 1973, 5 pp.

32. "The Benefit and Grace of This Time in History." *Reverend Moon Speaks.* Translated by Bo Hi Pak. Belvedere, N.Y., December 19, 1976, 11 pp.

33. "The Best Thing." *Reverend Moon Speaks.* Translated by Sang Kil Han. Belvedere, N.Y., January 4, 1981, 6 pp.

34. "Bicentennial Speeches." *Reverend Moon Speaks.* New York and Washington, D.C., June 1, 1976 and September 18, 1976, 9 pp.

35. "The Birth of Jesus and the Consummation of God's Will." *Reverend Moon Speaks.* Translated by Bo Hi Pak. Belvedere, N.Y., December 24, 1978, 13 pp.

36. "The Birth of a New Providence." *Reverend Moon Speaks.* Translated by Bo Hi Pak. World Mission Center, N.Y., February 18, 1983, 6 pp.

37. "Blessed Family." *Reverend Moon Speaks.* Translated by Bo Hi Pak. Belvedere, N.Y., June 20, 1982, 14 pp.

38. "The Boundary Point of History." *Master Speaks.* MS-467. Translated by Won Pok Choi. Tarrytown, N.Y., March 2, 1975, 8 pp.

39. "Breaking the Barrier." *Reverend Moon Speaks.* Translated by Bo Hi Pak. Belvedere, N.Y., December 10, 1978, 11 pp.

40. "The Building and Creation of the Fatherland" and "Creation of the Fatherland and God's Day." *Reverend Moon Speaks.* Translated by Bo Hi Pak. World Mission Center, N.Y., January 11, 1985, Midnight and Morning, 10 pp.

41. "The Burden of Destiny." *Reverend Moon Speaks.* Translated by Bo Hi Pak. Belvedere, N.Y., February 19, 1978, 17 pp.

42. "The Burden on Our Shoulders." *Reverend Moon Speaks.* Translated by Sang Kil Han. London, England, June 11, 1978, 15 pp.

43. "Cain-Abel Relationships." *Master Speaks.* MS-462. Translated by Won Pok Choi. Barrytown, N.Y., March 15, 1975, 8 pp.

44. "CAUSA Seminar Speech." *Reverend Moon Speaks.* Translated by Bo Hi Pak. Manhattan Center, N.Y., August 29, 1985, 10 pp.

45. "Central Figure." *Master Speaks.* MS-415. Translated by San Kil Han. Belvedere International Training Center, N.Y., February 13, 1974. 8 pp.

46. "Change of Blood Lineage I." *Master Speaks.* MS-318. Translated by Won Pok Choi. Belvedere, N.Y., January 18, 1973, 5 pp.

47. "Change of Blood Lineage II." *Master Speaks.* MS-319. Translated by Won Pok Choi. Tarrytown, N.Y., January 19, 1973, 8 pp.

48. "Change of Blood Lineage III." *Master Speaks.* MS-321. Translated by Won Pok Choi. Tarrytown, N.Y., January 21, 1973, 13 pp.

49. "Children's Day." *Reverend Moon Speaks.* Translated by Bo Hi Pak. World Mission Center, N.Y., November 5, 1983, 14 pp.

50. "Children's Day." *Master Speaks.* MS-441. Translated by Bo Hi Pak. Tarrytown, N.Y., August 4, 1974, 14 pp.

51. "Children's Day and Tradition." *Reverend Moon Speaks.* Translated by Bo Hi Pak. Los Angeles, November 20, 1979, 15 pp.

52. "The Children's Day We Have Been Longing For." *Reverend Moon Speaks.* Translated by Bo Hi Pak. Manhattan Center, N.Y., November 11, 1977, 17 pp.

53. "Christmas in Heart." *Master Speaks.* MS-405. Translated by Bo Hi Pak. Belvedere International Training Center, N.Y., December 25, 1973, 7 pp.

54. "Complete Restoration." *Master Speaks.* MS-479. Translated by Won Pok Choi. Tarrytown, N.Y., June 2, 1975, 7 pp.

55. "The Completion of Our Responsibility." *Master Speaks.* MS-445. Translated by Won Pok Choi and David Kim. Barrytown, N.Y., October 28, 1974, 9 pp.

56. "Completion of the Providence and Parents' Day." *Reverend Moon Speaks.* Translated by Bo Hi Pak. World Mission Center, N.Y., April 15, 1980, 13 pp.

57. "The Completion Period for the Dispensation." *Reverend Moon Speaks.* Translated by Bo Hi Pak. Belvedere, N.Y., November 12, 1978, 14 pp.

58. "Concluding Remarks." *Master Speaks.* MS-384. Translated by David Kim. Belvedere, N.Y., July 5, 1973, 4 pp.

59. "The Contrast between Secular People and Us." *Reverend Moon Speaks.* Translated by Bo Hi Pak. Belvedere, N.Y., December 23, 1979, 13 pp.

60. "Core Love and Indemnity." *Reverend Moon Speaks.* Translated by Bo Hi Pak. World Mission Center, N.Y., October 22, 1981, 16 pp.

61. "The Core of Unification." *Reverend Moon Speaks.* Translated by Bo Hi Pak. Belvedere, N.Y., October 9, 1977, 15 pp.

62. "The Course of Life and Restoration by Indemnification." *Reverend Moon Speaks.* Translated by Bo Hi Pak. Belvedere, N.Y., February 26, 1978, 22 pp.

63. "Creation of the Fatherland." *Reverend Moon Speaks.* Translated by Bo Hi Pak. World Mission Center, N.Y., January 1, 1984 (midnight), 9 pp.

64. "Creation of the Fatherland and God's Day." *Reverend Moon Speaks.* Translated by Bo Hi Pak. World Mission Center, N.Y., January 1, 1984 (morning), 4 pp.

65. "The Critical Turning Point of the Dispensation of God." *Reverend Moon Speaks.* Translated by Bo Hi Pak. Belvedere, N.Y., December 31, 1978, 16 pp.

66. "Crossing over the Boundary Line." *Reverend Moon Speaks.* Translated by Bo Hi Pak. Belvedere, N.Y., June 1, 1980, 11 pp.

67. "Crossroads of Life and Death." *Reverend Moon Speaks.* Translated by Bo Hi Pak. Belvedere, N.Y., December 17, 1978, 11 pp.

68. "Day of All Things." *Master Speaks.* MS-425. Translated by Won Pok Choi. Tarrytown, N.Y., June 20, 1974, 9 pp.

69. "The Day of All Things." *Reverend Moon Speaks.* Translated by Sang Kil Han. London, England, June 6, 1978, 9 pp.

70. "Day of All Things." *Reverend Moon Speaks.* Translated by Bo Hi Pak. World Mission Center, N.Y., May 26, 1979, 9 pp.

71. "Day of All Things." *Reverend Moon Speaks.* Translated by Bo Hi Pak. Belvedere, N.Y., June 13, 1980, 9 pp.

72. "Day of All Things 1984." *Reverend Moon Speaks.* Translated by Bo Hi Pak. World Mission Center, N.Y., May 31, 1984, 10 pp.

73. "Day of Heavenly Victory." *Reverend Moon Speaks.* Translated by Sang Kil Han. Belvedere, N.Y., October 4, 1983, 10 pp.

74. "The Day of the Love of God." *Reverend Moon Speaks.* Translated by Bo Hi Pak. Belvedere, N.Y., May 20, 1984, 13 pp.

75. "Day of the Resolution of Victory." *Master Speaks.* MS-422. Translated by Won Pok Choi. Tarrytown, N.Y., July 1, 1974, 8 pp.

76. "The Day of the Victory of Heaven." *Reverend Moon Speaks.* Translated by Bo Hi Pak. Belvedere, N.Y., October 4, 1976, 16 pp.

77. "Day of the Victory of Heaven." *Reverend Moon Speaks.* Translated by Bo Hi Pak. World Mission Center, N.Y., October 4, 1979, 13 pp.

78. "Day of Victory of Heaven." *Reverend Moon Speaks.* Translated by Sang Kil Han. Belvedere, N.Y., October 4, 1980, 7 pp.

79. "The Day of Victory over Resentment." *Master Speaks.* MS-418. Translated by Won Pok Choi. Tarrytown, N.Y., May 19, 1974, 10 pp.

80. "The Day We Have Been Longing For." *Reverend Moon Speaks.* Translated by Bo Hi Pak. Manhattan Center, N.Y., November 11, 1977, 17 pp.

81. "Declaration of the Ceremony of Unity between Spirit World and Physical World." *Reverend Moon Speaks.* Translated by Sang Kil Han. Belvedere, N.Y., March 28, 1982, 6 pp.

82. "The Deep Desire of Our Original Nature." *Reverend Moon Speaks.* Translated by Sang Kil Han. Belvedere, N.Y., February 14, 1982, 9 pp.

83. "The Desire of All Things." *Reverend Moon Speaks.* Translated by Bo Hi Pak. Manhattan Center, N.Y., June 17, 1977, 10 pp.

84. "The Desire of God." *Reverend Moon Speaks.* Translated by Bo Hi Pak. Belvedere, N.Y., June 19, 1977, 11 pp.

85. "Dialogue and Alliance." *Founder's Address.* Assembly of the World's Religions. McAfee, New Jersey, November 15, 1985, 7 pp.

86. "The Dignity of God and Man." *Reverend Moon Speaks* . Translated by Bo Hi Pak. World Mission Center, N.Y., April 1, 1977 (midnight), 11 pp.

87. "Directives to Foreign Missionaries." *Master Speaks.* MS-471. Translated by David Kim. Barrytown, N.Y., March 20, 1975, 12 pp.

88. "Dispensation of Restoration and Myself." *Reverend Moon Speaks.* Translated by Sang Kil Han. Belvedere, N.Y., April 6, 1980, 14 pp.

89. "The Dividing Peak of Restoration." *Reverend Moon Speaks.* Translated by Bo Hi Pak. Belvedere, N.Y., January 15, 1978, 26 pp.

90. "Divine Providence and the Turning Point of History." *Master Speaks.* MS-205. n.tr. Washington, D.C., December 23, 1971, 7 pp.

91. "Do Not Be Discouraged." *Reverend Moon Speaks.* Translated by Bo Hi Pak. Belvedere, N.Y., November 11, 1979, 11 pp.

92. "Emergency Time Period." *Reverend Moon Speaks.* Translated by Sang Kil Han. Belvedere, N.Y., December 12, 1982, 9 pp.

93. "Eternal Happiness." *Reverend Moon Speaks.* Translated by Sang Kil Han. Belvedere, N.Y., February 25, 1979, 24 pp.

94. "Eve of Departure from United States." *Leader's Address.* Translated by Bo Hi Pak. N.p., June 30, 1965, 4 pp.

95. "Evening Address-Direction to Leaders." *Master Speaks.* MS-383. Translated by David Kim. Belvedere, N.Y., July 4, 1973, 10 pp.

96. "Farewell Speech." *Reverend Moon Speaks.* Translated by Bo Hi Pak. East Garden, N.Y., July 20, 1984, 6 pp.

97. "Faith and Reality." *Master Speaks.* MS-347. Translated by Won Pok Choi. N.p., March 18, 1973, 5 pp.

98. "The Fight Has Begun." *Master Speaks.* MS-218. Translated by Won Pok Choi. San Francisco, January 9, 1972, 4 pp.

99. "The Final Warning Concerning Good and Evil." *Reverend Moon Speaks.* Translated by Bo Hi Pak. Belvedere, N.Y., December 26, 1976, 11 pp.

100. "The Formula for God's Providence." *Master Speaks.* MS-203. Translated by Won Pok Choi. Los Angeles, December 14, 1971, 6 pp.

101. "For the Future." *Reverend Moon Speaks.* Translated by Sang Kil Han. London, England, September 10, 1978, 16 pp.

102. "Generation Record of the True Parent's Love." *Reverend Moon Speaks.* Translated by Bo Hi Pak. Belvedere, N.Y., April 22, 1984, 10 pp.

103. "The Glorious Sortie." *Reverend Moon Speaks.* Translated by Sang Kil Han. London, England, August 1, 1978, 14 pp.

104. "God and His Kingdom." *Master Speaks.* MS-429. Translated by Won Pok Choi. Tarrytown, N.Y., August 11, 1974, 10 pp.

105. "God and the Building of the Kingdom of God." *Reverend Moon Speaks.* Translated by Bo Hi Pak. Belvedere, N.Y., April 17, 1977, 18 pp.

106. "God and Us." *Reverend Moon Speaks.* Translated by Bo Hi Pak. World Mission Center, N.Y., February 1, 1982, 10 pp.

107. "God Depends on Us Alone." *Reverend Moon Speaks.* Translated by David Kim. Belvedere, N.Y., June 1, 1977, 11 pp.

108. "God, Myself, and the Country of My Assignment." *Master Speaks.* MS-476. Translated by Won Pok Choi. Barrytown, N.Y., April 21, 1975, 9 pp.

109. "God of Lamentation." *Reverend Moon Speaks.* Translated by Bo Hi Pak. Belvedere, N.Y., October 21, 1979, 11 pp.

110. "God's Day." *Reverend Moon Speaks.* Translated by Bo Hi Pak. World Mission Center, N.Y., January 1, 1983 (morning), 12 pp.

111. "God's Day." *Reverend Moon Speaks.* Translated by Bo Hi Pak. World Mission Center, N.Y., January 1, 1977, 12 pp.

112. "God's Day." *Reverend Moon Speaks.* Translated by Bo Hi Pak. Manhattan Center, N.Y., January 1, 1978 (morning), 11 pp.

113. "God's Day Address." *Master Speaks.* MS-410. Translated by Won Pok Choi. Tarrytown, N.Y., January 1, 1974, 8 pp.

114. "God's Day and My Congratulations." *Reverend Moon Speaks.* Translated by Sang Kil Han. World Mission Center, N.Y., January 1, 1981, 8 pp.

115. "God's Day Midnight Address." *Master Speaks.* MS-314. Translated by Won Pok Choi. Tarrytown, N.Y., January 1, 1973, 3 pp.

116. "God's Day 1984." *Reverend Moon Speaks.* Translated by Bo Hi Pak. World Mission Center, N.Y., January 1, 1984 (morning), 9 pp.

117. "God's Day Speech." *Master Speaks.* MS-315. Translated by Won Pok Choi. Tarrytown, N.Y., January 1, 1973, 10 pp.

118. "God's Grief." *Master Speaks.* MS-326. Translated by Won Pok Choi. Belvedere, N.Y., January 27, 1973, 7 pp.

119. "God's Will and Christmas. *Reverend Moon Speaks.* Translated by Bo Hi Pak. Manhattan Center, N.Y., December 25, 1976, 11 pp.

120. "Good Day." *Reverend Moon Speaks.* Translated by Bo Hi Pak. Belvedere, N.Y., July 3, 1977, 14 pp.

121. "Grateful God's Day." *Reverend Moon Speaks.* Translated by Bo Hi Pak. World Mission Center, N.Y., January 1, 1980 (morning), 10 pp.

122. "The Greatest of All Is Love." *Reverend Moon Speaks.* Translated by Bo Hi Pak. Belvedere, N.Y., March 20, 1977, 15 pp.

123. "Happy Unification Church Members." *Reverend Moon Speaks.* Translated by Bo Hi Pak. Belvedere, N.Y., May 22, 1977, 15 pp.

124. "The Harvest Season for God's Providence." *Reverend Moon Speaks.* Translated by Bo Hi Pak. Belvedere, N.Y., September 19, 1982, 15 pp.

125. "Heart." *Master Speaks.* MS-349. Translated by Won Pok Choi. N.p., March 30, 1973, 4 pp.

126. "The Heart of Reunion." *Reverend Moon Speaks.* Translated by Bo Hi Pak. Belvedere, N.Y., September 11, 1977, 10 pp.

127. "The Heavenly Procession." *Reverend Moon Speaks.* Translated by Sang Kil Han. World Mission Center, N.Y., June 3, 1984, 10 pp.

128. "Heavenly Tradition." *Master Speaks.* Translated by Won Pok Choi. N.p., January 20, 1973, 7 pp.

129. "Heaven's Side and Satan's Side." *Reverend Moon Speaks.* Translated by Bo Hi Pak. Belvedere, N.Y., February 20, 1983, 10 pp.

130. "Heavy Burden." *Reverend Moon Speaks.* Translated by Sang Kil Han. Belvedere, N.Y., May 7, 1978, 10 pp.

131. "Historical Children's Day." *Reverend Moon Speaks.* Translated by Bo Hi Pak. World Mission Center, N.Y., October 28, 1981, 10 pp.

132. "Historical View of the Dispensation." *Reverend Moon Speaks.* Translated by Bo Hi Pak. Belvedere, N.Y., September 18, 1979, 13 pp.

133. "History and Our Responsibility." *Reverend Moon Speaks.* Translated by Sang Kil Han. London, England, July 16, 1978, 12 pp.

134. "History of the Providence through Restoration by Indemnity." *Reverend Moon Speaks.* Translated by Bo Hi Pak. World Mission Center, N.Y., February 10, 1981, 12 pp.

135. "The History of the Struggle of Good and Evil and Oneself." *Reverend Moon Speaks.* Translated by Bo Hi Pak. Belvedere, N.Y., March 1, 1984, 10 pp.

136. "History of the Unification Church." *Master Speaks.* MS-208. Translated by Won Pok Choi. Washington, D.C., December 27, 1971, 10 pp.

137. "History of the Unification Church (Continued)." *Master Speaks.* MS-209. Translated by Won Pok Choi. Washington, D.C., December 28, 1971, 4 pp.

138. "History of the Unification Church (Continued)." *Master Speaks.* MS-210. Washington, D.C., December 29, 1971, 13 pp.

139. "The Holy Water Ceremony." *Reverend Moon Speaks.* Translated by Bo Hi Pak. Belvedere, N.Y., August 20, 1985, 9 pp.

140. "Home Church and the Battle of Love." *Reverend Moon Speaks.* Translated by Bo Hi Pak. Belvedere, N.Y., January 7, 1979, 11 pp.

141. "Home Church and the Completion of the Kingdom of Heaven." *Reverend Moon Speaks.* Translated by Bo Hi Pak. World Mission Center, N.Y., January 1, 1979, 18 pp.

142. "Home Church Is My Kingdom of Heaven." *Reverend Moon Speaks.* Translated by Sang Kil Han. World Mission Center, N.Y., January 1, 1981, 8 pp.

143. "Home Church Is the Base of the Kingdom of Heaven." *Reverend Moon Speaks.* Translated by Bo Hi Pak. World Mission Center, N.Y., January 1, 1980 (midnight), 11 pp.

144. "Home Church Is Our Land of Settlement." *Reverend Moon Speaks.* Translated by Bo Hi Pak. World Mission Center, N.Y., January 1, 1983 (midnight), 12 pp.

145. "Hope of Youth." *Master Speaks.* MS-427. Translated by Sang Kil Han. Barrytown, N.Y., July 26, 1974, 22 pp.

146. "Host of the Future." *Reverend Moon Speaks.* Translated by Bo Hi Pak. Belvedere, N.Y., October 23, 1977, 16 pp.

147. "House of Providence." *Reverend Moon Speaks.* Translated by Bo Hi Pak. Belvedere, N.Y., December 9, 1979, 15 pp.

148. "How Can We Become One with God?" *Master Speaks.* MS-220. Translated by Won Pok Choi. New York, January 15, 1972, 3 pp.

149. "How God Is Pursuing His Restoration Providence." *Master Speaks.* MS-204. Washington, D.C., December 22, 1971, 12 pp.

150. "How to Witness: To State Leaders." *Reverend Moon Speaks.* Translated by Sang Kil Han. Gracemere, N.Y., April 1, 1977, 12 pp.

151. "How Will the Unified World Be Established on This Earth?" *Master Speaks.* MS-221. Reconstructed from notes and partial transcriptions. Washington, D.C., December 21, 1972, 5 pp.

152. "Human Death." *Master Speaks.* MS-489. Translated by Won Pok Choi. Barrytown, N.Y., July 21, 1975, 8 pp.

153. "Human Life." *Master Speaks.* MS-450. Translated by Won Pok Choi. Tarrytown, N.Y., December 1, 1974, 19 pp.

154. "Human Relationships." *Master Speaks.* MS-469. Translated by Won Pok Choi. Tarrytown, N.Y., March 9, 1975, 6 pp.

155. "I Proclaim That I Know." *Reverend Moon Speaks.* Translated by Sang Kil Han. World Mission Center, N.Y., April 1, 1978, 15 pp.

156. "Ideal Family, Ideal World." *Reverend Moon Speaks.* Translated by Sang Kil Han. Belvedere, N.Y., June 6, 1982, 13 pp.

157. "Ideal Home." *Reverend Moon Speaks.* Translated by Bo Hi Pak. Belvedere, N.Y., November 4, 1979, 9 pp.

158. "Ideal Nation of God." *Reverend Moon Speaks.* Translated by Bo Hi Pak. World Mission Center, N.Y., February 21, 1980, 9 pp.

159. "The Ideal World." *Master Speaks.* MS-200. Translated by Young Whi Kim. Los Angeles, December 11, 1971, 5 pp.

160. "The Ideal World of Adam." *Reverend Moon Speaks.* Translated by Bo Hi Pak. Belvedere, N.Y., June 1, 1982, 10 pp.

161. "The Ideal World of Subject and Object." *Reverend Moon Speaks.* Translated by Bo Hi Pak. Belvedere, N.Y., February 13, 1977, 13 pp.

162. "The Importance of Heavenly Heart." *Master Speaks.* MS-211. Translated by Won Pok Choi. Washington, D.C., December 30, 1971, 6 pp.

163. "The Importance of Prayer." *Reverend Moon Speaks.* Translated by Bo Hi Pak. Belvedere, N.Y., April 15, 1979, 10 pp.

164. "Important Person." *Master Speaks.* MS-377r. Translated by Won Pok Choi. Belvedere, N.Y., June 10, 1973, 9 pp.

165. "In Search of Our Home." *Reverend Moon Speaks.* Translated by Sang Kil Han. Belvedere, N.Y., July 11, 1982, 17 pp.

166. "Individual Course of Life." *Reverend Moon Speaks.* Translated by Sang Kil Han. Belvedere, N.Y., January 20, 1980, 14 pp.

167. "Instructions to IOWC Commanders and Team Members." *Master Speaks.* MS-411. Translated by Bo Hi Pak. Washington, D.C., January 31, 1974, 9 pp.

168. "Jacob's Course and Our Life of Faith." *Master Speaks.* MS-372r. Translated by Won Pok Choi. Tarrytown, N.Y., May 27, 1973, 14 pp.

169. "The Kingdom of God on Earth and the Ideal Family." *Reverend Moon Speaks.* Translated by Bo Hi Pak. New Yorker Hotel, N.Y., January 1, 1977 (midnight), 12 pp.

170. "Korea and the World." *Master Speaks.* MS-480. n.trans. Seoul, Korea, June 7, 1975, 7 pp.

171. "The Last Front-Line." *Master Speaks.* MS-339. Translated by Won Pok Choi. Washington, D.C., February 25, 1973, 11 pp.

172. "Leader Speaks on America." *Leader's Address.* N.p., n.d., 14 pp.

173. "Leader's Address on Opening Night." *Master Speaks.* MS-316. Translated by Won Pok Choi. Belvedere, N.Y., January 15, 1973, 1 p.

174. "Leadership: To the MFT Captains." *Reverend Moon Speaks.* Translated by Bo Hi Pak. World Mission Center, N.Y., March 16, 1977, 9 pp.

175. "Let This Be a Good Year." *Reverend Moon Speaks.* Translated by Bo Hi Pak. World Mission Center, N.Y., January 2, 1983, 23 pp.

176. "Let Us Be Grateful." *Reverend Moon Speaks.* Translated by Sang Kil Han. London, England, June 18, 1978, 10 pp.

177. "Let Us Cross over the Hill." *Master Speaks.* MS-443. Translated by Won Pok Choi. Tarrytown, N.Y., September 29, 1974, 6 pp.

178. "Let Us Establish the Kingdom of Heaven." *Master Speaks.* MS-455. Chungpa Dong, Seoul, Korea, January 1, 1975, 6 pp.

179. "Let Us Follow the Will of God." *Leader's Address.* N.p., n.d., 7 pp.

180. "Let Us Give Thanks." *Reverend Moon Speaks.* Translated by Bo Hi Pak. Belvedere, N.Y., November 23, 1980, 6 pp.

181. "Let Us Go over the Boundary Line." *Master Speaks.* MS-444. Translated by Won Pok Choi. Tarrytown, N.Y., October 6, 1974, 15 pp.

182. "Let Us Go over the Hill." *Reverend Moon Speaks.* Translated by Bo Hi Pak. World Mission Center, N.Y., February 7, 1984, 11 pp.

183. "Let Us Know Ourselves." *Reverend Moon Speaks.* Translated by Sang Kil Han. Belvedere, N.Y., September 30, 1979, 11 pp.

184. "Let Us Know the Heart of God." *Master Speaks.* MS-490. Translated by Won Pok Choi. Tarrytown, N.Y., April 20, 1975, 7 pp.

185. "Let Us March Forward to Our Heavenly Father." *Reverend Moon Speaks.* Translated by David Kim. Belvedere, N.Y., November 13, 1977, 10 pp.

186. "Let Us Meet Opportunity Well." *Reverend Moon Speaks*. Translated by Bo Hi Pak. World Mission Center, N.Y., January 2, 1977, 9 pp.

187. "Let Us Protect Ourselves." *Reverend Moon Speaks*. Translated by Sang Kil Han. Belvedere, N.Y., May 1, 1982, 11 pp.

188. "Let Us Repay Our Debts." *Master Speaks*. MS-464. Translated by Won Pok Choi. Barrytown, N.Y., March 10, 1975, 5 pp.

189. "Let Us Restore the Homeland and the Fatherland." *Reverend Moon Speaks*. Translated by Bo Hi Pak. Belvedere, N.Y., January 14, 1979, 13 pp.

190. "Let Us Set the Record." *Master Speaks*. MS-431. Translated by Bo Hi Pak. New York, N.Y., September 11, 1974, 10 pp.

191. "Let Us Set the Record." *Reverend Moon Speaks*. Translated by Bo Hi Pak. Belvedere, N.Y., October 12, 1980, 9 pp.

192. "Let Us Set the Tradition." *Master Speaks*. MS-455. Translated by Won Pok Choi. Tarrytown, N.Y., November 17, 1974, 10 pp.

193. "Let Us Thank God." *Reverend Moon Speaks*. Translated by Bo Hi Pak. Belvedere, N.Y., May 29, 1977, 12 pp.

194. "Let Us Think." *Reverend Moon Speaks*. Translated by Bo Hi Pak. Belvedere, N.Y., May 6, 1979, 10 pp.

195. "Let Us Think Once More." *Reverend Moon Speaks*. Translated by Bo Hi Pak. Belvedere, N.Y., June 12, 1977, 12 pp.

196. "Let Us Turn This Historical Moment into a Great Victory." *Master Speaks*. MS-437. Translated by Bo Hi Pak. Tarrytown, N.Y., September 8, 1974 , 7 pp.

197. "Life of Experience in the Realm of Heart." *Reverend Moon Speaks*. Translated by Sang Kil Han. Belvedere, N.Y., March 15, 1981, 8 pp.

198. "Line of Limitation." *Reverend Moon Speaks*. Translated by Bo Hi Pak. Belvedere, N.Y., January 27, 1980, 9 pp.

199. "Liquidation and Blessing." *Reverend Moon Speaks*. Translated by Bo Hi Pak. Belvedere, N.Y., May 18, 1980, 12 pp.

200. "Living Sacrifice." *Reverend Moon Speaks*. Translated by Bo Hi Pak. Belvedere, N.Y., May 8, 1977, 13 pp.

201. "London Conference Address." *Master Speaks*. MS-451. Translated by Bo Hi Pak. London, England, November 25, 1974, 14 pp.

202. "Love Forever." *Reverend Moon Speaks.* Translated by Sang Kil Han, January 22, 1984, 7 pp.

203. "Mainstream of the Dispensation of God." *Reverend Moon Speaks.* Translated by Bo Hi Pak. Belvedere, N.Y., November 19, 1978, 24 pp.

204. "Mankind and the Ideal World." *Reverend Moon Speaks.* Translated by Bo Hi Pak. Belvedere, N.Y., April 29, 1979, 9 pp.

205. "The Master Speaks on Bible Interpretation." *Master Speaks.* MS-7. N.p., 1965, 6 pp.

206. "The Master Speaks on Bible Interpretation." *Master Speaks.* MS-7(2). Second Series. N.p., June, 1967, 2 pp.

207. "The Master Speaks on the Blessing and Witnessing." *Master Speaks.* MS-2. N.p., 1965, 20 pp.

208. "The Master Speaks on the Blessing and Witnessing." *Master Speaks.* MS-2(2). Second series. N.p., December, 1967, 6 pp.

209. "The Master Speaks on Creation." *Master Speaks.* MS-5. Compiled, various locations, 1965, 6 pp.

210. "The Master Speaks on the Lord of the Second Advent." *Master Speaks.* MS-1. Various locations, 1965, 8 pp.

211. "The Master Speaks on the Lord of the Second Advent." *Master Speaks.* MS-1(2). Second series. N.p., December, 1967, 8 pp.

212. "The Master Speaks on Prayer and the Spirit World." *Master Speaks.* MS-3. Various locations, 1965, 28 pp.

213. "The Master Speaks on Prayer and the Spirit World." *Master Speaks.* MS-3(2). Second series. N.p., December, 1967, 9 pp.

214. "The Master Speaks on Restoration and Judgement." *Master Speaks.* MS-4. Various locations, 1965, 14 pp.

215. "The Master Speaks on Restoration and Judgement." *Master Speaks.* MS-4(2). Second series. N.p., June, 1967, 14 pp.

216. "The Master Speaks on Restoration and Judgement." *Master Speaks.* MS-4(2a) Second series a. N.p., December, 1967, 2 pp.

217. "The Master Speaks on Satan, the Fall, and Evil." *Master Speaks.* MS-6. Various locations, 1965, 4 pp.

218. "The Master Speaks on Satan, the Fall, and Evil." *Master Speaks*. MS-6(2). Second series. N.p., December, 1967, 1 p.

219. "Master Speaks to the 100-Day Trainees after Lecture." *Master Speaks*. MS-371. Belvedere, N.Y., May 26, 1973, 6 pp.

220. "Master's Remarks." *Master Speaks*. MS-345. Translated by David Kim. Belvedere, N.Y., March 5, 1973, 11 pp.

221. "May God Protect Us on Our Way of Destiny." *Master Speaks*. MS-376r. Belvedere, N.Y., June 3, 1973, 5 pp.

222. "May the Fatherland Shine Forth." *Reverend Moon Speaks*. n.trans. Seoul, Korea, October 19, 1978, 12 pp.

223. "Men Are Destined to Go the Road of Restoration--Returning Home." *Leader's Address*. Various locations. N.d. 10 pp.

224. "Men of God." *Reverend Moon Speaks*. Translated by Bo Hi Pak. Belvedere, N.Y., September 23, 1979, 13 pp.

225. "Men of Justice, Rise Up." *Reverend Moon Speaks*. Translated by Bo Hi Pak. World Mission Center, N.Y., May 21, 1977, 14 pp.

226. "Message to the American People." *Master Speaks*. MS-361. Translated by Won Pok Choi. Washington, D.C., May 1, 1973, 4 pp.

227. "Mind the Environment in Advancing Forward." *Master Speaks*. MS-370. Translated by Won Pok Choi. N.p., May 25, 1973, 9 pp.

228. "The Mission We Are Undertaking." *Master Speaks*. MS-440. Translated by Won Pok Choi. Tarrytown, N.Y., March 16, 1975, 14 pp.

229. "Mission of Our Life." *Reverend Moon Speaks*. Translated by Bo Hi Pak. Belvedere, N.Y., April 22, 1979, 9 pp.

230. "My Life." *Reverend Moon Speaks*. Translated by Bo Hi Pak. Belvedere, N.Y., March 12, 1978, 16 pp.

231. "My New Self." *Reverend Moon Speaks*. Translated by Sang Kil Han. Belvedere, N.Y., October 2, 1983, 8 pp.

232. "Myself." *Reverend Moon Speaks*. Translated by Sang Kil Han. Belvedere, N.Y., January 13, 1980, 11 pp.

233. "The Necessity for the Day of Victory of Love." *Reverend Moon Speaks*. Translated by Bo Hi Pak. Belvedere, N.Y., January 15, 1984, 14 pp.

234. "The Necessity of Prayer." *Reverend Moon Speaks*. Translated by Bo Hi Pak. Belvedere, N.Y., June 22, 1980, 11 pp.

235. "A Needed Man." *Master Speaks*. MS-484. Translated by Won Pok Choi. Barrytown, N.Y., July 16, 1975, 8 pp.

236. "A New Breed of People." *Master Speaks*. MS-449. Translated by Bo Hi Pak. Tarrytown, N.Y., September 15, 1974, 9 pp.

237. "New Morning of Glory." *Reverend Moon Speaks*. Translated by Bo Hi Pak. Belvedere, N.Y., January 22, 1978, 17 pp.

238. "New York City Center" [from notes of Majorie Hill]. *Leader's Address*. New York, N.Y., May 1, 1965, 9 pp.

239. New York Church Leaders Director's Meeting with Father. N.trans., n.p., March 5, 1975, 6 pp.

240. "Noble Dream." *Reverend Moon Speaks*. Translated by Bo Hi Pak. Belvedere, N.Y., December 1, 1981, 9 pp.

241. "On Approaching God." *Master Speaks*. MS-461. Translated by Sang Kil Han. Barrytown, N.Y., March 3, 1975, 9 pp.

242. "On Jesus' Family." *Master Speaks*. MS-206. Washington, D.C., December 25, 1971, 6 pp.

243. "On Leadership." *Master Speaks*. MS-400. Translated by Won Pok Choi. Atlanta, Ga., November 9, 1973, 8 pp.

244. "On Unification Philosophy." *Master Speaks*. MS-368. Translated by Won Pok Choi. N.p., May 19, 1973, 2 pp.

245. "On Witnessing." *Master Speaks*. MS-216. Translated by Young Whi Kim. Washington, D.C., January 3, 1972, 4 pp.

246. "One Age, One Generation." *Reverend Moon Speaks*. Translated by Sang Kil Han. London, England, September 3, 1978, 14 pp.

247. "The Ones Who Can Receive God's Love." *Reverend Moon Speaks*. Translated by Bo Hi Pak. Pasadena, Calif., October 1, 1977, 3 pp.

248. "One World." *Master Speaks*. MS-447. Translated by Won Pok Choi. Tarrytown, N.Y., October 13, 1974, 8 pp.

249. "One Year Anniversary of the Seunghwa Ceremony of Heung-jin Moon." *Reverend Moon Speaks*. Translated by Bo Hi Pak. World Mission Center, N.Y., January 1, 1985, 7 pp.

250. "Opening of the Training Session." *Master Speaks.* MS-300. Translated by Won Pok Choi. Washington, D.C., December 9, 1972, 14 pp.

251. "Opening Talk-Morning Session." *Master Speaks.* MS-382. Translated by David Kim. Belvedere, N.Y., July 4, 1973, 7 pp.

252. "Opportunity for Happiness or Unhappiness." *Master Speaks.* MS-468. Translated by Won Pok Choi. Tarrytown, N.Y., March 2, 1975, 9 pp.

253. "Original Base of Cosmic Completion." *Reverend Moon Speaks.* Translated by Bo Hi Pak. Belvedere, N.Y., December 16, 1979, 12 pp.

254. "Original Eden, Centering on True Love." *Reverend Moon Speaks.* Translated by Sang Kil Han. Belvedere, N.Y., May 27, 1984, 11 pp.

255. "The Original I." *Master Speaks.* MS-342. Translated by Won Pok Choi. N.p., March 3, 1973, 5 pp.

256. "Original Place of Utmost Happiness." *Reverend Moon Speaks.* Translated by Sang Kil Han. Belvedere, N.Y., December 1, 1983, 9 pp.

257. "Original Way of God's Will." *Reverend Moon Speaks.* Translated by Sang Kil Han. Belvedere, N.Y., July 8, 1984, 9 pp.

258. "Our Advancement and Retreat." *Master Speaks.* MS-348. Translated by Won Pok Choi. Washington, D.C., March 22, 1973, 7 pp.

259. "Our Attitude." *Master Speaks.* MS-322. Translated by Won Pok Choi. Tarrytown, N.Y., January 26, 1973, 8 pp.

260. "Our Basic Attitude." *Reverend Moon Speaks.* Translated by Bo Hi Pak. Belvedere, N.Y., March 13, 1983, 13 pp.

261. "Our Desire." *Master Speaks.* MS-323. Translated by Won Pok Choi. Tarrytown, N.Y., January 23, 1973, 4 pp.

262. "Our Destined Relationship." *Reverend Moon Speaks.* Translated by Bo Hi Pak. Belvedere, N.Y., November 6, 1977, 16 pp.

263. "Our Determination to Win." *Master Speaks.* MS-340. Translated by Won Pok Choi. Belvedere, N.Y., March 1, 1973, 7 pp.

264. "Our Duty, Our Mission." *Reverend Moon Speaks.* Translated by Sang Kil Han. Belvedere, N.Y., October 5, 1980, 23 pp.

265. "Our Family in the Light of the Dispensation, Part I." *Reverend Moon Speaks.* Translated by Sang Kil Han. Belvedere, N.Y., March 1, 1977, 18 pp.

266. "Our Family in the Light of the Dispensation, Part II." *Reverend Moon Speaks.* Translated by Bo Hi Pak. Belvedere, N.Y., March 6, 1977, 13 pp.

267. "Our Fatherland." *Master Speaks.* MS-317. Translated by Won Pok Choi. Belvedere, N.Y., January 17, 1973, 5 pp.

268. "Our Future Path of Advancement." *Master Speaks.* MS-328. Translated by Won Pok Choi. Belvedere, N.Y., January 30, 1973, 9 pp.

269. "Our Hope." *Master Speaks.* MS-435. Translated by Won Pok Choi. Barrytown, N.Y., August 20, 1974, 20 pp.

270. "Our Ideal Home, Part I." *Reverend Moon Speaks.* Translated by Sang Kil Han. Belvedere, N.Y., June 19, 1983, 7 pp.

271. "Our Ideal Home, Part II." *Reverend Moon Speaks.* Translated by Sang Kil Han. Belvedere, N.Y., June 26 1983, 9 pp.

272. "Our Ideal Home, Part III." *Reverend Moon Speaks.* Translated by Bo Hi Pak. Belvedere, N.Y., September 11, 1983, 14 pp.

273. "Our Identity." *Reverend Moon Speaks.* Translated by Sang Kil Han. Belvedere, N.Y., April 1, 1981, 7 pp.

274. "Our Leader's Talk." *Master Speaks.* MS-344. Translated by Won Pok Choi. Belvedere, N.Y., March 5, 1973, 6 pp.

275. "Our Life in the Kingdom Of God." *Master Speaks.* MS-327. Translated by Won Pok Choi. Belvedere, N.Y., January 28, 1973, 6 pp.

276. "Our Mission Is Great." *Leader's Address.* N.p., July 17, 1965, 4 pp.

277. "Our Newborn Selves." *Reverend Moon Speaks.* Translated by Bo Hi Pak. Belvedere, N.Y., November 1, 1977, 16 pp.

278. "Our One Life." *Reverend Moon Speaks.* Translated by Sang Kil Han. Belvedere, N.Y., March 4, 1979, 9 pp.

279. "Our Pledge." *Reverend Moon Speaks.* Translated by Bo Hi Pak. Belvedere, N.Y., November 21, 1982, 15 pp.

280. "Our Position." *Reverend Moon Speaks.* Translated by Bo Hi Pak. World Mission Center, N.Y., January 2, 1979, 13 pp.

281. "Our Present Mission." *Master Speaks.* MS-428. Translated by Won Pok Choi. Tarrytown, N.Y., August 4, 1974, 13 pp.

282. "Our Pride." *Reverend Moon Speaks.* Translated by Bo Hi Pak. Belvedere, N.Y., June 5, 1977, 19 pp.

283. "Our Road to Go." *Master Speaks.* MS-217. Translated by Won Pok Choi. Washington, D.C., January 9, 1972, 8 pp.

284. "Our Shame (Instead of Honor)." *Master Speaks.* MS-346. Translated by Won Pok Choi. Belvedere, N.Y., March 11, 1973, 5 pp.

285. "Our Situation." *Master Speaks.* MS-335r. Translated by Won Pok Choi. Belvedere, N.Y., February 17, 1973, 4 pp.

286. "Our Standard." *Reverend Moon Speaks.* Translated by Bo Hi Pak. Belvedere, N.Y., March 1, 1981, 10 pp.

287. "Our Tradition." *Reverend Moon Speaks.* Translated by Sang Kil Han. Belvedere, N.Y., June 15, 1980, 11 pp.

288. "Parents, Children and the World Centered upon Oneself." *Reverend Moon Speaks.* Translated by Bo Hi Pak. Belvedere, N.Y., June 5, 1983, 12 pp.

289. "Parent's Day." *Leader's Address.* Translated by Bo Hi Pak. Washington, D.C., April 2, 1965, 13 pp.

290. "Parent's Day." *Reverend Moon Speaks.* Translated by Bo Hi Pak. Manhattan Center, N.Y., April 8, 1978, 16 pp.

291. "Parent's Day." *Reverend Moon Speaks.* Translated by Bo Hi Pak. World Mission Center, N.Y., April 7, 1985, 13 pp.

292. "Parent's Day Address." *Master Speaks.* MS-352. Translated by Won Pok Choi. Belvedere, N.Y., April 3, 1973, 6 pp.

293. "Parent's Day 1984." *Reverend Moon Speaks.* Translated by Bo Hi Pak. Belvedere, N.Y., April 1, 1984, 11 pp.

294. "Parent's Day 1974." *Master Speaks.* MS-416. Translated by Bo Hi Pak. Jackson, Miss., March 24, 1974, 9 pp.

295. "The Participants in Celebrating Christmas." *Reverend Moon Speaks.* Translated by Sang Kil Han. Manhattan Center, N.Y., December 25, 1977, 10 pp.

296. "Past and Future Generations." *Reverend Moon Speaks.* Translated by Bo Hi Pak. Tarrytown, N.Y., August 1, 1976, 12 pp.

297. "The Path of Abel." *Master Speaks.* MS-343. Translated by Won Pok Choi. Belvedere, N.Y., March 4, 1973, 11 pp.

298. "Path of Advancement for Our Faith." *Master Speaks.* MS-338. Translated by Won Pok Choi. Washington, D.C., February 23, 1973, 6 pp.

299. "The Path of the Chosen." *Reverend Moon Speaks.* Translated by Sang Kil Han. London, England, July 9, 1978, 12 pp.

300. "The Path That We Tread." *Master Speaks.* MS-430. Translated by Won Pok Choi. New York, August 25, 1974, 11 pp.

301. "Perfection and Gratitude." *Reverend Moon Speaks.* Translated by Bo Hi Pak. Belvedere, N.Y., October 10, 1976, 17 pp.

302. "Perfection of Restoration by Indemnity through Human Responsibility." *Reverend Moon Speaks.* Translated by Sang Kil Han, March 1, 1983, 16 pp.

303. "Persecution and Blessing." *Reverend Moon Speaks.* Translated by Sang Kil Han. Belvedere, N.Y., May 1, 1980, 11 pp.

304. "Perseverance and Contemplation." *Reverend Moon Speaks.* Translated by Sang Kil Han. London, England, August 27, 1978, 17 pp.

305. "Person of Central Value." *Master Speaks.* MS-434. Translated by Won Pok Choi. Barrytown, N.Y., August 16, 1974, 17 pp.

306. "The Person Who Worries about God's Nation." *Master Speaks.* MS-453. Translated by David Kim. Tarrytown, N.Y., September 1, 1974, 8 pp.

307. "The Pinnacle of Suffering." *Reverend Moon Speaks.* Translated by Bo Hi Pak. Belvedere, N.Y., June 26, 1977, 10 pp.

308. "Portland Director's Conference." *Master Speaks.* MS-417. Translated by Bo Hi Pak. Portland, Oregon, April 14, 1974, 12 pp.

309. "Prayer." *Reverend Moon Speaks.* Translated by Sang Kil Han. Belvedere, N.Y., March 29, 1981.

310. "The Present and the Future." *Master Speaks.* MS-458. Translated by Won Pok Choi. Tarrytown, N.Y., December 15, 1974, 11 pp.

311. "The Present Situation, Centering upon the Will of God." *Reverend Moon Speaks.* Translated by Bo Hi Pak. Belvedere, N.Y., May 23, 1982, 12 pp.

312. "The Present Time." *Reverend Moon Speaks*. Translated by Bo Hi
     Pak. Belvedere, N.Y., February 4, 1979, 10 pp.

313. "The Price of the Dispensation." *Master Speaks*. MS-420. Translated
     by Won Pok Choi. Tarrytown, N.Y., June 9, 1974, 13 pp.

314. "Process of Restoration." *Leader's Address*. Translated by Bo Hi
     Pak. N.p., February 13, 1965, 9 pp.

315. "The Providence of God in Relation to the Human Viewpoint." *Master
     Speaks*. MS-446. Translated by Bo Hi Pak. Barrytown, N.Y.,
     August 21, 1974, 6 pp.

316. "Providential Time Limits." *Master Speaks*. MS-472. Translated by
     Won Pok Choi. Barrytown, N.Y., April 17, 1975, 13 pp.

317. "The Public and Private Way." *Reverend Moon Speaks*. Translated by
     Sang Kil Han. Belvedere, N.Y., January 11, 1981, 8 pp.

318. "Public Life." *Reverend Moon Speaks*. Translated by Bo Hi Pak.
     Belvedere, N.Y., April 1, 1982, 7 pp.

319. "Pure Way of Truth and Public Righteousness." *Reverend Moon
     Speaks*. Translated by Bo Hi Pak. Belvedere, N.Y., July 18,
     1982, 11 pp.

320. "The Purpose of Life, Coming and Going." *Reverend Moon Speaks*.
     Translated by Sang Kil Han. Belvedere, N.Y., January 8, 1984,
     11 pp.

321. "Questions and Answers." *Master Speaks*. MS-202. Translated by
     David Kim and Won Pok Choi. Los Angeles, December 12, 1971,
     7 pp.

322. "The Realm of Resurrection." *Reverend Moon Speaks*. Translated by
     Bo Hi Pak. Belvedere, N.Y., April 3, 1977, 15 pp.

323. "Record-Setter of History." *Reverend Moon Speaks*. Translated by
     Bo Hi Pak. Belvedere, N.Y., July 1, 1979, 9 pp.

324. "Reflection upon Life." *Reverend Moon Speaks*. Translated by Bo Hi
     Pak. Belvedere, N.Y., June 1, 1979, 11 pp.

325. "Relationship between Men and Women." *Master Speaks*. MS-369.
     Translated by Won Pok Choi. Belvedere, N.Y., May 20, 1973, 8
     pp.

326. "Renewed Pride." *Reverend Moon Speaks*. Translated by Bo Hi Pak.
     Washington, D.C., December 4, 1977, 14 pp.

327. "The Responsibility of Cain and Abel." *Reverend Moon Speaks.* Translated by Won Pok Choi. Belvedere, N.Y., November 1, 1976, 9 pp.

328. "The Restoration of Heart ('Shim Jung')." *Master Speaks.* MS-337. Translated by Won Pok Choi. Belvedere, N.Y., February 20, 1973, 7 pp.

329. "Restoration through Indemnity." *Master Speaks.* MS-474. Translated by Won Pok Choi. Barrytown, N.Y., April 19, 1975, 3 pp.

330. "Restored Family." *Reverend Moon Speaks.* Translated by Bo Hi Pak. Belvedere, N.Y., January 21, 1979, 15 pp.

331. "Resurrected Kingdom of God." *Reverend Moon Speaks.* Translated by Bo Hi Pak. Belvedere, N.Y., March 26, 1978, 21 pp.

332. "The Resurrection of Jesus and Ourselves." *Reverend Moon Speaks.* Translated by Bo Hi Pak. Belvedere, N.Y., April 10, 1977, 17 pp.

333. "Return to Home Town." *Reverend Moon Speaks.* Translated by Bo Hi Pak. Belvedere, N.Y., March 18, 1979, 12 pp.

334. "The Return to Tears." *Reverend Moon Speaks.* Translated by Bo Hi Pak. Belvedere, N.Y., October 16, 1977, 18 pp.

335. "The Road of Religion and the Will of God." *Reverend Moon Speaks.* Translated by Bo Hi Pak. Belvedere, N.Y., April 24, 1977, 13 pp.

336. "Safeguard the United Front." *Master Speaks.* MS-212. Translated by Won Pok Choi. Washington, D.C., December 31, 1971, 6 pp.

337. "The Secret of Total Success." *Reverend Moon Speaks.* Translated by Bo Hi Pak. Belvedere, N.Y., December 19, 1982, 8 pp.

338. "Seeking the True Master." *Reverend Moon Speaks.* Translated by Bo Hi Pak. Belvedere, N.Y., November 29, 1981, 10 pp.

339. "Self Reflection." *Reverend Moon Speaks.* Translated by Won Pok Choi. Belvedere, N.Y., December 1, 1976, 19 pp.

340. "Seven-Day Fast." *Master Speaks.* MS-436. Translated by Won Pok Choi. Barrytown, N.Y., October 20, 1974, 20 pp.

341. "The Significance of God's Day." *Master Speaks.* MS-213. Translated by Won Pok Choi. Washington, D.C., January 1, 1972, 5 pp.

342. "The Significance of the IOWC in Japan." *Master Speaks.* MS-457. Translated by Bo Hi Pak. Tokyo, Japan, January 22, 1975, 7 pp.

343. "The Significance of July 1st, 1973." *Master Speaks.* MS-381. Translated by Bo Hi Pak. Belvedere, N.Y., July 1, 1973, 9 pp.

344. "Significance of Madison Square Garden Success." *Master Speaks.* MS-442. Translated by Bo Hi Pak. Tarrytown, N.Y., September 19, 1974, 5 pp.

345. "Significance of the Training Session." *Master Speaks.* MS-366. Translated by Won Pok Choi. Belvedere, N.Y., May 17, 1973, 12 pp.

346. "The Significance of Victory in Korea." *Master Speaks.* MS-483. Translated by Won Pok Choi. Barrytown, N.Y., July 1, 1973, 13 pp.

347. "The Sound of the Bell of the Mind." *Reverend Moon Speaks.* Translated by Bo Hi Pak. Belvedere, N.Y., January 28, 1979, 12 pp.

348. "Sorrow and Tears." *Reverend Moon Speaks.* Translated by Bo Hi Pak. Belvedere, N.Y., March 1, 1978, 16 pp.

349. "Speech at Foley Square." New York, October 22, 1981.

350. "Speech on True Parent's Birthday." *Master Speaks.* MS-456. Translated by Won Pok Choi. Tarrytown, N.Y., February 16, 1975, 10 pp.

351. "Speech to Los Angeles Family." *Master Speaks.* MS-475. Translated by Won Pok Choi. Los Angeles, March 24, 1975, 6 pp.

352. "The Spirit World and the Physical World." *Reverend Moon Speaks.* Translated by Bo Hi Pak. Belvedere, N.Y., February 6, 1977, 23 pp.

353. "Spring." *Reverend Moon Speaks.* Translated by David Kim. Belvedere, N.Y., April 16, 1978, 7 pp.

354. "Spring Season of the Providence." *Reverend Moon Speaks.* Translated by Bo Hi Pak. Belvedere, N.Y., April 1, 1979, 10 pp.

355. "The Standard of Hope, Common to God and Man." *Leader's Address.* Translated by Young Oon Kim. Los Angeles, February 19, 1965, 4 pp.

356. "Standing in the Presence of God." *Reverend Moon Speaks.* Translated by Sang Kil Han. Belvedere, N.Y., November 7, 1982, 9 pp.

357. "The Start of the Forty-Day Witnessing Condition." *Reverend Moon Speaks*. Translated by Sang Kil Han. London, England, July 4, 1978, 11 pp.

358. "Starting Point of Good and Evil." *Master Speaks*. MS-378r. Translated by Won Pok Choi. Belvedere, N.Y., June 24, 1973, 6 pp.

359. "Statement on Jews and Israel." New York: HSA-UWC, August 10, 1976. 1 p.

360. "Stony Path of Death." *Reverend Moon Speaks*. Translated by Bo Hi Pak. Belvedere, N.Y., April 27, 1980, 12 pp.

361. "Textbook of Love." *Reverend Moon Speaks*. Translated by Bo Hi Pak. Belvedere, N.Y., February 5, 1984, 11 pp.

362. "Thanksgiving to God's Will." *Reverend Moon Speaks*. Translated by Bo Hi Pak. Belvedere, N.Y., July 8, 1979, 12 pp.

363. "Things Found Most Important in Leading a Life of Faith." *Master Speaks*. MS-201. Translated by Won Pok Choi. Los Angeles, December 12, 1971, 4 pp.

364. "Things That Are Important to You." *Reverend Moon Speaks*. Translated by Bo Hi Pak. Belvedere, N.Y., February 1, 1981, 8 pp.

365. "Things That Belong to God and Things That Belong to Man." *Reverend Moon Speaks*. Translated by Bo Hi Pak. Belvedere, N.Y., May 15, 1977, 15 pp.

366. "The Things We Want to Be Proud Of." *Reverend Moon Speaks*. Translated by Sang Kil Han. Belvedere, N.Y., October 25, 1981, 7 pp.

367. "Thinking Back Historically." *Reverend Moon Speaks*. Translated by Sang Kil Han. Belvedere, N.Y., December 28, 1980, 7 pp.

368. "Thirtieth Anniversary of the Unification Church." *Reverend Moon Speaks*. Translated by Bo Hi Pak. World Mission Center, New York, May 1, 1984, 14 pp.

369. "The Third Seven Year Course--The Perfection Period." *Master Speaks*. MS-482. Tarrytown, N.Y., July 6, 1975, 8 pp.

370. "Those Who Are Left." *Master Speaks*. MS-424. Translated by Won Pok Choi. Tarrytown, N.Y., June 23, 1974, 10 pp.

371. "Those Who Will Prevail." *Master Speaks*. MS-463. Translated by Won Pok Choi. Barrytown, N.Y., March 12, 1975, 4 pp.

372. "Time and Our Destined Relationship." *Reverend Moon Speaks.*
     Translated by Bo Hi Pak. World Mission Center, N.Y., April 2,
     1978, 12 pp.

373. "To Belvedere Trainees." *Master Speaks.* MS-448. Translated by
     David Kim. Tarrytown, N.Y., August 29, 1974, 11 pp.

374. "To Foreign Missionaries." *Master Speaks.* MS-475. Translated by
     Won Pok Choi. Tarrytown, N.Y., April 19, 1975, 6 pp.

375. "To Para Study Group." *Leader's Address.* Translated by Bo Hi Pak.
     Washington, D.C., April 21, 1965, 8 pp.

376. "To the MFT." *Reverend Moon Speaks.* Translated by Bo Hi Pak.
     World Mission Center, N.Y., January 2, 1980, 13 pp.

377. "To Whom Do I Belong?" *Reverend Moon Speaks.* Translated by Bo
     Hi Pak. Belvedere, N.Y., January 16, 1977, 10 pp.

378. "Today in the Light of Dispensational History." *Reverend Moon
     Speaks.* Translated by Bo Hi Pak. World Mission Center, N.Y.,
     February 23, 1977, 17 pp.

379. "Total Completion of the Ideal." *Reverend Moon Speaks.* Translated
     by Sang Kil Han. Belvedere, N.Y., February 28, 1982, 12 pp.

380. "Total Self Re-evaluation." *Reverend Moon Speaks.* Translated by Bo
     Hi Pak. Belvedere, N.Y., September 14, 1980, 16 pp.

381. "Tradition Centered on God." *Master Speaks.* MS-214. Translated by
     Won Pok Choi. Washington, D.C., January 2, 1972, 5 pp.

382. "The Tradition of the Unification Church." *Reverend Moon Speaks.*
     Translated by Bo Hi Pak. Belvedere, N.Y., December 11, 1977,
     16 pp.

383. "True Couple." *Reverend Moon Speaks.* Translated by Bo Hi Pak.
     World Mission Center, N.Y., May 27, 1979, 9 pp.

384. "True Faith." *Master Speaks.* Translated by Won Pok Choi.
     Tarrytown, N.Y., April 1, 1973, 6 pp.

385. "A True Man--A Man of Truth." *Leader's Address.* Translated by
     Young Oon Kim. N.p., February 12, 1965, 5 pp.

386. "True Meaning of Christmas." *Reverend Moon Speaks.* Translated by
     Bo Hi Pak. World Mission Center, N.Y., December 25, 1979, 7
     pp.

387. "True Parent's Birthday." *Reverend Moon Speaks.* Translated by Bo
     Hi Pak. Belvedere, N.Y., February 25, 1985, 10 pp.

388. "True Parents Day." *Reverend Moon Speaks.* Translated by Bo Hi Pak. World Mission Center, N.Y., March 25, 1982, 6 pp.

389. "True Parents Day and Our Family." *Reverend Moon Speaks.* Translated by Bo Hi Pak. World Mission Center, N.Y., March 28, 1979, 11 pp.

390. "True Parents' Day from the Historical Point of View." *Reverend Moon Speaks.* Translated by Bo Hi Pak. Manhattan Center, N.Y., April 18, 1977, 22 pp.

391. "True Parents' Mission." *Reverend Moon Speaks.* Translated by Bo Hi Pak. Belvedere, N.Y., April 20, 1980, 11 pp.

392. "True Path of Restoration." *Master Speaks.* MS-219. Translated by Won Pok Choi. San Francisco, January 11, 1972, 17 pp.

393. "The True Pattern of Family Life." *Master Speaks.* MS-459. Translated by Won Pok Choi. Barrytown, N.Y., March 7, 1975, 9 pp.

394. "True Way of Life." *Reverend Moon Speaks.* Translated by Bo Hi Pak. Belvedere, N.Y., July 1, 1984, 14 pp.

395. "The Trust Placed in Us." *Reverend Moon Speaks.* Translated by Bo Hi Pak. Belvedere, N.Y., June 3, 1979, 10 pp.

396. "25th Anniversary of the Unification Church." *Reverend Moon Speaks.* Translated by Sang Kil Han. Belvedere, N.Y., May 1, 1979, 12 pp.

397. "The 25th Year of the Unification Church." *Reverend Moon Speaks.* Translated by David Kim. Belvedere, N.Y., May 1, 1978, 11 pp.

398. "The 23rd Anniversary of the Unification Church." *Reverend Moon Speaks.* Translated by Bo Hi Pak. Belvedere, N.Y., May 1, 1977, 21 pp.

399. "The Two Worlds of Good and Evil." *Reverend Moon Speaks.* Translated by Bo Hi Pak. Belvedere, N.Y., February 15, 1981, 7 pp.

400. "Unification Church and Heavenly Law." *Reverend Moon Speaks.* Translated by Sang Kil Han. Belvedere, N.Y., March 1, 1979, 9 pp.

401. "Untitled." *Master Speaks.* MS-215. Translated by David Kim. Washington, D.C., January 3, 1972, 3 pp.

402. "Untitled Address on Training Plans." *Master Speaks.* MS-363. Translated by Won Pok Choi. Belvedere, N.Y., May 7, 1973, 6 pp.

403. "Untitled Address to Conference of U.S. and International Leaders." *Reverend Moon Speaks.* Translated by Bo Hi Pak. Tarrytown, N.Y., September 20, 1976, 12 pp.

404. "The Vibration of True Love." *Reverend Moon Speaks.* Translated by Bo Hi Pak. World Mission Center, N.Y., January 30, 1982, 9 pp.

405 "The Victorious Day." *Reverend Moon Speaks.* Translated by Sang Kil Han. Belvedere, N.Y., June 29, 1980, 9 pp.

406. "Victory Celebration." *Reverend Moon Speaks.* Translated by Bo Hi Pak. Belvedere, N.Y., August 21, 1985, 7 pp.

407. "Victory of Home Church." *Reverend Moon Speaks.* Translated by Bo Hi Pak. World Mission Center, N.Y., January 1, 1982, 16 pp.

408. "Victory or Defeat." *Master Speaks.* MS-350. Translated by Won Pok Choi. Belvedere, N.Y., March 31, 1973, 7 pp.

409. "Victory throughout Three Ages." *Reverend Moon Speaks.* Translated by Bo Hi Pak. Belvedere, N.Y., March 20, 1983, 20 pp.

410. "Waiting to Live in the Kingdom of Heaven." *Reverend Moon Speaks.* Translated by Bo Hi Pak. Belvedere, N.Y., December 20, 1981, 11 pp.

411. "Washington Monument." *Reverend Moon Speaks.* Translated by Bo Hi Pak. London, England, September 18, 1978, 12 pp.

412. "The Way." *Master Speaks.* Translated by Won Pok Choi. Tarrytown, N.Y., May 30, 1974, 10 pp.

413. "Way of Life." *Master Speaks.* MS-335. Belvedere, N.Y., February 16, 1973, 7 pp.

414. "Way of Original Form." *Reverend Moon Speaks.* Translated by Bo Hi Pak. Belvedere, N.Y., June 8, 1980, 16 pp.

415. "The Way of Prosperity and Defeat." *Reverend Moon Speaks.* Translated by Sang Kil Han. Belvedere, N.Y., March 11, 1979, 11 pp.

416. "Way of Tuna." *Reverend Moon Speaks.* Translated by Bo Hi Pak. Belvedere, N.Y., July 13, 1980, 10 pp.

417. "The Way to True Happiness." *Master Speaks.* MS-460. Translated by Sang Kil Han. Barrytown, N.Y., March 5, 1975, 7 pp.

418. "We Who Have Been Called to Do God's Work." *Reverend Moon Speaks*. Translated by Sang Kil Han. London, England, July 23, 1978, 9 pp.

419. "Welcome, Arthur Ford Sitting." *Leader's Address*. Translated by Bo Hi Pak. Washington, D.C., April 21, 1965, 2 pp.

420. "What Kind of Thought Do You Have?" *Reverend Moon Speaks*. Translated by Bo Hi Pak. Belvedere, N.Y., June 10, 1979, 11 pp.

421. "What Shall We Do?" *Reverend Moon Speaks*. Translated by Bo Hi Pak. Belvedere, N.Y., February 11, 1979, 12 pp.

422. "What the Unification Church Is Trying to Solve after Taking the Responsibility of Jesus on Earth." *Master Speaks*. MS-207. Washington, D.C., December 26, 1971, 6 pp.

423. "Where Are You Bound?" *Master Speaks*. MS-324. Translated by Won Pok Choi. Belvedere, N.Y., January 24, 1973.

424. "When Are We Satisfied? *Reverend Moon Speaks*. Translated by Sang Kil Han. World Mission Center, N.Y., April 9, 1978, 11 pp.

425. "Where Do We Go?" *Reverend Moon Speaks*. Translated by Bo Hi Pak. London, England, September 17, 1978, 10 pp.

426. "Where God Resides and His Course." *Reverend Moon Speaks*. Translated by Sang Kil Han. Belvedere, N.Y., March 19, 1978, 17 pp.

427. "Where We Are Situated Now." *Master Speaks*. MS-452. Translated by Won Pok Choi. Tarrytown, N.Y., September 22, 1974, 13 pp.

428. "Who Am I?" *Reverend Moon Speaks*. Translated by Bo Hi Pak. Belvedere, N.Y., January 23, 1977, 15 pp.

429. "Who Is God and Who Am I?" *Reverend Moon Speaks*. Translated by Bo Hi Pak. Belvedere, N.Y., January 25, 1981, 10 pp.

430. "Who Was I?" *Reverend Moon Speaks*. Translated by Bo Hi Pak. Belvedere, N.Y., March 13, 1977, 11 pp.

431. "Who Will Be Responsible for the Providence of God?" *Master Speaks*. MS-470. Translated by Won Pok Choi. Barrytown, N.Y., March 23, 1975, 8 pp.

432. "The Whole and Myself." *Master Speaks*. MS-419. Translated by Won Pok Choi. Tarrytown, N.Y., May 26, 1974, 7 pp.

433. "Why Father Goes to Sea." *Master Speaks*. MS-491. Barrytown, N.Y., August 23, 1975, 8 pp.

434. "The Will of God." God and Freedom Banquet. Washington, D.C., August 20, 1985. 6pp.

435. "The Will of God and the Ideology America Must Follow." *Leader's Address*. Dallas, Tex., n.d. 4 pp.

436. "The Will of God and Individual Perfection." *Reverend Moon Speaks*. Translated by Bo Hi Pak. Belvedere, N.Y., February 27, 1977, 15 pp.

437. "The Will of God and Thanksgiving." *Reverend Moon Speaks*. Translated by Bo Hi Pak. Manhattan Center, N.Y., February 12, 1978, 11 pp.

438. "Word and Deed." *Reverend Moon Speaks*. Translated by Bo Hi Pak. Belvedere, N.Y., January 30, 1977, 15 pp.

439. "The World Age and Our Mission." *Master Speaks*. MS-438. Translated by Won Pok Choi. Tarrytown, N.Y., November 3, 1974, 13 pp.

440. "World Day." *Leader's Address*. Translated by Bo Hi Pak. Washington, D.C., May 31, 1965, 8 pp.

441. "World Day." *Master Speaks*. MS-372r. Belvedere, N.Y., June 1, 1973, 10 pp.

442. "Yesterday and Today." *Reverend Moon Speaks*. Translated by Sang Kil Han. Belvedere, N.Y., April 30, 1978, 11 pp.

443. "Young Generation." *Master Speaks*. MS-334. Belvedere, N.Y., February 15, 1973, 5 pp.

444. "Youth Must Have Hope." *Master Speaks*. MS-492. Translated by Won Pok Choi. Barrytown, N.Y., September 11, 1975, 7 pp.

B. THEOLOGICAL DOCTRINE

While there exists no single authoritative edition of the Reverend Moon's speeches and statements, there exist several official editions of UC theological doctrine. These make up a substantial body of material which is published in separate doctrinal texts. UC theological doctrines derive primarily from the teachings of Rev. Moon and address traditional topics of God, humanity, sin, divine providence, etc. These teachings, known as The Principle, are said to have been first systematized by Rev. Moon in the early 1950s, a point challenged by some critics alleging more original sources. Regardless of conflicting claims, however, neither an original manuscript nor a more primary text has been forthcoming, at least in English. What is available are a number of texts written by early followers as systematic formulations of Rev. Moon's teaching. In English, these texts are variously titled *Explanation of The Principle, Discourse on The Principle, The Divine Principles, Divine Principle, Divine Principle and Its Application, Outline of The Principle* and *Interpretation of the Principles*. Though varying in part, all of these texts contain four common assertions. First, they all claim The Principle to be a new revelation. A second and related assertion is that The Principle has world-transforming implications. A third common assertion relates to confessed inadequacies of individual texts to fully convey The Principle, and a fourth assertion, stemming from the third, is that more of The Principle remains to be published, or revealed.

Though all editions of The Principle have the above assertions in common, it is also the case that specific formulations have been shaped by the context within which they were written. This would include factors of environment, Church ethos and personal orientations of editors and translators. The transition, for example, from a 1950s Korean milieu to the environment of the United States has been significant as was the founding of a seminary and the convening of conferences in which theological claims have been debated and discussed. In short, the development of theological doctrine has been subject to a variety of influences although universalizing and ecumenical trends are apparent in later English editions. For example, whereas the earlier Korean-language editions posited Korean as the coming universal language, the first official English translation refers only to the necessity for the unity of languages, and the latest official edition drops the matter entirely. Similar development is apparent in attitudes expressed toward other religions, particularly Judaism and Islam as well as changes in terminology reflective of sensitivity to feminists. These changes can be viewed in one of two ways. On the one hand, they could reflect strategic concessions or abridgements and, thereby, be subject to future reversals. On the other hand, they could signify ongoing theological development fully in accord with the Church's basic teaching or Principle.

Prior to 1972, editions of The Principle in English were the work of early missionaries. These included works published by Young Oon Kim [454-62], David S.C. Kim [452-53], and Bo Hi Pak [470]. Their volumes were authoritative within their respective missionary groupings. Since 1972, the two major texts of The Principle in English have been *Divine Principle* [445-49] and *Outline of The Principle: Level Four* [468-69]. *Divine Principle* is a slightly edited translation of *Wol-li Kang-ron* [Discourse on The Principle] (Seoul, Korea: Segye Kiddokyo Tong-il Silyong Hyophoe, 1966) written by Hyo Won Eu. This translation went through five editions (three of which are reprints) between 1973-77. *Outline of the Principle: Level Four* utilizes *Wol-li Kang-ron* as a point of departure but is not a literal translation. It was written by Chung Hwan Kwak, the UC's international director of education, as the fourth in a series of lecture outlines beginning with two-hour, four-hour and six-hour lectures (the first three "levels") in 1977 [465-67]. *Divine Principle Home Study Course* [450] and *Introduction to The Principle: An Islamic Perspective* [451] also were written under the aegis of Rev. Kwak.

445. *Divine Principle.* 1st ed. Washington, D.C.: HSA-UWC, 1973. 643 pp.

446. ———. 2nd ed. Washington, D.C.: HSA-UWC, 1973. 536 pp.

447. ———. 3rd ed. Reprint. 1974, c1973.

448. ———. 4th ed. Reprint. c1973.

449. ———. 5th ed. New York: HSA-UWC, 1977, c1973.

450. *Divine Principle Home Study Course.* 6 vols. New York: HSA-UWC, 1980.

451. *Introduction to The Principle: An Islamic Perspective.* New York: HSA-UWC, 1980. 197 pp.

452. Kim, David S.C. *Individual Preparation for His Coming Kingdom: Interpretation of the Principles.* Portland, Oreg.: United Chapel of Portland, 1964. 191 pp.

453. ———. *Individual Preparation for His Coming Kingdom: Interpretation of the Principles.* Rev. ed. Portland, Oreg.: United Chapel of Portland, 1968.

454. Kim, Young Oon. *The Divine Principles.* Seoul, Korea: HSA-UWC, 1956. 184 pp.

455. ———. *The Divine Principles.* 1st ed. San Francisco: HSA-UWC, 1960. 241 pp.

456. _____. *The Divine Principles*. 2nd rev. ed. San Francisco: HSA-UWC, 1962, c1960. 216 pp.

457. _____. *The Divine Principles*. 3rd ed. San Francisco: HSA-UWC, 1963. 219 pp.

458. _____. *The Divine Principles*. 4th ed.

459. _____. *The Divine Principles*. 5th ed. Study Course.

460. _____. *The Divine Principles*. 6th ed. Study Guide. 1968.

461. _____. *The Divine Principle and Its Application*. 7th ed. Washington, D.C.: HSA-UWC, 1969. 197 pp.

462. _____. *Divine Principle and Its Application*. 8th ed. Washington, D.C.: HSA-UWC, 1972. 197 pp.

463. [Kim, Young Whi]. *The Divine Principle Study Guide*. Part I. Tarrytown, N.Y.: HSA-UWC, 1973. 199 pp.

464. _____. *The Divine Principle Study Guide*. Part II. Translated by Tadaaki Shimmyo. New York: HSA-UWC, 1975. 135 pp.

465. [Kwak, Chung Hwan]. *Divine Principle: Four Hour Lecture*. New York: HSA-UWC, 1977. 30 pp.

466. _____. *Divine Principle: Six Hour Lecture*. New York: HSA-UWC, 1977. 49 pp.

467. _____. *Divine Principle: Two Hour Lecture*. New York: HSA-UWC, 1977. 13 pp.

468. _____. *Outline of The Principle*, Level 4. New York: HSA-UWC, 1980. 214 pp.

469. _____. *Outline of The Principle*, Level 4. 2nd ed. New York: HSA-UWC, 1983. 316 pp.

470. [Pak, Bo Hi]. *Outline of Study: The Divine Principles*. Arlington, Va.: HSA-UWC, ca., 1964.

C. CHURCH PERIODICALS

Next in importance to the speeches of Rev. Moon and theological texts are Church periodicals. These are important not only as a record of activities but also as a source of UC cohesiveness and morale. Despite their documentary and communal significance, however, many of these periodicals are unknown outside the Church. Nonetheless, they constitute a bulk of primary source material that can be grouped into five major categories: 1) international missionary news magazines; 2) domestic news periodicals; 3) *ad hoc* evangelistic and local center publications; 4) "internal guidance" magazines; and 5) "alternative" publications.

The Way of the World [490], published from 1969-78, and *Today's World* [486] which succeeded it in 1980 are the UC's two main international missionary news magazines published in English. Taken together, they provide an indispensable account of international Church activities and have a number of characteristics in common. They both, for example, are relatively high budget, glossy publications which include sermons, reports from mission branches, testimonies, general news and extensive pictorials. At the same time, there are important differences. The chief one is that *The Way of the World* featured commentary on religion, culture, politics, economics and science. In addition, it was intended, at least initially, for outside distribution. *Today's World*, however, is restricted to intra-Church concerns and is internally circulated. It also includes expanded coverage of Rev. Moon, his family and Korean Church origins as well as reports from newly established missionary outposts in Africa, South America, the Middle East, Oceania and southern Asia. *New Age Frontiers* [477], although published under the auspices of the "Unified Family" for most of its run (see chap. 2, sec. A), is an important source of international UC activity during the sixties.

If there has been a trend toward internal coverage and distribution within international missionary magazines, UC domestic periodicals have moved in the opposite direction. That is, *New Hope News* [479], the American UC's major domestic news periodical during the seventies, was circulated internally while *Unification News* [489] which displaced it in 1982 is intended for an outside as well as an inside readership and contains commentary pieces on contemporary issues. Both of these domestic periodicals contain sermons as well as coverage of evangelistic campaigns, property purchases, conferences sponsored and legal battles. However, while *New Hope News* was limited to intra-Church issues, *Unification News* is oriented toward public relations with emphasis given to community service projects, defenses of religious liberty and membership testimonials.

Less important than either international or domestic news publications are *ad hoc* evangelistic and local UC periodicals. *Ad hoc* evangelistic periodicals accompanied particular "campaigns" and circulated internally. Examples are *Pioneer's Progress* [481], the *Director's Newsletter* [474], and *Witnessing News* [491]. Of these, the *Director's Newsletter* is particularly useful as it highlights behind-the-scenes administrative activities during the Church's early U.S. evangelistic crusades. Local Church periodicals frequently were published to capitalize on interest generated by evangelistic tours and to appeal to mass audiences. This was true of the *Ginseng Sun* [475] in Washington, D.C. and *The Light of Hope* [476] and *New Hope Herald* [478] in New York City. Because of financial costs as well as high transfer and turnover rates among local membership, these periodicals were short-lived. The only local UC periodical maintaining longer-term continuity was *Chicago's New Hope* [473] and, more recently, *U.C. News* [488] out of Washington, D.C.

"Internal guidance" magazines relate to issues of family life and spirituality. These include *Blessed Family* [471], *The Blessing Quarterly* [472], and *Principle Life* [482]. *The Blessing Quarterly* (1977-) is addressed to UC married couples and features sermons by Reverend Moon, articles on Church tradition, testimonies, practical guidance and "family news" including photos of new babies. *Blessed Family* (1984-), also quarterly, is less news-oriented and focuses each issue on a particular topic. *Principle Life* (1979-84) addressed issues of personal spirituality and consisted of testimonies and sermons.

Two "alternative" publications, *Our Network* [480] and *The Round Table* [484], emerged in 1984 and 1985 on the West and East coasts, respectively. Expressing varying opinions on Church policies and practices, these are independent periodicals begun by adherents as "forums for dialogue." Although there is some overlap between the two, *Our Network,* as the name implies, is primarily a support-group publication for members (and some former members) living outside Church centers. *The Round Table*, reformist in orientation, has attempted to initiate dialogue with UC leaders.

471. *Blessed Family: An International Journal for Blessed Families of the Unification Movement.* New York: HSA-UWC. Quarterly. 1984-.

472. *The Blessing Quarterly.* New York: HSA-UWC. Quarterly [irregular]. 1977-.

473. *Chicago's New Hope.* Chicago: Unification Church of Chicago. Monthly. 1972-83.

474. *Director's Newsletter.* Washington, D.C.: HSA-UWC. Biweekly [irregular]. 1972-74.

475. *The Ginseng Sun.* Washington, D.C.: HSA-UWC of Washington, D.C., 1973.

476. *The Light of Hope.* New York: Unification Church of New York. Monthly. 1974.

477. *New Age Frontiers.* Eugene, Oreg., San Francisco, and Washington, D.C.: HSA-UWC. Monthly. 1962-63, 1971-73. Published by the Unified Family. Monthly and biweekly, 1964-70.

478. *New Hope Herald.* New York: Unification Church of New York. Irregular. 1976.

479. *New Hope News.* Washington, D.C. and New York: HSA-UWC. Biweekly [irregular]. 1974-81.

480. *Our Network.* Palo Alto, Calif. Monthly. 1984-.

481. *Pioneer's Progress.* Washington, D.C.: Unification Church. Biweekly. 1972.

482. *Principle Life.* New York: HSA-UWC. Monthly. 1979-84.

483. *Providential Report.* Berkeley, Calif.: Unification Church of Northern California. Monthly. 1985-.

484. *The Round Table.* New York. Monthly. 1985-.

485. *Sunrise.* Los Angeles: Unification Church of Los Angeles. Monthly. 1977-79.

486. *Today's World.* New York: HSA-UWC. Monthly. 1980-.

487. *Truth and Love: A Newsletter for Home Members of the Unification Church.* Berkeley, Calif.: Home Church Association of Northern California. Monthly. 1981-82.

488. *U.C. News.* Washington, D.C.: Unification Church of Washington, D.C. Biweekly. 1984-.

489. *Unification News.* New York: Unification Church of America. Monthly. 1982-.

490. *The Way of the World.* Seoul, Korea and Washington, D.C.: HSA-UWC. Monthly. 1969-78.

491. *Witnessing News.* New York: HSA-UWC. Monthly. 1977-1978.

D. EDUCATIONAL MATERIALS

Educational materials published by the Church include public relations literature, works of spiritual instruction, and academic volumes. Public relations literature makes up a large bulk of this material and consists of rebuttals to outside criticism as well as attempts to portray the UC in a positive light. Works of spiritual instruction and edification, a category of material still in the process of development, include one major compilation of Church ceremonial practices, "internal guidance" lectures, hymnals and sermons. Academic volumes, generally not published directly by the UC but through its organizational affiliates, are primarily the work of Young Oon Kim.

Public relations literature is generated by the UC on an *ad hoc* basis, often to counter negative publicity, and reflects a plurality of approaches. Nonetheless, two general comments apply. First, public relations literature by no means has exhausted the Church's PR response. Published documents are only one prong of a multi-faceted network that has included PR teams and tours, public demonstrations, letter-writing campaigns, press conferences, employment of commercial advertising agencies, litigation, coalitions and alliances, academic conferences and the founding of daily newspapers. Second, in terms of content, UC public relations literature constitutes a distinct genre distinguished primarily by efforts to set the Church within a tradition of persecuted religious minorities.

Again, though public relations literature has not exhausted the Church's PR response, it does convey a sense of the UC's interaction with various sectors of the American public. In general, this interaction has produced strain on religious, political, economic and organizational grounds. Public relations literature represents the Church's attempt to address these strains. "Have Christians Forsaken the Words of Jesus" [497], for example, was an early effort to counter fundamentalist Christian opposition during evangelistic speaking tours while *The Unification Church: As Others See Us* [502], a compilation of testimonials to the UC by civic officials, was published in response to the Immigration and Naturalization Service's decision not to grant missionary visas to UC foreign nationals. Allegations of UC overseas political connections and, especially, a United States House of Representatives Subcommittee's inclusion of the Church in its "Koreagate" investigation of 1976-78 led to a plethora of UC public relations material. The most important are *Truth is My Sword* [516], a reprint of Col. Bo Hi Pak's testimony before the House Subcommittee, and *Our Response* [492], a point-by-point refutation of the Subcommittee's final report. Widespread reaction to UC street fundraising precipitated the "Unification Church National Policy of Fundraising" [528] while issues of organizational recruitment and lifestyle are addressed in a number of official statements, notably *The Reverend Sun Myung Moon and His Church: Excerpts From Letters of Parents and Friends* [521], *Statement of the Unification Church on the Guyana Tragedy* [524] and *The Truth About Reverend Sun Myung Moon* [525]. Although not precisely fitting any of the above-listed categories, Rev.

Moon's indictment, conviction, appeals and imprisonment on tax evasion charges sparked the Church's most sustained public relations offensive. However, besides "Reverend Moon: A Vindication for Justice" [519] and a number of ads purchased in major U.S. newspapers, the bulk of this literature was channeled through UC periodicals, notably *Unification News* [489], and through separately incorporated organizations affiliated with or funded by the Church.

Sermonic materials and academic volumes are less immediately prominent than public relations literature. There are several reasons for this. First, works of spiritual instruction (sermons and the like) commonly are incorporated within Church periodicals and, therefore, need not be published separately. Second, and more important, much of the spiritual guidance within the Church is as yet transmitted orally. With regard to academic works, as stated, most have not been published by the Church directly but through organizational affiliates. Nonetheless, both of these groupings contain significant material.

The most comprehensive single work of spiritual instruction is Chung Hwan Kwak's *The Tradition, Book One* [514]. A compilation of "ceremonial traditions associated with the Unification Church's life of faith" (ix), the volume supplies historical background on Church practices as well as illustrated guidelines for conducting UC rituals and ceremonies. In addition to this work, the Church has begun publishing sermons and "internal guidance" lectures by Church elders in book-length form. Examples are Won Pil Kim's *Father's Course and Our Life of Faith* [503], Young Whi Kim's *Guidance For Heavenly Tradition* [510], and Paul Werner's *From Heaven Down to Earth* [530]. John A. Sonneborn's *Unification Theology and Christian Tradition* [523], the first of a projected "Question and Answer Series," also has been published. Finally, the Church publishes a variety of hymnals and song books. *Holy Songs* [499], a collection of hymns composed by Rev. Moon and early Church followers, is the most important of these. A useful commentary, detailing specifics of composition, is *Holy Songs: Their Meanings and Historical Backgrounds* [511].

Academic works published by the Church are primarily those of Young Oon Kim, currently Professor of Theology at the Unification Theological Seminary. Her most important Church-published work is *Unification Theology* [509], a commentary on The Principle. Apologetic in orientation, this volume details "how often this new Korean theology is confirmed by professional theologians in the West" (iv). Other of her Church-published works include *An Introduction to Theology* [507] and *The Types of Modern Theology* [508].

492. Ad Hoc Committee of Members of the Unification Church. *Our Response: To the Report on October 31, 1978 on the Investigation of Korean-American Relations Regarding Reverend Sun Myung Moon and Members of the Unification Church*. New York: HSA-UWC, 1979. 279 pp.

493. *Analysis of the Present Day.* Washington, D.C.: HSA-UWC, 1973. 29 pp.

494. *Brainwashing, Deprogramming and the Unification Church Controversy.* New York: HSA-UWC, ca., 1976. 6 pp.

495. Durst, Mose. *Examining New Religious Movements.* New York: Unification Church of America, 1982. 3 pp.

496. _____.*Quality of Spiritual Life.* New York: HSA-UWC, 1980. 13 pp.

497. *Have Christians Forsaken the Words of Jesus?* New York: HSA-UWC, ca., 1974. 1 p.

498. *Help ... We are Being Persecuted.* Berkeley, Calif.: The Unification Church of Northern California, ca., 1977. 10 pp.

499. *Holy Songs.* Washington, DC: HSA-UWC, 1975. 58 pp.

500. *Humanitarian and Educational Projects Founded through the Vision of Reverend Sun Myung Moon.* New York: Public Affairs Department, Unification Church of America, 1983. 41 pp.

501. Jones, W. Farley. *A New Prophet for a New Age.* Washington, D.C.: The Unification Church, 1970. 15 pp.

502. _____, ed. *The Unification Church: As Others See Us.* Washington, D.C.: HSA-UWC, 1974. 156 pp.

503. Kim, Won Pil. *Father's Course and Our Life of Faith.* London, England: HSA-UWC, 1982. 149 pp.

504. _____. "Father's Testimony." New York: HSA-UWC, April 2, 1978. 21 pp.

505. _____. "How to Practice Father's Instruction on Home Church." New York: HSA-UWC, n.d. 11 pp.

506. Kim, Young Oon. *For God's Sake.* Washington, D.C.: The Unification Church, 1972. 34 pp.

507. _____. *An Introduction to Theology.* New York: HSA-UWC, 1983. 186 pp.

508. _____. *The Types of Modern Theology.* New York: HSA-UWC, 1983. 296 pp.

509. _____. *Unification Theology.* New York: HSA-UWC, 1980. 294 pp.

510. Kim, Young Whi. *Guidance for Heavenly Tradition.* London, England: HSA-UWC, 1984. 296 pp.

511. Kobayashi, Yoko, and Kathy Goldman Novalis, eds. *Holy Songs: Their Meanings and Historical Backgrounds.* Barrytown, N.Y.: Unification Church International Training Center, 1975. 43 pp.

512. Kwak, Chung Hwan. "The Blessing." New York: HSA-UWC, 1978. 28 pp.

513. _____. "The Meaning of Love." New York: HSA-UWC, 1978. 12 pp.

514. _____. *The Tradition, Book One.* New York: HSA-UWC, 1985. 225 pp.

515. *Ocean Church Training Program.* New York: Unification Church of America, n.d. 10 pp.

516. Pak, Bo Hi. *Truth Is My Sword: Testimony at the Korea Hearings, U.S. Congress.* New York: Unification Church of America, 1978. 68 pp.

517. *People Serving People: Projects of Reverend Sun Myung Moon and the Unification Movement.* New York: HSA-UWC, 1985. 54 pp.

518. *Religious Liberty and the Reverend Sun Myung Moon.* New York: The Unification Church of America, 1982.

519. *Reverend Moon: A Vindication for Justice.* New York: HSA-UWC, 1981. 16 pp.

520. *Reverend Sun Myung Moon.* Washington, D.C.: Unification Church, n.d. 28 pp.

521. *The Reverend Sun Myung Moon and His Church: Excerpts from Letters of Parents and Friends.* New York: HSA-UWC, 1976. 1 p.

522. *Reverend Sun Myung Moon and the Unification Church.* New York: Unification Church in America, n.d. 26 pp.

523. Sonneborn, John A. *Christian Tradition and Unification Theology.* Question and Answer Series, no. 1. New York: HSA-UWC, 1985. 79 pp.

524. *Statement of the Unification Church on the Guyana Tragedy.* New York: HSA-UWC, 1978. 3 pp.

525. *The Truth about the Reverend Sun Myung Moon: An Official Statement by the Unification Church of America.* New York: HSA-UWC, 1976. 1 p.

526. *21 Commonly Asked Questions about the Unification Church.* N.p.: The Unification Church of America, 1975. 10 pp.

527. *The Unification Church and the Ocean.* New York: The Unification Church of America, 1981.

528. "The Unification Church National Policy of Fundraising." Revised. New York: HSA-UWC, 1977. 2 pp.

529. *The Unification Church: People of the Quest.* New York: HSA-UWC, 1983. 39 pp.

530. Werner, Paul. *From Heaven Down to Earth.* Toronto, Canada: HSA-UWC, 1985. 377 pp.

531. *Word and Deed: The Unification Movement.* Rev. ed. New York: HSA Publications, 1985. 31 pp.

II.

PUBLICATIONS OF ORGANIZATIONAL AFFILIATES

A. EVANGELISTIC ASSOCIATIONS

Of those organizations affiliated with the Church, evangelistic affiliates have been the most volatile. The major reason for this is that these organizations are virtually interchangeable with the UC. That is, with few exceptions, membership in evangelistic affiliates has meant membership in the Church. Thus, rather than functioning as a buffer between the UC and American society, UC evangelistic organizations have heightened already existing tensions. Outside the Church, the virtual identification of separately incorporated evangelistic affiliates with the UC has led to charges of recruitment under false pretenses. From within, the same identification has provoked dissension over standards of belief and practice. To highlight the literature produced by evangelistic organizations, they may be grouped into three categories: 1) pre-1972 missionary organizations; 2) evangelistic affiliates established after 1972; and 3) student groups.

Four important missionary organizations predated Reverend Moon's more-or-less permanent 1972 arrival in the United States. These were the "Unified Family" led by Young Oon Kim; "United Faith, Inc." led by David S.C. Kim; the "International Re-Educational Foundation" (IRF) led by Sang Ik Choi; and the "Oakland Family," later known as "New Education Development Systems, Inc." (NEDS) and as the "Creative Community Project" (CCP) led by Onni and Mose Durst. In addition, Colonel Bo Hi Pak led a Washington, D.C.-based association that merged with Young Oon Kim's Unified Family in 1965. These organizations, all evangelistic in orientation, were incorporated separately due to differing missionary styles, early disagreements, and the sheer size of the United States. Continued jurisdictional disputes, tactical alliances and general grievances, however, hindered organizational consolidation during the sixties and early seventies.

Literature produced by these communities primarily included theological texts and organizational newsletters. The Unified Family, formally incorporated as the Holy Spirit Association for the Unification of World Christianity, published eight editions of Young Oon Kim's *The Divine Principles,* later *The Divine Principle and Its Application* [455-62] from 1960-72. It also published a monthly newsletter, *New Age Frontiers* [477] which is the best single source in English of UC activities during the sixties. United Faith, Inc. published two editions of *Individual Preparation for His Coming Kingdom: Interpretation of the Principles* [452-53] written by David S.C. Kim, as well as an important newsletter, *United Temple Bulletin* [565]. The International Re-Education Foundation published *The Principles of*

Education [533] originally written by Sang Ik Choi in Japan but utilized by IRF in San Francisco during the late sixties. This adaptation (not translation) of The Principle caused dissension within the Church as did the IRF community style as chronicled in the *Epoch Maker* [551] and *The Universal Voice* [566].

The Oakland Family, which emerged out of IRF, perpetuated this dissension and is a unique case. On the one hand, it was the only one of the missionary groupings to survive the early seventies. On the other hand, it has left a meager documentary record. The major reason for this is that the Oakland Family was able to draw on the resources of both IRF and the emerging national Church. Its evangelistic workshops, for example, combined introductory sessions based on Sang Ik Choi's *Principles of Education* and an advanced session teaching the newly translated *Divine Principle*. Similarly, though initiating several short-lived newsletters, the Oakland Family mainly relied on UC national publications. While this approach freed organizational energies from documentary responsibilities, it also created problems. The public at large charged that converts were being led into the Church deceptively. Those inside, but not part of the Oakland Family, questioned whether they were being led into the Church at all. NEDS' own dictum that it was "affiliated with, but independent of, the Unification Church" satisfied neither group of critics. As a result, the Oakland Family was a major locus of strain throughout the seventies, a situation, however, that has been largely resolved since Mose Durst was appointed president of the American Unification Church in 1980.

The most important evangelistic organizations established after 1972 were the International One World Crusade (IOWC) and the Barrytown Training Program. The IOWC, originally the One World Crusade (OWC), was set up in 1972 and consisted of mobile teams that supported UC evangelistic crusades. By stressing non-sectarian issues such as patriotism, morality and international fellowship, the IOWC sought to bridge gaps between the UC and American culture and at the same time gain a hearing for the Church's theological claims. In general, the IOWC was successful, winning numerous civic testimonials and a stream of new converts. Following the cessation of major evangelistic tours in 1976, American IOWCs faded but were reinstated in 1983 when UC wives were asked to join mobile units. These proliferated to more than fifty teams by the end of that year.

The IOWC produced two important works. First was a two-volume *Day of Hope in Review* [535-36] that chronicled Reverend Moon's early American ministry. Compiled by David S.C. Kim, these massive limited-edition folios contain innumerable photographs, newspaper clippings (pro and con) and reproductions of memorabilia as well as editorial introductions and excerpts from Rev. Moon's speeches. A third volume, not yet released, carries the account forward from 1975. The second important IOWC-published work was Yo Han Lee's *Faith and Life* [538], a three-volume set of lectures. Although delivered in Japan and translated into English, these are helpful in understanding the IOWC ethos and spirituality.

The Barrytown Training Program, unlike the IOWC, moved in a sectarian direction. Originally set up in 1975 for the first American wave of UC foreign missionaries, the program was commissioned to re-train UC domestic missionaries as well and did so in successive four-month (120-day) training sessions. These, however, were evangelistic and public relation disasters. On the one hand, with many of their best leaders overseas, UC domestic "pioneers" faltered badly. On the other hand, extra-doctrinal interpretations (including a doctrine of "heavenly deception") alleged to be contained in program director Ken Sudo's *120-Day Lectures* [544] were later repudiated by the Church [912]. This manual, however, was widely-used by UC foreign and domestic missionaries in the mid-seventies. The other important publication of the Barrytown Training Program was *Pioneer News* [563], a newsletter that included sermons, exhortations, testimonies and news from the field.

Student groups make up a final category of evangelistic affiliates. While Unified Students, Students for World Unification (SWU), Students for New Age Unification (SNAU) and Students for an Ethical Society (SES) were set up by missionary groups, the only student affiliate maintaining continuity and producing a body of literature is the Collegiate Association for the Research of Principles (CARP). Originally founded in the Orient, CARP USA was organized in 1973 but remained relatively inactive until the late seventies when the UC committed resources and personnel toward its development. During the early eighties, CARP has been active on major college campuses, most prominently in demonstrations against the USSR. CARP campus publications include *Global Insight* [553], the *World Student Times* [568], and the *World University Times* [569]. Internally-circulated publications include *CARP Monthly* [550], *Front Line* [552], *New Pioneer* [560] and *Pioneer* [562].

Monographs

532. *Bicentennial God Bless America Festival Statement of Purpose.* New York: Bicentennial God Bless America Committee, 1976, 16 pp.

533. Choi, Sang Ik. *The Principles of Education.* 2 vols. San Francisco: Re-Education Foundation, 1969.

534. Cowin, James Y. *El Salvador: The Real Story.* New York: CARP Committee to Save El Salvador, April 20, 1981. 26 pp.

535. Kim, David S.C. *Day of Hope in Review.* Part I. Tarrytown, N.Y.: IOWC, 1974. 412 pp.

536. _____. *Day of Hope in Review.* Part II. Tarrytown, N.Y.: IOWC, 1975. 951 pp.

*   _____. *Individual Preparation For His Coming Kingdom-Interpretation of the Principles.* 2 eds. Cited above as items 452-53.

*   Kim, Young Oon. *The Divine Principles.* 8 eds. Cited above as items 455-62.

537.   Lawson, Josie. *Unificationism as a Response to Modernity.* CARP Contemporary Issues Series 1. N.p., n.d. 12 pp.

538.   Lee, Yo Han. *Faith and Life.* 3 vols. N.p.: IOWC, 1977.

539.   *Prospectus for the Establishment of the International Ideal City under the Re-Education Movement.* San Francisco: Re-Education Center, 1970. 11 pp.

540.   *Prospectus for the Establishment of the International Pioneer Academy.* San Francisco: International Re-Education Foundation, 1971. 6 pp.

541.   *Prospectus for the Establishment of the International Re-Education Foundation.* San Francisco: International Re-Education Foundation, n.d. 6 pp.

542.   Seuk, Joon Ho. *Unificationism.* New York: CARP, 1983. 10 pp.

543.   [Seuk, Joon Ho]. *Wonhwa-Do: The Unified Martial Art.* Edited by Gerry Servito. New York: CARP, 1984. 120 pp.

544.   Sudo, Ken. *120-Day Lectures.* Barrytown, N.Y.: Barrytown Publication Department, 1975. 236 pp.

545.   _____. *Pioneer Manual (Part I).* Barrytown, N.Y.: American Pioneer Program (Special Projects and Research Department), June 1, 1976. 71 pp.

546.   _____. *Pioneer Witnessing Approach Book.* Barrytown, N.Y.: American Pioneer Program, 1975. 22 pp.

547.   _____. *21-Day Manual.* Barrytown, N.Y.: American Pioneer Program, December, 1975.

548.   *The Unified Family Center Guide.* Washington, D.C.: The Unified Family 1968. 30 pp.

Periodicals

549. *The Bridge Builder.* San Francisco: Creative Community Project.
     Biweekly, 1975.

550. *CARP Monthly.* New York: CARP. Monthly. 1980-82.

551. *Epoch Maker.* San Francisco: Re-Education Center and International
     Re-Education Foundation. Monthly. 1969-72.

552. *Front Line.* New York: CARP. Quarterly [irregular]. 1984-.

553. *Global Insight.* Washington, D.C.: CARP. Monthly. 1982-83.

554. *God Bless America Festival News.* Washington, D.C.: God Bless
     America Committee. 1 issue. 1976.

555. *God Bless America News.* New York: Bicentennial God Bless
     America Committee. 4 issues. 1976.

556. *International Chinese Association Newsletter.* New York: International
     Chinese Association. Quarterly [irregular]. 1984-.

557. *Lightning Flashes: A Bulletin for Members of the Unified Family in
     the United States.* Washington, D.C.: Unified Family. Irregular.
     1964-69.

558. *NED's News.* Berkeley, Calif.: New Education Development.
     Monthly. 1974-75.

*   *New Age Frontiers.* Cited above as item 477.

559. *New Perspectives.* New York: CARP. 1 issue. 1984.

560. *New Pioneer.* New York: CARP. Bimonthly. 1983-.

561. *Pacific Student Times.* San Francisco: CARP. Biweekly. 1978-79.

562. *Pioneer.* Washington, D.C.: CARP. Monthly. 1982.

563. *Pioneer News.* Barrytown, N.Y.: Pioneer Program Office. Irregular.
     1975-76.

564. *The Positive Voice.* Berkeley, Calif.: New Education Development.
     Monthly. 1978.

565. *United Temple Bulletin.* Portland, Oreg.: United Faith Chapel and
     United Faith. Monthly. 1961-72.

566. *The Universal Voice.* San Francisco: Re-Education Center and
     International Re-Education Foundation. Monthly. 1968-73.

567. *Wonhwa-Do Newsletter.* New York: International Wonhwa-Do Association. Quarterly. 1984-.

568. *World Student Times.* New York: CARP. Monthly and biweekly [irregular]. 1973-84.

569. *World University Times.* New York: CARP. Monthly and biweekly [irregular]. 1984-.

570. *YES* [newsletter]. New York: Youth for an Ethical Society. Quarterly [irregular]. 1985-.

B. ANTI-COMMUNIST FOUNDATIONS

UC anti-communist affiliates derive in part from the Church's Korean origins and have been set up in accordance with the its call for "a worldwide ideological offensive to counter the global threat of communism." These affiliates, incorporated as non-profit educational and research foundations, have organized conferences, sponsored seminars and issued publications in efforts to educate and influence policy-makers in the U.S. and elsewhere. At the same time, the Church has underwritten a number of alliances, coalitions and committees designed to combat a perceived erosion of civil and religious liberties in communist nations and in the West. These organizations also have been utilized to defend the UC.

The Freedom Leadership Foundation (FLF) was the UC's chief anti-communist affiliate during the seventies. It was set up in 1969 as the American branch of the International Federation for Victory over Communism (IFVOC) previously organized by the UC in Japan and Korea. Although FLF supported some lobbying efforts through *ad hoc* coalitions and committees (and thereby did not violate its tax-exempt status), its primary thrust was ideological. FLF, for example, published Sang Hun Lee's *Communism: A Critique and Counterproposal* [578] which became a standard UC text. This volume, a translation of an earlier version in Korean, criticizes Marxist theories of value, dialectics and history. It also elaborates a counterproposal based on UC doctrines. FLF, itself, attempted to cultivate allies and influence public opinion. Its chief vehicle to do so was *The Rising Tide* [599]. Billed as "America's fastest growing freedom newspaper," *The Rising Tide* maintained 7-8,000 biweekly press runs and occasional runs of 60-80,000 on issues deemed crucial. With news, commentary and theoretical critiques of Marxist-Leninism, it is the best single source for understanding the UC's political orientation during the seventies. Other FLF publications included *Korea: Vortex of Global Confrontation* [585] and *Communism: Promise and Practice* [591].

CAUSA International and the CAUSA Institute, an interdisciplinary research and teaching center, displaced FLF as the UC's major anti-communist affiliates during the eighties. Under the leadership of Bo Hi Pak, CAUSA (from the Latin word for "cause") has attained widespread visibility due to its access to high-ranking government officials in several Latin American countries, its alleged monetary contributions to conservative political-action organizations and its well-attended seminars in the United States. These latter conferences featured multi-media presentations of material subsequently published as the *CAUSA Lecture Manual* [582] and *Introduction to the CAUSA Worldview* [583]. Essentially updated and more fully documented versions of Sang Hun Lee's work, these promulgate "Godism" as an alternative to communism and to "confusion in the Western system of values." Additionally, CAUSA, in conjunction with its Center for International Security (CIS) and International Security Council (ISC), has sponsored seminars on global trouble spots. Proceedings from these seminars are published in hard-cover and booklet form. See the *CAUSA* [593] and *CAUSA USA Report* [595] for overviews of activities.

Related to it's anti-communist critique, the UC has underwritten a number of alliances, coalitions and committees designed to combat a perceived worldwide erosion of civil and religious liberties. These have included the American Committee for Human Rights of Japanese Wives of North Korean Repatriates, the International Committee Against Racial and Religious Intolerance, Minority Alliance International, the Committee to Defend the U.S. Constitution, and the Coalition for Religious Freedom. Of these, the Coalition for Religious Freedom generated the most publicity. Its activities, which included strong support for Rev. Moon in his tax case, are covered in *Religious Freedom Alert* [597].

Monographs

571. *CAUSA Manifesto*. New York: CAUSA International, n.d. 13 pp.

572. *The Geopolitics of Southwestern Africa*. CAUSA International Seminar Proceedings. New York: CAUSA International, 1984. 18 pp.

573. *First Amendment/Symposium on Religious Liberty*. Washington, D.C.: Committee to Defend the First Amendment Research Institute, 1979. 87 pp.

574. *The Foundation for Peace*. New York: CAUSA International, 1983. 24 pp.

575. Henze, Paul, Assad Homayoun, and Martin Sicker. *The Geopolitics of South Arabia and the Horn of Africa*. CAUSA International, International Security Council Seminar. New York: CAUSA International, 1985. 25 pp.

576. *If I Had Wings Like a Bird I Would Fly Across the Sea*. Washington, D.C.: The American Committee for Human Rights of Japanese Wives of North Korean Repatriates, 1974. 167 pp.

577. Kim, David S.C. *Victory over Communism and the Role of Religion*. New York: Vantage Press, 1972. 166 pp.

578. Lee, Sang Hun. *Communism: A Critique and Counterproposal*. Washington, D.C.: Freedom Leadership Foundation, 1973. 240 pp.

579. _____. *Communism: A New Critique and Counterproposal, Questions and Answers*. Washington, D.C.: Freedom Leadership Foundation, 1975. 51 pp.

580. *Main VOC Activities 1976.* Seoul, Korea: International Federation for Victory over Communism, 1976. 82 pp.

581. *Nuclear Balance: Challenge and Response.* CAUSA International Seminar Proceedings. New York: CAUSA International, 1985. 33 pp.

582. [Pak, Bo Hi, Thomas Ward, and William Lay.] *CAUSA Lecture Manual.* New York: CAUSA Institute, 1985. 264 pp.

583. ———. *Introduction to the CAUSA Worldview.* New York: CAUSA International, 1985. 405 pp.

584. *Proceedings of the 1st CAUSA International Pan-American Convention.* New York: CAUSA International, 1984. 35 pp.

585. Salonen, Neil A. *Korea: Vortex of Global Confrontation.* Washington, D.C.: Freedom Leadership Foundation, 1975. 133 pp.

586. *The Soviet Challenge in Central America and the Caribbean.* CAUSA Position Paper No. 2. New York: CAUSA International, 1985. 16 pp.

587. *The Soviet Union Challenge in East Asia.* CAUSA Position Paper No. 1. New York: CAUSA International, 1984. 17 pp.

588. *The Soviet Union and the Middle East.* Center for International Security and CAUSA International Seminar. New York: CAUSA Publications, 1984. 31 pp.

589. *Sun Myung Moon: His Work and His Vision* (Su Obra y Su Vision). New York: CAUSA International, 1981. 87 pp.

590. *Victory for Freedom: Portrait of a Movement for Freedom.* Washington, D.C.: Committee to Defend the Constitution, 1985. 143 pp.

591. Wilson, Andrew M. *Communism: Promise and Practice.* Washington, D.C.: Freedom Leadership Foundation, 1975. 137 pp.

592. *Women's VOC Activities.* Seoul, Korea: International Women's Federation for Victory over Communism, 1976. 50 pp.

Periodicals

593. *CAUSA.* New York: CAUSA Institute. Quarterly. 1981-.

594. *CAUSA International Military Alliance* [newsletter]. New York: CAUSA. Quarterly [irregular]. 1985-.

595. *CAUSA USA Report.* Washington, D.C.: CAUSA USA. Monthly.
    1984-.

596. *The ICARRI Report.* Jamaica, N.Y.: International Committee against
    Racial and Religious Intolerance. Irregular. 1982-84.

597. *Religious Freedom Alert.* Washington, D.C.: Coalition for Religious
    Freedom. Monthly. 1984-.

598. *The Religious Freedom Record.* Washington, D.C.: Ad Hoc
    Committee for Religious Freedom. Irregular. 1984.

599. *The Rising Tide.* Washington, D.C.: Freedom Leadership Foundation.
    Biweekly. 1971-83.

600. *The Weekly Computer Newsletter.* New York: CAUSA International.
    Weekly. 1985.

C. ACADEMIC SOCIETIES

Academic, scientific and cultural organizations affiliated with the Church stem from its anti-communist affiliates. That is, while UC anti-communist affiliates seek to combat communism, academic, scientific, and cultural affiliates embody a counterproposal. In general, this counterproposal has meant two things. First, it has meant the establishment and sponsorship of organizations promoting internationalist, multi-disciplinary and generally theistic approaches to the crises of contemporary civilization. Second, it has meant the development of a philosophical system not only as an alternative to Marxist-Leninism but also as the ideological basis for UC monetary support of ongoing conferences and symposia, publishing concerns, academic exchanges, research funding, good-will tours, public forums and academic prizes.

The International Cultural Foundation (ICF) is the umbrella organization for UC affiliates addressing problems of modern society. Set up in Japan in 1968 to promote "academic, scientific, and cultural exchange among the countries of the world," ICF funds a number of activities and organizations. The most important are the International Conference on the Unity of the Sciences (ICUS), the Professors World Peace Academy (PWPA), the Washington Institute for Values in Public Policy (WI), and Paragon House Publishers (PHP).

ICUS, first convened in 1972, attracts scientists and scholars to annual meetings on science and "absolute" values. Although these gatherings have been controversial and large, the current trend is away from larger meetings and toward smaller conferences with more focused attention given to committee work and publications. Papers and proceedings of meetings are published under such titles as *Absolute Values and the New Cultural Revolution* [602-3], *Absolute Values and the Search for the Peace of Mankind* [604], *The Centrality of Science and Absolute Values* [607], *Modern Science and Moral Values* [647], and *The Responsibility of the Academic Community in the Search for Absolute Values* [655]. These volumes include more than twelve titles in all.

PWPA, founded in 1973 but not organized in the United States until 1979, is an international association of scholars pursuing a broad range of "peace" studies. Its most important single publication is the *International Journal on World Peace* [688]. Including articles, often accompanied by opposing viewpoints and rejoiners, summaries of peace-related news and book reviews, the journal is published quarterly out of New York. In addition to publications generated by PWPA-USA, PWPA national affiliates publish materials in English. PWPA-Japan has been the most active, publishing a journal, *The Academician* [685], monographs such as *Challenging the Future* [608] and project reports [623]. Also prominent are published proceedings of the International Conference on World Peace

(ICWP), sponsored on a rotating basis by PWPA chapters in Korea, Nationalist China and Japan since 1974.

The Washington Institute for Values in Public Policy was set up in 1983 by a group of academics associated with PWPA-USA. Organized to offer "nonpartisan analyses exploring ethical values underlying public policy issues," the Institute sponsors research and conferences on nuclear energy policy, aggression and war, East-West relations, arts and humanities and foreign affairs. Published monographs include *Central America in Crisis: A Policy for Action* [606], *One Nation...Indivisible? The English Language Amendment* [620], *Global Policy: The Challenge of the 80's* [632], and *Reflections on Religion and Public Policy* [663]. The Institute also publishes regular "white paper reports" on a variety of topics.

Activities of ICUS, PWPA and the Washington Institute are reported on in the quarterly *ICF Report* [687]. Additionally, Paragon House Publishers (PHP) was organized in 1982 as an outgrowth of ICF. Books authored in connection with ICF-related organizations now are published by Paragon House as imprint series, i.e., ICUS Books, PWPA Books, Washington Institute Books. Paragon also publishes a general line of fiction, criticism and scholarly works as well as New ERA Books, an imprint of the New Ecumenical Research Association (see chap. 2, sec. D).

The key UC affiliate developing a philosophical orientation to counter Marxist theory and to provide the ideological foundation for UC support of ICF is the Unification Thought Institute (UTI). With branches in Seoul, Tokyo, and New York, UTI has pursued these dual objectives primarily through publication of Sang Hun Lee's *Unification Thought* [639], later updated as *Explaining Unification Thought* [638]. Although these volumes have not circulated widely, if at all, outside the Church, they argue for a final synthesis of all sciences and philosophies under the "Unification Principle" as the basis for a new world order. The volumes, themselves, include chapters on Ontology, Original Human Nature, Epistemology, Axiology, Ethics, History, Logic, Education, Art and Methodology. These topics and others are addressed in the *Unification Thought Quarterly* [689]. An early sounding board for Unification Thought was the New World Forum organized in 1975 as an outgrowth of the UC's United Nations mission. Its monthly journal, *Unified World* [690], included excerpts from *Unification Thought* and articles from the staff of UTI.

Monographs

601. *Absolute Values and the Creation of the New World.* Proceedings of the 11th International Conference on the Unity of the Sciences. 2 vols. New York: International Cultural Foundation, 1983. 1487 pp.

602. *Absolute Values and the New Cultural Revolution.* A Commemorative
    Volume of the 12th International Conference on the Unity of the
    Sciences. New York: ICUS Books, 1984. 284 pp.

603. *Absolute Values and the New Cultural Revolution.* A Commemorative
    Volume of the 13th International Conference on the Unity of the
    Sciences. New York: ICUS Books, 1985. 377 pp.

604. *Absolute Values and the Search for the Peace of Mankind.* Proceedings
    of the 9th International Conference on the Unity of the Sciences. 2
    vols. New York: International Cultural Foundation, 1981. 1201
    pp.

605. Celmina, Helene. *Women in Soviet Prisons.* New York: Paragon
    House, 1985.

606. *Central America in Crisis: A Program for Action.* Washington, D.C.:
    Washington Institute for Values in Public Policy, 1982. 295 pp.

607. *The Centrality of Science and Absolute Values.* 2 vols. Proceedings of
    the 4th International Conference on the Unity of the Sciences.
    Tarrytown, N.Y.: International Cultural Foundation, 1975. 1345
    pp.

608. *Challenging the Future: Thoughts and Actions of PWPA-Japan.*
    Tokyo, Japan: Professors World Peace Academy of Japan, 1982.
    112 pp.

609. Cline, Ray S. "Domestic Society: First and Fourth Amendments."
    White Paper Report. Washington, D.C.: Washington Institute for
    Values in Public Policy, 1985. 11 pp.

610. Comfort, Alex. *Reality and Empathy: Physics, Mind and Science in
    the 21st Century.* New York: Paragon House, 1985. 272 pp.

611. Dougherty, Jude. *The Good Life and Its Pursuit.* New York: Paragon
    House, 1984. 296 pp.

612. Eccles, John, ed. *Mind and Brain: The Many-Faceted Problem.* New
    York: Paragon House, 1982.

613. *Education, Culture, and Development in Africa.* Proceedings of the 1st
    Seminar of the PWPA of English Speaking West Africa. New
    York: Professors World Peace Academy, 1985. 109 pp.

614. *Emerging Asia-The Role of Japan.* Proceedings of the 11th
    International Conference on World Peace. Tokyo: Professors
    World Peace Academy, 1983. 307 pp.

615. *Future Aspects of Asia in the Changing World.* Proceedings of the 4th International Conference on World Peace. Seoul, Korea: Professors World Peace Academy, 1976. 201 pp.

616. Gold, Philip. *Evasions: The American Way of Military Service.* New York: Paragon House, 1985. 188 pp.

617. Haag, Ernest van den. "Must the American Criminal Justice System Be Impotent?" *White Paper Report.* Washington, D.C.: Washington Institute for Values in Public Policy, 1985. 15 pp.

618. Hartshorne, Charles. *Creativity in American Philosophy.* New York: Paragon House, 1985. 299 pp.

619. Haskell, Edward, ed. *Moral Orientation of the Sciences.* Proceedings of the 1st International Conference on Unified Science. N.p., 1974.

620. Hayakawa, S.I. *One Nation...Indivisible? The English Language Amendment.* Washington, D.C.: Washington Institute for Values in Public Policy, 1985. 19 pp.

621. *ICUS Into the 80's.* New York: International Cultural Foundation Press, 1980. 28 pp.

622. *Interdisciplinary Approaches to Peace.* Canberra, Australia: Professors World Peace Academy, 1983. 131 pp.

623. *International Highway.* Japan-Korea Tunnel Project 1st Report. Tokyo, Japan: PWPA International Highway Research Center, 1982. 16 pp.

624. Jain, Girilal. *Indo-U.S. Relations and Rajiv Gandhi's India.* Washington, D.C.: Washington Institute for Values in Public Policy, 1985. 34 pp.

625. Jiminez, Juan Ramon. *Platero and I.* New York: Paragon House, 1985. 162 pp.

626. _____. *Stories of Life and Death.* New York: Paragon House, 1985. 176 pp.

627. Kaplan, Morton A. "Ethics of Nuclear Strategy." *White Paper Report.* Washington, D.C.: Washington Institute for Values in Public Policy, 1984. 11 pp.

628. _____. *A Proposal to End the Danger of War in Europe.* Washington, D.C.: Washington Institute for Values in Public Policy, 1982. 18 pp.

629. _____. *Science, Language and the Human Condition.* New York: Paragon House, 1984. 394 pp.

630. _____. *United States Foreign Policy and the China Problem.* New York: International Cultural Foundation, 1982. 31 pp.

631. _____, ed. *Global Policy: The Challenge of the 80's.* From the Proceedings of the First Annual Conference of PWPA-USA, 1981. New York: PWPA-USA, 1982. 51 pp.

632. _____. *Global Policy: The Challenge of the 80's.* Washington, D.C.: Washington Institute for Values in Public Policy, 1982. 272 pp.

633. Kataoka, Tetsuya. *Japan's Defense Non-Buildup: What Went Wrong?* Washington, D.C.: Washington Institute for Values in Public Policy, 1985. 28 pp.

634. *Korea: A Model of a Semi-Developed Country.* Proceedings of the 9th International Conference on World Peace. Seoul, Korea: Professors World Peace Academy, 1980. 612 pp.

635. Kurland, Philip B. "The Constitutional Impact on Public Policy: From the Warren to the Burger Court and Beyond." *White Paper Report.* Washington, D.C.: Washington Institute for Values in Public Policy, 1984. 21 pp.

636. Lawrence, Richard, and Gordon Summer. *Challenge to U.S. Intelligence Capabilities in Central America.* Washington, D.C.: Washington Institute for Values in Public Policy, 1985. 36 pp.

637. Lee, Sang Hun. *The End of Communism.* New York: Unification Thought Institute, 1985. 459 pp.

638. _____. *Explaining Unification Thought.* New York: Unification Thought Institute, 1981. 357 pp.

639. _____. *Unification Thought.* New York: Unification Thought Institute, 1973. 300 pp.

640. _____. *Unification Thought Study Guide.* New York: Unification Thought Institute, 1974. 59 pp.

641. _____. *Unification Thought: A New Philosophy.* San Francisco: Unification Thought Institute, 1973. 26 pp.

642. _____. *The Way to Happiness: An Abstract of Unification Thought.* New York: Unification Thought Institute, 1975.

643. Li, Jeanne Tchong Koei, ed. *Asian Regional Security and the Free World.* Taipei, Taiwan: Pacific Cultural Foundation, 1978. 226 pp.

644. Lincoln, Victoria. *Theresa: A Woman.* New York: Paragon House, 1985. 440 pp.

645. Long, Eugene T. *Existence, Being and God: An Introduction to the Philosophy of John Maquarrie.* New York: Paragon House, 1985. 144 pp.

646. Matsushita, Masatoshi, ed. *Strategy for Peace.* Proceedings of the 5th International Conference on World Peace. Tokyo, Japan: Professors World Peace Academy, 1975. 229 pp.

647. *Modern Science and Moral Values.* Proceedings of the 2nd International Conference on the Unity of the Sciences. Tarrytown, N.Y.: International Cultural Foundation, 1973. 591 pp.

*   Moon, Sun Myung. *Science and Absolute Values.* Cited above as item 13.

648. *National Culture and World Peace.* Proceedings of the 6th International Conference on World Peace. Seoul, Korea: Professors World Peace Academy, 1977. 189 pp.

649. *The Ninoy Aquino Phenomenon: Its Significance to the National Search for Peace with Justice.* Conference Proceedings. Manila, Philippines: Professors World Peace Academy, 1984. 64 pp.

650. Norton, Augustus Richard. *External Intervention and the Politics of Lebanon.* Washington, D.C.: Washington Institute for Values in Public Policy, 1984. 16 pp.

651. *The Pacific Era-Issues for the 1980s and Beyond.* Proceedings of the 8th International Conference on World Peace. Tokyo, Japan: Professors World Peace Academy, 1978. 620 pp.

652. Pino-Marina, Nester. "Strategic Importance of Central America to the United States." *White Paper Report.* Washington, D.C.: Washington Institute for Values in Public Policy, 1985. 19 pp.

653. *Proceedings of the 13th International Conference on World Peace.* Taipei: Professors World Peace Academy, 1984. 339 pp.

654. *The Re-Evaluation of Existing Values and The Search for Absolute Values.* Proceedings of the 7th International Conference on the Unity of the Sciences. 2 vols. New York: International Cultural Foundation, 1979. 1150 pp.

655. *The Responsibility of the Academic Community in the Search for Absolute Values.* Proceedings of the 8th International Conference on the Unity of the Sciences. 2 vols. New York: International Cultural Foundation, 1980. 1028 pp.

656. Rivero, Emilio Adolfo. "Central America 1985: A Contest of Wills." *White Paper Report.* Washington, D.C.: The Washington Institute for Values in Public Policy, 1985. 25 pp.

657. *The Role of Academics and Human Relationships in Southern Africa.* Papers from a Conference of the South African PWPA. Johannesburg, South Africa: Professors World Peace Academy, 1985. 35 pp.

658. *The Role of African Academics in the Development of Africa.* Proceedings of the 4th Seminar of the Eastern, Central, and Southern African PWPA. New York: Professors World Peace Academy, 1983. 88 pp.

659. *The Role of East Asia in World Peace.* Proceedings of the 14th International Conference on World Peace. Manila, Philippines: Professors World Peace Academy, 1985. 434 pp.

660. *The Role of Technology in the Development of the Caribbean.* Proceedings of a Conference of the Professors World Peace Academy of Guyana. New York: Professors World Peace Academy, 1985. 38 pp.

661. Rosenau, James N. *Beyond Imagery: The Long-Run Adaptation of Two Chinas.* Washington, D.C.: Washington Institute for Values in Public Policy, 1985. 24 pp.

662. Rubenstein, Richard L. "Lessons of Grenada and Military Intervention." *White Paper Report.* Washington, D.C.: The Washington Institute for Values in Public Policy, 1984. 20 pp.

663. _____. *Reflections on Religion and Public Policy.* Washington, D.C.: Washington Institute for Values in Public Policy, 1984. 20 pp.

664. _____, ed. *Modernization: The Humanist Response to Its Promise and Problems.* Washington, D.C.: Paragon House, 1982. 393 pp.

665. *Science and Absolute Values.* Proceedings of the 3rd International Conference on the Unity of the Sciences, 2 vols. Tarrytown, N.Y.: International Cultural Foundation, 1974. 1453 pp.

666. *The Search for Absolute Values and the Creation of the New World.* Proceedings of the 10th International Conference on the Unity of the Sciences. 2 vols. New York: International Cultural Foundation, 1982. 1457 pp.

667. *The Search for Absolute Values: Harmony among the Sciences.*
     Proceedings of the 5th International Conference on the Unity of the
     Sciences. 2 vols. New York: International Cultural Foundation,
     1977. 1037 pp.

668. *The Search for Absolute Values in a Changing World.* Proceedings of
     the 6th International Conference on the Unity of the Sciences. 2
     vols. New York: International Cultural Foundation, 1978. 1277
     pp.

669. Simon, Sheldon W. *The Great Powers and Southeast Asia: Cautious
     Minuet or Dangerous Tango?* Washington, D.C.: The Washington
     Institute for Values in Public Policy, 1985. 31 pp.

670. Singh, Igbal. *U.S. Defense Policy and Power Projection in
     Southwest Asia.* Washington, D.C.: Washington Institute for
     Values in Public Policy, 1984. 60 pp.

671. Sonnenfeldt, Helmut. *The Soviet Style in International Politics.*
     Washington, D.C.: Washington Institute for Values in Public
     Policy, 1985. 28 pp.

672. Sours, Martin H. *Service Enterprises in the Pacific Community.*
     Washington, D.C.: Washington Institute for Values in Public
     Policy, 1985. 30 pp.

673. Steffy, Joan Marie. *The San Francisco Peace Movement: A Survey.*
     Monograph Series. New York: Professors World Peace Academy,
     1985. 76 pp.

674. Stromas, Alexander. *To Fight Communism: Why and How.*
     Monograph Series. New York: Professors World Peace Academy,
     1985. 32 pp.

675. *Sun Myung Moon: The Man and His Ideal.* Seoul, Korea: Future
     Civilization Press, 1981. 186 pp.

     Contains items 1460, 1591, 1618, 1644.

676. Thornton, Richard C. *Is Detente Inevitable?* Washington, D.C.:
     Washington Institute for Values in Public Policy, 1985. 24 pp.

677. _____. *Soviet Asian Strategy in the Brezhnev Era and Beyond.*
     Washington, D.C.: Washington Institute for Values in Public
     Policy, 1985. 77 pp.

678. Turner, Fredrick. *Natural Classicism.* New York: Paragon House,
     1985. 277 pp.

679. *Unification Thought Charts.* N.Y.: Unification Thought Institute, n.d. 37 pp.

680. *Vision for Asian Peace in the Eighties.* Proceedings of the 12th International Conference on World Peace. Seoul, Korea: Professors World Peace Academy, 1982. 332 pp.

681. Weinberg, Alvin, ed. *The Nuclear Connection.* Washington Institute for Values in Public Policy. New York: Paragon House, 1984. 295 pp.

682. *West European Pacifism and the Strategy for Peace.* London, England: Professors World Peace Academy, 1983.

683. *What ICUS Is.* New York. International Cultural Foundation Press, 1978. 28 pp.

684. *Youth Attack on Values.* Symposium in Nice, France. New York: International Cultural Foundation, 1978. 205 pp.

Periodicals

685. *The Academician: A Journal of Japan's Views and Visions in Defense of Free Civilization.* Japan: Professors World Peace Academy. Semiannually, nos. 1 and 2. Quarterly, no. 3 on. 1982-.

686. *Focus-New World Forum.* New York: New World Forum. Monthly [irregular]. 1978-81.

687. *ICF Report.* New York: International Cultural Foundation. Bimonthly. 1983-.

688. *International Journal on World Peace.* New York: Professors World Peace Academy. Quarterly. 1984-.

689. *The Unification Thought Quarterly.* New York: Unification Thought Research Institute. Quarterly [irregular]. 1981-.

690. *Unified World.* New York: New World Forum. Bimonthly. 1976-78.

D. INTERRELIGIOUS BODIES

Ecumenical, interfaith and social service organizations affiliated with the Church are primarily outgrowths of UC evangelistic affiliates but with two important differences. First, unlike UC-related evangelistic organizations, they have been able to involve a broad range of intellectuals and church professionals in a variety of ongoing relationships. Second, whereas evangelistic organizations have been oriented toward conversion, UC ecumenical, interfaith and social service affiliates are oriented more toward dialogue. In general, this dialogue has involved exchanges with Christian theologians, interfaith work and initiatives in the area of religion and society.

The UC's most important ecumenical organizations have been Unification Theological Seminary (UTS) and the New Ecumenical Research Foundation (New ERA). Unification Theological Seminary, founded at Barrytown, New York in 1975, has related ecumenically to the Christian community in at least three ways. First, and most significantly, UTS was organized along the lines of mainline Christian seminaries. This is evident in its Religious Studies and Divinity programs as well as in efforts to gain recognition from the American Association of Theological Schools. Second, the seminary installed a faculty of mostly mainstream Protestant and Catholic scholars. Third, UTS sponsors numerous conferences and dialogues with interested theologians both at the seminary and regionally throughout the United States. In 1979, UTS hosted a summer seminar on "Unification Theology" which led to the formation of New ERA, an association of scholars who had participated in this conference and others. Formally established in 1980, New ERA has worked conjointly with the seminary to sponsor conferences, seminars and publications.

Literature produced by Unification Theological Seminary and New ERA is varied. The best source for the makeup and orientation of the seminary is its catalogue [740]. It includes lists of faculty, course offerings, summaries of the seminary's history, stated goals and descriptions of its community life. Ongoing UTS activities are well-documented in its monthly, student-run newsletter, *The Cornerstone* [734]. While the seminary's early interaction with Christian theologians was stimulated by Young Oon Kim's *Unification Theology and Christian Thought* [711-12], subsequent dialogues and conferences resulted in a series of volumes published by the seminary and by New ERA Books. A number of these titles derive from the UC's interaction with professional theologians. *Proceedings of the Virgin Islands Seminar on Unification Theology* [694], *Hermeneutics and Unification Theology* [696], *Exploring Unification Theology* [697], *Restoring the Kingdom* [703], *Hermeneutics and Horizons: The Shape of the Future* [706], and *Ten Theologians Respond to the Unification Church* [724] all examine facets of UC doctrines as they relate to various schools of Christian thought. *Evangelical-Unification Dialogue* [722] and *Orthodox-Unification*

Dialogue [730] contain proceedings and papers from conferences held with practicioners of particular traditions. *The Family and the Unification Church* [709] and *Lifestyle: Conversations with Members of the Unification Church* [721] explore issues of spirituality and social organization. Other conferences which did not result in books are reported on in *New ERA* [738], a bimonthly newsletter.

A number of UC-related organizations including UTS and New ERA engage in interfaith work. The most important of these are the Global Congress of the World's Religions (GCWR) and the International Religious Foundation (IRF). GCWR was initiated by the faculty of the Unification Theological Seminary as "a response to the quantum leap in religious pluralism around the world in the past few decades." Its major emphasis to date has been the sponsorship of interfaith consultations and conferences. Proceedings of conferences convened prior to 1980 are published in *Towards a Global Congress of World's Religions* [714-15] and *Towards a Global Congress of the World's Religions* [716]. Proceedings from 1980-82 are published in *The Global Congress of the World's Religions* [727]. Since 1981, the organization also has published a newsletter [739].

The International Religious Foundation, incorporated in 1982 as an umbrella organization for virtually all the UC's interreligious activities, quickly eclipsed the GCWR in importance. IRF's major project to date has been an Assembly of the World's Religions, held for the first time in late 1985 and planned for 1989 and 1993. This project was an outgrowth of IRF annual conferences on God convened since 1981. Papers from the first of these meetings were published under the title, *God, the Contemporary Discussion* [726]. Subsequent "God Conferences" produced *God and Temporality* [699], *God and Global Justice* [704] and *The Defense of God* [725], among other titles. In addition to GCWR and IRF, Unification Theological Seminary fosters interfaith work through guest lectureships and regular courses utilizing Young Oon Kim's 3 vol. *World Religions* [713]. Finally, New ERA in conjunction with the seminary and IRF sponsors an annual international sociology conference on contemporary religious movements. Papers from the first two of these are published as *The Social Impact of New Religious Movements* [732] and *Alternatives to American Mainstream Churches* [705].

In the area of religion and society, important UC affiliates have been the Society for Common Insights (SCI) and the National Council for the Church and Social Action (NCCSA). SCI, originally a group of UC and UC-related scientists interested in "common insights and methodologies of science and religion in their social context," increasingly emphasized the social dimension. This emphasis was evident in the *Journal of the Society for Common Insights* [736] and in SCI's decision to help establish and later affiliate with the National Council for the Church and Social Action. Active primarily among black churches, NCCSA expanded to include more than two dozen chapters after 1977. Although basically a social service organization, it produced some literature. Noteworthy are proceedings from two national conferences "On the Church and Social Problems" [719-20] and local chapter newsletters such as the Washington, D.C. *WCSA Housing Monitor* [741].

In 1982, NCCSA became one of the constellation of organizations under IRF which subsequently convened "Interdenominational Conferences for Clergy with Emphasis on Ecumenism and Social Action." UC overseas social work is channeled through the International Relief Friendship Foundation (IRFF) headquartered in New York. Its activities which include emergency relief aid, farm projects and mobile medical teams are covered in IRFF's quarterly *Frontiers in Development* [735]. In addition to these organizations, Unification Theological Seminary involves itself in the area of religion and society through student internships and, for several years, through publication of a community-service newsletter, *The Mid-Hudson Tide* [737].

Monographs

691. Bettis, Joseph, and Stanley K. Johannesen, eds. *The Return of the Millenium.* A New ERA Book. New York: Paragon House, 1984. 233 pp.

692. Bisher, Frank, Michael L. Mickler, Robert McCauley and Bob Schmidt, eds. *Signs of Presence, Love & More: Poetry of the Unification Movement.* Barrytown, N.Y.: Unification Theological Seminary, 1977.

693. Boslooper, Thomas. *The Image of Woman.* New York: Rose of Sharon Press, 1980. 228 pp.

694. Bryant, M. Darrol, ed. *Proceedings of the Virgin Islands' Seminar on Unification Theology.* Conference Series no. 6. Barrytown, N.Y.: Unification Theological Seminary, 1980. 323 pp.

695. Bryant, M. Darrol, and Donald Dayton, eds. *The Coming Kingdom: Essays in American Millennialism and Eschatology.* Barrytown, N.Y.: International Religious Foundation, 1983. 246 pp.

     Contains item 1404.

696. Bryant, M. Darrol, and Durwood Foster, eds. *Hermeneutics and Unification Theology.* Conference Series no. 5. Barrytown, N.Y.: Unification Theological Seminary, 1980. 154 pp.

697. Bryant, M. Darrol, and Susan Hodges, eds. *Exploring Unification Theology.* New York: Edwin Mellen, 1978; Conference Series no. 1. Barrytown, N.Y.: Unification Theological Seminary, 1978.

     Contains items 1410, 1418, 1493, 1616.

698. Bryant, M. Darrol, and Rita H. Mataragnon, eds. *The Many Faces of Religion and Society.* God, the Contemporary Discussion Series. A New ERA Book. New York: Paragon House, 1985. 200 pp.

699. Clarke, Bowman L., and Eugene T. Long, eds. *God and Temporality.* God, the Contemporary Discussion Series. A New ERA Book. New York: Paragon House, 1984. 189 pp.

700. *Conference on Christianity, Crisis and Community Change.* New York: National Council For the Church and Social Action, 1982. 40 pp.

701. Duerlinger, James, ed. *Ultimate Reality and Spiritual Discipline.* God, the Contemporary Discussion Series. A New ERA Book. New York: Paragon House, 1984. 239 pp.

   Contains item 1407.

702. Durst, Mose. *International Renaissance for Resources: An End to World Hunger.* Policy Statement for the 1980s. Oakland, Calif.: Project Volunteer, 1980. 1 p.

703. Ferm, Deane William. *Restoring the Kingdom.* A New ERA Book. New York: Paragon House, 1984. 226 pp.

   Contains items 1403, 1413, 1420, 1425, 1427-28, 1438, 1449, 1472-73, 1475-76, 1479, 1499, 1501, 1641.

704. Ferre, Fredrick, and Rita H. Mataragnon, eds. *God and Global Justice: Religion and Poverty in an Unequal World.* God, the Contemporary Discussion Series. A New ERA Book. New York: Paragon House, 1985. 214 pp.

   Contains item 1402.

705. Fichter, Joseph H., ed. *Alternatives to American Mainline Churches.* Conference Series no. 14. Barrytown, N.Y.: Unification Theological Seminary, 1983. 201 pp.

   Contains item 1553.

706. Flinn, Frank K., ed. *Hermeneutics and Horizons: The Shape of the Future.* Conference Series no. 11. Barrytown, N.Y.: Unification Theological Seminary, 1982. 445 pp.

   Contains items 1405-6, 1408, 1423-24, 1429, 1434, 1436-37, 1445, 1447-48, 1456, 1465, 1477, 1483, 1490, 1498, 1500.

707. Foster, Durwood, and Paul Mojzes, eds. *Society and Original Sin: Ecumenical Essays on the Impact of the Fall.* A New ERA Book. New York: Paragon House, 1985. 193 pp.

   Contains items 1433, 1443, 1454, 1495-96.

708. *God Who Unifies All Things.* The First International Conference for Super-Denomination. Seoul, Korea: The Christian Association for Super-Denomination, 1978. 297 pp.

709. James, Gene, ed. *The Family and the Unification Church.* Conference Series no. 15. Barrytown, N.Y.: Unification Theological Seminary, 1983. 269 pp.

    Contains items 1430, 1440, 1442, 1474, 1489, 1494, 1503-4, 1510, 1552, 1554, 1589, 1621, 1632.

710. Johnson, Kurt, and M. Craig Johnson, eds. *The Scientific Basis of Divine Principle.* New York: Society for Common Insights, 1980, 1981.

711. Kim, Young Oon. *Unification Theology and Christian Thought.* New York: Golden Gate, 1975. 289 pp.

712. _____. *Unification Theology and Christian Thought.* Rev. ed. New York: Golden Gate, 1976. 320 pp.

713. _____. *World Religions.* 3 vols. New York: Golden Gate, 1976.

714. Lewis, Warren, ed. *Towards a Global Congress of World Religions.* Proceedings at San Francisco, Barrytown, and Bristol, England. Conference Series no. 2. Barrytown, N.Y.: Unification Theological Seminary, 1978. 297 pp.

715. _____. *Towards a Global Congress of World Religions.* Proceedings at Boston. Conference Series no. 4. Barrytown, N.Y.: Unification Theological Seminary, 1979. 63 pp.

716. _____. *Towards a Global Congress of the World's Religions.* Proceedings at Los Angeles. Conference Series no. 5. Barrytown, N.Y.: Unification Theological Seminary, 1980. 78 pp.

717. Moon, Ye-jin. *Mind Garden.* New York: Rose of Sharon Press, 1979. 189 pp.

718. Nyangoni, Wellington W. *United States Policy and South Africa.* New York: Society for Common Insights, 1981. 316 pp.

719. *Proceedings of the First National Conference on the Church and Social Problems.* Published as vol. 2, no. 1 of the *Journal of the Society for Common Insights* (item 736), Nov. 10, 1977. 154 pp.

720. *Proceedings of the Second National Conference on the Church and Social Action.* Published as vol. 2, no. 2 of the *Journal of the Society* for *Common Insights* (item 736), Nov. 10, 1978. 144 pp.

721. Quebedeaux, Richard, ed. *Lifestyle: Conversations with Members of the Unification Church.* Conference Series no. 13. Barrytown, N.Y.: Unification Theological Seminary, 1982. 214 pp.

Contains item 1568.

722. Quebedeaux, Richard, and Rodney Sawatsky. *Evangelical-Unification Dialogue.* Conference Series no. 3. Barrytown, N.Y.: Unification Theological Seminary, 1979. 374 pp.

723. *Research on the Unification Principle: Seminar of Korean Scholars on Unification Theology.* Seoul, Korea: Sunghwa Press, 1981. 304 pp.

Contains items 1414-17, 1439, 1451-52, 1502, 1663.

724. Richardson, Herbert, ed. *Ten Theologians Respond to the Unification Church.* Conference Series no. 10. Barrytown, N.Y.: Unification Theological Seminary, 1981. 199 pp.

Contains items 1419, 1431, 1435, 1455, 1458, 1466, 1481, 1484, 1488.

725. Roth, John K., and Fredrick Sontag, eds. *The Defense of God.* God, the Contemporary Discussion Series. A New ERA Book. New York: Paragon House, 1985. 172 pp.

Contains item 1421.

726. Sontag, Fredrick, and M. Darrol Bryant, eds. *God, the Contemporary Discussion.* Conference Series no. 12. Barrytown, N.Y.: Unification Theological Seminary, 1982. 419 pp.

Contains items 1453, 1459.

727. Thompson, Henry O., ed. *The Global Congress of the World's Religions.* Proceedings 1980-1982. Barrytown, N.Y.: Unification Theological Seminary 1982. 365 pp.

728. _____. *Unity in Diversity: Essays in Religion by Members of the Faculty of the Unification Theological Seminary.* Barrytown, N.Y.: Unification Theological Seminary, 1984. 435 pp.

Contains items 1409, 1422, 1441, 1444, 1446, 1450, 1461, 1478, 1486, 1491, 1497, 1634, 1686.

729. *Toward Our Third Century.* Barrytown, N.Y.: Unification Theological Seminary, 1976.

730. Tsirpanlis, Constantine. *Orthodox-Unification Dialogue.* Conference Series no. 8. Barrytown, N.Y.: Unification Theological Seminary, 1981. 139 pp.

    Contains items 1426, 1469-70, 1492.

731. *Unification Theological Affirmations.* Barrytown, N.Y.: Unification Theological Seminary, 1976. 4 pp.

732. Wilson, Bryan. *The Social Impact of New Religious Movements.* Conference Series no. 9. Barrytown, N.Y.: Unification Theological Seminary, 1981. 235 pp.

    Contains items 1516, 1620.

Periodicals

733. *Church and Social Action.* Washington, D.C.: National Council for the Church and Social Action. Irregular. ca., 1982.

734. *The Cornerstone.* Barrytown, N.Y.: Unification Theological Seminary. Monthly. 1976-.

735. *Frontiers in Development.* New York: International Relief Friendship Foundation. Quarterly. 1984-.

736. *Journal of the Society for Common Insights.* New York: Society for Common Insights. Irregular. 1976-78.

737. *Mid-Hudson Tide.* Barrytown, N.Y.: Unification Theological Seminary. Monthly. 1979-83.

738. *New ERA.* Barrytown, N.Y.: New Ecumenical Research Assocation. Bimonthly. 1981-85.

739. *Newsletter.* Chicago and Barrytown, N.Y.: Global Congress of the World's Religions. Monthly and semiannually. 1978-.

740. *Unification Theological Seminary Catalogue.* Barrytown, N.Y.: Unification Theological Seminary. Annually. 1978-.

741. *WCSA Housing Counseling Monitor.* Washington, D.C.: Washington Church for Social Action. Quarterly. 1980-82.

742. *Youth Seminar on World Religions.* Barrytown, N.Y.: Unification Theological Seminary. Quarterly. 1983-85.

E. MEDIA OUTLETS

Literature published by UC media affiliates includes metropolitan newspapers, conference proceedings and material generated by a motion picture company. The organizations producing this literature have been set up and funded by the Church for three major reasons. First, the creation of media outlets stems from a stated commitment to the values of a free press. In this respect, the UC has been willing to employ large numbers of non-church professionals and to fund outlets over which it has had only indirect control. Second, as public hostility against the UC has been reflected in press reports, media affiliates were created to counter this trend and portray the Church in a more favorable, or at least more "objective," light. In addition, since most UC media outlets were established in New York City or Washington, D.C., these organizations enabled the Church to make important contacts and advance its perspective in major centers of the American communications industry. Third, and a factor not to be overlooked despite reportedly huge operating losses, most UC media-related affiliates have been set up as profit-making business ventures.

News World Communications, Inc. coordinates the UC's media network. In New York, it publishes the *The New York City Tribune* [753], a New York daily newspaper (formerly *The News World* [754]); *International Report* [751], a news service; *Noticias Del Mundo* [755], a Spanish-language daily (also published in Los Angeles); and *Saege Shimbo* [756], a Korean-language daily. Some of these are identifiable as UC operations and reflect Church views. *The News World*, for example, defended the UC on religious liberty grounds, maintained an ideological offensive against communism and promoted wholesome moral values. *Noticias Del Mundo* enabled the UC to make important contacts in Latin America. In 1982, the UC purchased facilities of the newly defunct *Washington Star* and began operations there, but with a different approach. Hiring ex-*Washington Star* writers and non-UC editors, some of whom had autonomy clauses written into their contracts, *The Washington Times* [758] reflects conservative, though not necessarily UC, perspectives. As the "flagship" of UC media affiliates, it published a national edition in 1984 and in 1985 began *Insight* [750], a weekly newsmagazine.

Besides news outlets, the UC's two most important media organizations are the World Media Conference and One Way Productions, Inc. The World Media Conference, originally sponsored in conjunction with *Sekai Nippo* [757], the UC's Tokyo daily, is held annually. Proceedings from the first conference are published under the title, *World Crisis and the Mission of Journalism* [747]. One Way Productions, Inc., the UC's incipient motion picture company, has produced one feature film and has others planned. "Inchon," released through United Artist theatres in the United States, depicted an amphibious landing directed by General Douglas MacArthur during the Korean War. Although estimates of its total cost ranged from $40-60 million, "Inchon" was not successful at the box office nor was it favorably reviewed by film critics [796, 1266].

Monographs

743. *Kim Il Sung's 30-year Deception.* Tokyo, Japan: World Daily News, 1976. 36 pp.

744. Moore, Robin. *Oh! Inchon.* N.p.: One Way Productions, 1981. 291 pp.

745. *The New York City Tribune, The Contemporary Newspaper.* New York: News World Communications, 1984. 62 pp.

746. Warder, Michael Young. *Another Watchdog.* New York: News World Communications, 1978. 62 pp.

747. *World Crisis and the Mission of Journalism.* Proceedings of the 1st International World Conference of Journalists. Tokyo, Japan: Sekai Nippo, 1978. 348 pp.

Periodicals

748. *Accord: The Magazine of Human Dignity.* New York: Accord Monthly. 1984-85.

749. *Harlem Weekly.* New York: News World Communications. Weekly. 1979-82.

750. *Insight.* Washington, D.C.: News World Communications. Weekly. 1985-.

751. *International Report.* New York: Free Press International. Biweekly. 1976-.

752. *The Middle East Times.* Cyprus: News World Communications. Weekly. 1983-.

753. *The New York City Tribune.* New York: News World Communications. Daily. 1983-.

754. *The News World.* New York: News World Communications. Daily. 1975-83.

755. *Noticias del Mundo.* New York and Los Angeles: News World Communications. Daily. 1980-.

756. *Saegae Shinbo.* New York: News World Communications. Daily. 1982-.

757. *Sekai Nippo.* Tokyo, Japan: Sekai Nippo. Daily. 1975-.

758. *The Washington Times.* Washington, D.C.: News World Communications. Daily. 1982-.

III.

RESPONSES TO THE CHURCH: RELIGIOUS

A. THE PROTESTANT RESPONSE

Protestant responses to the UC are varied. Ranging from polemical attacks and apostate accounts to descriptive analyses, general reportage, ecumenical overtures and "official" position papers, these treatments can be grouped into conservative, liberal and denominational categories. In general, conservative materials are dominated by doctrinal concerns while liberal publications are preoccupied with sociopolitical issues. Responses in denominational house organs have reflected both doctrinal and sociopolitical emphases in attempting to make sense of the UC to their membership constituencies.

CONSERVATIVE

Conservative Protestant responses to the UC include polemical, descriptive and ecumenical approaches. Of these, polemical materials predominate and include direct frontal attacks, apostate accounts and treatments of the UC within the context of opposition to "cults" in general. Although varying in specifics, conservative anti-UC polemics share three common presuppositions. First, they presuppose that the UC represents a distinct threat. In some accounts, the UC is portrayed as one of a whole litany of dangers including liberalism, Eastern mysticism, communism, immorality, etc. In other accounts, the UC is singled out. In either case, these treatments maximize rather than minimize the UC's alleged disruptive potential. Second, conservative anti-UC polemics presuppose that there is a clear, definable "Christian" position over against which the UC can be measured primarily in terms of its deviance. This typically is established through point-by-point refutations of UC doctrines although UC deviations from standards of Christian morality are sometimes alleged. Third, these materials presuppose that there is an appropriate "Christian" response to the UC. While sympathy with kidnapping and "deprogramming" is not absent, the predominant emphases are on prayer, patience, evangelism and self-reform. A significant portion of this literature is of the self-help variety with practical suggestions, sample witnessing strategies and suggested Biblical proof-texts.

Given these common presuppositions, much of this material is redundant. Some treatments, however, are more carefully drawn than others.

Of those accounts which can be classified as direct frontal attacks, that is, polemical diatribes dealing exclusively and in their entirety with the UC, J. Isamu Yamamoto's *The Puppet Master* [1017] is the most comprehensive and useful, particularly in its collation of historical materials. Other less helpful examples of this genre are John Allan's *The Rising of the Moon* [762], James Bjornstad's *The Moon is Not the Son* [783], Zola Levitt's *The Spirit of Sun Myung Moon* [883] and Park, Young-Kwan's *Unification Church* [950].

Apostate accounts comprise a second category of conservative Protestant polemics against the UC. Basically testimonies of former UC adherents who have become evangelical Christians, these accounts differ from the above-described material in that they are more experiential. This is especially true of Deanna Durham's *Life Among the Moonies* [807] and Steve Kemperman's *Lord of the Second Advent* [867]. Durham, a divorced mother during her stay in the Church, depicts family separations imposed within particular UC communal settings while Kemperman, who joined the Church from a university campus, describes the sacrifice of his college education. Chris Elkins' *Heavenly Deception* [811] is less intensely personal. Though moderately critical of the UC for stressing what he termed "results" over "methods," Elkins account is of note for the strong stance he takes against deprogramming. At the same time, as consultant to the Southern Baptist Convention Home Missions Board, Elkins advocated evangelizing UC members. He developed this position in *What Do You Say to a Moonie?* [814].

Treatments of the UC within the context of opposition toward cults in general make up a final category of conservative Protestant polemics. By and large, these are introductory overviews and range from the moderate to the militant. Moderate treatments, such as chapters on the UC in Kenneth Boa's *Cults, World Religions and You* [785], James Hefley's *The Youthnappers* [838], and William J. Petersen's *Those Curious New Cults* [954] are informational. Militant treatments such as *Walter Martin's Cult Reference Bible* [905], Pat Means' *The Mystical Maze* [913], Robert and Gretchen Passantino's *Answers to the Cultist at Your Door* [951], James Sire's *Scripture Twisting* [979], and Jack Sparks' *The Mindbenders* [988] supplement information with strategies for evangelization. A mix of militant and moderate approaches is evident in the work of "Christian sociologist" Ronald Enroth. Though his *Youth, Brainwashing and the Extremist Cults* [818] sounded an early alarmist cry, subsequent reaction against "born-again" Christians and accumulating scholarship on the UC and other new religions moderated his tone and vocabulary in *The Lure of the Cults* [817] and *A Guide to Cults and New Religions* [819].

In addition to polemics, conservative Protestant responses to the UC include descriptive and ecumenical approaches. In terms of general coverage, the evangelical magazine *Christianity Today* (CT) has been the most complete. In fact, by piecing together its news articles, one could construct a substantial documentary record of the UC's emergence and development during the seventies and early eighties. Its coverage is especially strong on early UC evangelistic crusades, the deprogramming controversy, interaction with evangelicals and ongoing UC development.

Ecumenical responses to the UC are less evident among conservative Protestants although there are some examples. Irving Hexham and Myrtle Langley in "Cracking the Moonie Code" [841], state they "have met some individual Moonies who were very definitely Christians" (25). In distinguishing, however, between "beliefs of the members and the official teachings of the group," Hexham and Langley posit dialogue as a means of conversion or, in their words, "to win Moonies for Christ" (27). Author and evangelical trend-watcher Richard Quebedeaux [805] maintained a more consistently ecumenical posture in depicting the UC as "a Korean form of Christianity" (12). Quebedeaux also organized several dialogues between evangelical Christians and UC seminarians. One of these brought together some fifteen evangelicals and a like number of UC adherents [722]. Another assembled UC seminarians and the Church's most prominent evangelical critics [912]. A final, if confusing, ecumenical response to the UC was that of former Black Panther turned evangelical Christian, Eldridge Cleaver. A rumored UC convert, Cleaver spent six weeks at a UC retreat camp and supported the Church in its anti-communist work on college campuses. Although his involvement became increasingly tangential, Cleaver's comment that he'd "rather be with the littlest Moonie than with Billy Graham" circulated widely [911].

LIBERAL

Liberal Protestant responses to the UC also include polemical, descriptive and ecumenical approaches. Further, as with conservatives, polemical materials predominate although from the liberal side they typically attack the UC on sociopolitical rather than doctrinal grounds. Nonetheless, liberal polemics against the UC share the basic presuppositions that characterize conservative approaches. First, they portray the UC as a distinct threat. In some accounts, the Church is linked to the Korean government or religious fundamentalism. In other treatments, the UC is singled out in ways that maximize its alleged disruptive potential. Second, though usually implicit, liberal polemics presume there is a normative Christian posture over against which the UC is hopelessly deviant. In this respect, liberal critiques flay the UC for alleged political and intra-organizational authoritarianism. Third, liberal polemics against the UC presuppose an appropriate Christian response. For antagonistic liberals, however, this has not resulted in calls to evangelize but rather in admonitions to ignore the UC and shun participation with it. A corollary approach has been to "unmask" and expose UC efforts to gain legitimation.

As with conservative Protestant polemics, the above-described presuppositions have led to repetitious and sometimes unsubstantiated claims. Critiques of the UC on political grounds, for example, charge the Church with complicity in human rights abuses of South Korea, with lobbying for the South Korean government in the United States and with exploiting politics to its own advantage. These charges are maintained in Frank Baldwin's "The Korea Lobby" [768], the Institute on the Church in Urban Industrial Society's select bibliography on "Religion on the Right in South Korea: Moon, Sun Myung, etc." [961] and James Stentzel's "Reverend

Moon and His Bicentennial Blitz" [993]. S. Mark Heim's " 'Divine Principle' and the Second Advent" [839], while not directly alleging collusion with "Korean agents in the U.S.," criticizes the UC's political orientation on the basis of an analysis of its primary doctrinal text. Other articles such as "Moon's Credibility Game" [934] and Dan Peerman's "Korean Moonshine" [952] supplement opposition to the UC on political grounds with organizational critiques. At the same time, a late seventies resurgence of religious and political conservatism, UC accomodations and a desire not to sound "shrill and shrewish" moderated the positions of some commentators such as American church historian Martin Marty. Although in earlier treatments such as "I Dreamed I Went to Seminary in Its Maiden-term. Rah!" [907] and "Say It Ain't So, Roger!" [909] Marty "named names" in an effort to discourage participation in UC-sponsored events, by 1979 he [908] acknowledged having "long since stopped making such inquiries" (214).

Aside from polemics, liberal Protestant responses include descriptive and ecumenical approaches, though of a ambiguous bent. For example, *The Christian Century,* a liberal Protestant weekly, frequently reported on the UC in objective terms but covered mainly stories that cast the Church in a questionable light. This is evident in such titles as "Moon Called unChristian" [921], "Moonie Tactics in New York ... and Minnesota" [930], "Moonies Arrested" [932], and "Moonies Buy Bank" [933]. Similarly, Jean Caffey Lyles, in "Letting Go: Everybody Has the Right to Be Wrong" [892] and "The Religious Rights of the Unlovely" [893] carefully distances support for the UC on libertarian grounds from the necessity for any further analysis of, or interaction with, the Church. In this respect, Harvard theologian Harvey Cox's "The Real Threat of the Moonies" [799], which recounts his experience at a UC "weekend workshop," departs from other liberal Protestant responses on at least two counts. First, Cox was willing to acknowledge positive appeals of the UC. These he listed as "(1) Unification's bid to transcend the particularism of historical Christianity and combine the great religions into one; (2) Its programmatic effort to go beyond the dichotomy between religion and science; and (3) Its vision of a *novus ordo seculorum* guided in its economic and cultural life by religious teachings" (260). Second, although concluding that "Moon's theology is not my cup of ginseng tea," Cox was willing to be self-critical. As he put it, "the attraction of the Moon movement to naive idealistic youth is not the result of sinister brainwashing but an inevitable consequence of the utter vacuum that now exists on what might be called the 'Christian left' " (263).

DENOMINATIONAL

Although polemics are not lacking, Protestant denominations have responded to the UC in a manner that is at once more open-ended and more agonized than the responses of conservatives or liberals. This is the case for several reasons. First, because denominations represent not only ideological and social postures but also active membership constituencies, their responses tend to be more fluid and varied. Second, since denominations operate in the American religious marketplace, they are more likely to have been challenged directly by UC outreach. Third, as discrete organizational entities, they are required at times to take official stands. Protestant denominations have responded to these pressures both formally and informally as well as in ways that recapitulate approaches already discussed.

Denominational polemics against the UC combine doctrinal and sociopolitical emphases characteristic of conservative and liberal approaches. That is, denominational publications of a conservative or confessional orientation typically attack the UC on doctrinal grounds. Examples are Robert L. Gram's "Unification Theology and Gnostic Thought" [829], Donald S. Tingle and Richard A. Fordyce's *Phases and Faces of the Moon* [1000], and Lyle Vander Werff's "Moon and Christian Orthodoxy" [1005]. Standard liberal critiques include Joel A. McCollum's "The Unification Church" [897], Jane Day Mook's "The Unification Church" [920], and Lowell Streiker's chapter on the UC in *The Cults Are Coming!* [994].

Formal and official denominational responses to the UC are of two types. The first, which is barely distinguishable, if at all, from polemical broadsides, consists of resource materials prepared by denominational "cult" experts. Examples include sections on the UC in Harris Langford's *Traps: A Probe of the Strange New Cults* [878], James N. Lewis' *The Christian Confronting the Cults* [885], and Phillip Lochlass' *How to Respond to ... the New Christian Religions* [888]. The second type of formal materials consists of responses to direct UC initiatives. The most prominent example is the Commission on Faith and Order of the National Council of the Churches of Christ in the U.S.A.'s official study document on the UC. Entitled, *A Critique of the Theology of the Unification Church as Set Forth in the Divine Principle* [798], the eleven-page study document was issued "to clarify the claim to Christian identity made by the Unification Church" (1). Although disregarding UC "statements of self-clarification" and acknowledging "diversity in Christian belief and theology and, thus, internal disagreement," the commission concluded the UC "is not a Christian Church" based on three points: "1. Its doctrine of the nature of the triune God is erroneous. 2. Its Christology is incompatible with Christian teaching and belief. 3. Its teaching on salvation and the means of grace is inadequate and faulty" (11).

More open-ended than official pronouncements are a variety of unofficial interpretations. Frequently written by academics in seminary newsletters or denominational journals, these include several types. One type consists of interviews conducted with UC members attending mainline Christian seminaries. Examples are Paul Jeffrey's "By the Light of the Reverend Moon: Unification Church Members at PSR [Pacific School of Religion]" [858] and Loraine Karcz's "Members of Rev. Moon's Church Enroll at HDS [Harvard Divinity School]" [865]. A second category consists of responses from academics who have attended UC-sponsored seminars or visited its seminary. Unconstrained by pressures to represent their denominations as a whole, these scholars have set UC beliefs in social and theological context, questioned conventional wisdom about the Church and speculated about the UC's future. Examples include Cliff Edwards' "Son [sic] Myung Moon and the Scholars" [808], Brian Gaybbes' "A Week Spent with the Moonies" [825], Barbara Hargrove's "Some Advice for the Moonstruck" [836], Ray Jennings' "Moonies: A Movement in Search of a Theology" [859], Leo Sandon, Jr.'s *True Family: Korean Communitarianism and American Loneliness* [969] and Rodney Sawatsky's "Dialogue with the Moonies" [970].

A final category of unofficial denominational responses consists of treatments by academics who have had more extensive interaction with the Church. These include Richard Quebedeaux's "Korean Missionaries to America" [960] and Fredrick Sontag's *Sun Myung Moon and the Unification Church* [985]. Quebedeaux's article, which examines the UC cross-culturally, is a useful overview of the Church's theology and practices but mixes description with advocacy. Sontag's book, however, has been criticized for being "obsessively" objective. Concluding only that "(1) The origins of the movement are genuinely humble, religious, and spiritual (which many doubt), and (2) the adaptability and solidarity of the movement are such that we are dealing with a movement here to stay" (12), Sontag includes a detailed apologia of "How and Why This Book Was Written," long verbatim quotations from members and opponents, a thirty-two page interview with Rev. Moon and a long list of mostly unanswered research questions. In this sense, his volume is of use as much as a case study of how one goes about studying a new religious movement as it is for specific conclusions about the UC.

759. Aagaard, Pernille. "Sun Myung Moon and the Third World War."
     New Religious Movements Up-Date 2 (April 1978): 38-42.

760. Aikawa, Takaaki, "Current Scene." *The Japanese Christian Quarterly*
     41 (Spring 1975): 114-15.

761. Alcorn, Wallace. "Escape from Sun Myung Moon." *Moody Monthly*
     76 (May 1976): 56-59.

762. Allan, John. *The Rising of the Moon: An Examination of Sun Myung
     Moon and His Unification Church.* Leicester, England:
     Intervarsity, 1980. 62 pp.

763. "Also in the News." *Presbyterian Journal* 38 (October 17, 1979): 5.

764. Anderson, Kerby. "Why Follow Moon?" *Insight* [Probe Ministries
     International, Religion Series], 1979, 1-9.

765. Austin, Charles M. "Sun Myung Moon: Korean Moon Rises with the
     Super-sell of Madison Avenue and the Fervor of a Sawdust Trail
     Revivalist." *Christian Herald* 97 (December 1974): 14-20.

766. Backes, N. "One More Shot at Sun Myung Moon--from the Inside."
     Moody Monthly 78 (November 1977): 122-23, 128-33.

767. Baker, John W. "Views of the Wall." *Report from the Capital 35*
     (July 1980): 6-.

768. Baldwin, Frank. "The Korea Lobby." *Christianity and Crisis* 36 (July 19, 1976): 162-68.

769. Ball, George H. "Jonestown Checklist: One Year Later." *The Christian Century* 96 (November 21, 1979): 1148-50.

770. "Baptist Pastor Resigns as Head of Religious Freedom Group." *Christianity Today* 29 (June 4, 1985) 56.

771. Barnes, Vickie. "Growth of Cults." *Accent* 10 (May 1980): 16-.

772. Bayly, Joseph. "The Church's Taxing Future." *Eternity* 35 (October 1984): 72.

773. ———. "The Dark Side of the Moon Case." *Eternity* 6 (January 1985): 55-56.

774. ———. From Danbury Prison--Sincerely, Sun Myung Moon." *Eternity* 36 (June 1985): 11.

775. Beach, Charles. "How to Witness to Moonies." *Laymen's Quarterly Bulletin* 8 (Summer 1980).

776. Benne, Robert. "Response to David Earle Anderson." *Dialog* 21 (Winter 1982): 56-59.

777. Berry, Harold J. *Moon's Unification Church: Is It Biblical?* Lincoln, N.Dak.: Back To the Bible, 1976. 22 pp.

778. ———. "Unification Church: Not a Biblical Unity." *Good News Broadcaster* 34 (December 1976): 10-11.

779. ———. "Unmasking the Man in the Moon." *Good News Broadcaster* 34 (November 1976).

780. "BJC Brief Opposes Law; Would Regulate Religion." *Report from the Capital* 36 (November 1981): 8-.

781. Bjornstad, James. "Can Unification Theology Become Christian?" *Contemporary Christianity*, January-February 1980, 1-3.

782. ———. *Counterfeits at Your Door*. Glendale, Calif.: Royal Books, 1979. 160 pp.

783. ———. *The Moon is Not the Son: (A Close Look at the Religion of Sun Myung Moon)*. Minneapolis: Bethany Fellowship, 1977. 125 pp.

784. _____. *Sun Myung Moon and the Unification Church.* Minneapolis:
      Bethany House, 1984. 57 pp.

785. Boa, Kenneth. "The Unification Church." In *Cults, World Religions
      and You,* 167-77. Wheaton, Ill.: Victor Books, 1977.

786. Bowers, Margaret. "Sun Myung Moon Has Taken Our Daughter."
      Eternity 27 (April 1976): 27-30, 59-62.

787. Burrell, Maurice C. "The Unification Church." Chap. 4 in *The
      Challenge of the Cults,* 52-72. Grand Rapids, Mich.: Baker Book
      House, 1981.

788. Carey, E.F. "The Park Regime." The *Christian Century* 93
      (November 3, 1976): 950-51.

789. "Challenge to Christians: The Unification Church." *Accent on Youth*
      10 (November 1977): 1-.

790. Chandler, Russell. "Fighting Cults: The Tucson Tactic." *Christianity
      Today* 21 (February 4, 1977): 57-61.

791. _____. "By the Light of the 'Saviorly' Moon." *Christianity Today* 18
      (March 1, 1974): 101-2.

792. "A Christian and a Cultist: How the I.R.S. Brought Them Together."
      New Life Magazine 2 (August 1984) 11-12.

793. Christian World Liberation Front. "Prophet? A Challenge to Sun
      Myung Moon." *Radical Religion* 1 (Summer-Fall 1974): 67-68.

794. "Church Leaders in Korea Have Declared That the Unification Church
      Is Not a Sect of the Christian Church.'" *Christianity Today* 23
      (October 5, 1979): 73.

795. Clapp, Rodney. "The Moonies Seek a Niche in American Religion."
      Christianity Today 26 (March 5, 1982): 44-48.

796. _____. "Moon's Movie Disaster: To Describe Inchon, the Critics
      Hauled Out New Adjectives." *Christianity Today* 26 (October 22,
      1982): 63.

797. Clarkson, Fred. "'Father', Theocracy, and Other People's Money."
      Christianity and Crisis 45 (October 28, 1985): 424-28.

798. Commission on Faith and Order. *A Critique of the Theology of the
      Unification Church as Set Forth in the Divine Principle.* An Official
      Study Document. New York: National Council of the Churches of
      Christ in the U.S.A, June 1977. 11 pp.

799. Cox, Harvey. "The Real Threat of the Moonies." *Christianity and Crisis* 37 (November 14, 1977): 258-63.

800. Crim, Keith. "The Unification Church" and "Moon, Sun Myung." In *The Abingdon Dictionary of Living Religions,* edited by Keith Crim. Nashville: Abingdon, 1981.

801. "Cult Probe Criticized." The *Christian Century* 96 (September 26, 1979): 914.

802. Deedy, John. "The Church in the World: The Unification Church and the City of Gloucester." *Theology Today* 37 (January 1981): 480-86.

803. "Deprogramming: The Cults Fight Back." *Christianity Today* 21 (June 17, 1977): 36-37.

804. "Deprogramming Suit (Unification Church Member Thomas Ward's Suit against His Parents)." *Christian Century* 99 (February 3, 1982): 112.

805. "Door Interviews: Lewis Rambo, Richard Quebedeaux, Ron Enroth." *The Wittenberg Door* 59 (February-March 1981): 8-18.

806. Duncan, Paul. *Who is Sun Myung Moon?* Cleveland, Tenn.: Pathway. 21 pp.

807. Durham, Deanna. *Life Among the Moonies.* Plainfield, N.J.: Logos International, 1981. 202 pp.

808. Edwards, Cliff. "Son [sic] Myung Moon and the Scholars." *Dialog* 21 (Winter 1982): 56-59.

809. Eidsmoe, John. "The Christian and the Cults." Chap. 18 in *The Christian Legal Adviser,* 325-39. Milford, Mich.: Mott Media, 1984.

810. Elkins, Chris. "Following the Cults: Why I Joined a Cult and Why I Left." *His* 44 (May 1984): 8-10.

811. _____. *Heavenly Deception.* Wheaton, Ill.: Tyndale, 1980. 142 pp.

812. _____. "How to Answer a Moonie." *Christian Life* 42 (August 1980): 36-37, 55.

813. _____. "Responding to a Moon Disciple." *Royal Service* 1 (August 1978): 12.

814. _____. *What Do You Say to a Moonie?* Wheaton, Ill.: Tyndale, 1981. 95 pp.

815. Elkins, Kay. "God Gave Us Back Our Son." *Home Missions* 49 (April 1978): 13-.

816. Enroth, Ronald M. "Cults/Counter-cult." *Eternity* 28 (November 1977): 18-22, 32-35.

817. _____. *The Lure of the Cults.* Chappaqua, N.Y.: Christian Herald Books, 1979. 139 pp.

818. _____. *Youth, Brainwashing and the Extremist Cults.* Grand Rapids, Mich.: Zondervan, 1977. 221 pp.

819. Enroth, Ronald M., ed. *A Guide to Cults and New Religions.* Downers Grove, Ill.: Intervarsity, 1983.

Contains item 1018.

820. Enroth, Ronald M., and J. Gordon Melton. *Why Cults Succeed Where the Church Fails.* Elgin, Ill.: Brethren Press, 1985. 133 pp.

821. Fellman, E. "A Day without Miracles." *Moody Monthly* 81 (April 1981): 39-40.

822. Franklin, Carol B. "Sun Myung Moon Seeks Worldwide Takeover." *Report From the Capital* 34 (January 1979): 8-.

823. Gallagher, Sharon. "A Serious Talk with Moon's Followers." *Spiritual Counterfeits Project Newsletter* 5 (January-February 1979).

824. Gallup, George, and David Poling. "The Yearnings of Youth." Chap. 1 in *The Search for America's Faith,* 15-39. Nashville: Abingdon, 1980.

825. Gaybbe, Brian. "A Week Spent with the Moonies." *Theologia Evangelica* 15 (1982): 29-35.

826. Gittings, James. "Genri Undo." *The Japan Christian Quarterly* 34 (Summer 1968): 194-98.

827. Glissman, Dan. "Heavenly Deceit." *Christianity Today* 23 (October 20, 1978): 9-10.

828. "God is Alive and Working for President Park; Profile: Rev. Moon Sun Myung." *AMPO: Japan Christian Quarterly* 7 (April-June 1975): 5 pp.

829. Gram, Robert L. "Unification Theology and Gnostic Thought." *Reformed Review* 31 (Spring 1978): 143-47.

830. Green, Michael. "The Unification Church." In *I Believe in Satan's Downfall,* 150-56. Grand Rapids, Mich.: Eerdmans, 1981.

831. "Guidelines on Cult Debate Scheduled by Europeans." *Report from the Capital* 39 (April 1984): 12.

832. Gruss, Edmond C. "Reverend Sun Myung Moon and the Unification Church." *The Discerner* 8 (April-June 1976): 7-12.

833. ———. "Sun Myung Moon and the Unification Church." Chap. 15 in *Cults and the Occult,* rev. ed., 132-41. Grand Rapids, Mich.: Baker Book House, 1980.

834. Haack, Freidrich W. "New Youth Religions, Psychomutation and Technological Civilization." *International Review of Mission* 67 (October 1978): 436-47.

835. Handberg, Hugo. "Who Are the Moonies?" *The Discerner* 11 (July-September 1984): 5-8.

836. Hargrove, Barbara. "Some Advice for the Moon-Struck." *Reflection* [Yale Divinity School] 75 (April 1978): 4-7.

837. Hastey, Stan L. "Supreme Court Takes Church-State Actions." *Report from the Capital* 33 (October 1978): 5-.

838. Hefley, James C. "New Moon Rising." Chap. 2 in *The Youthnappers,* 12-32. Wheaton, Ill.: SP Publications, 1970.

839. Heim, S. Mark. "Divine Principle and the Second Advent." *The Christian Century* 94 (May 11, 1977): 448-51.

840. Henry, Brenda. "Leaving Sun Myung Moon" (An Interview with Brooks Alexander). *Radix* 8 (September-October 1976): 3-5.

841. Hexham, Irving, and Myrtle Langley. "Cracking the Moonie Code." *Crux* 15 (September 1979): 25-28.

842. "High Priced PR." *The Christian Century* 102 (April 17, 1985): 376.

843. Hitt, Russell T. "'Moonies' Cash and Class Upgrade Image." *Eternity* 31 (January 1980): 9-16.

844. Hondorp, Catherine. "Not Father, Not Son, Just Moon." *The Church Herald,* April 21, 1978, 4-5.

845. Hopkins, Joseph, M. "Are Moonies in a New Phase? Raiders and Koreanization." *Christianity Today* 24 (June 27, 1980): 60.

846. _____. "4000 Moonies Married." *Eternity* 33 (October 1982): 19.

847. _____. "Is Forum Integrity Eclipsed by Moon?" *Christianity Today* 23 (January 19, 1979): 38-39.

848. _____. "Meeting the Moonies on Their Territory." *Christianity Today* 22 (August 18, 1978): 40-42.

849. "How Moonies Win Friends and Influence People." *Christianity Today* 26 (January 1, 1982): 50.

850. "How to Spot a Cult." *Moody Monthly* 77 (July-August 1977): 32-33.

851. Hunt, Dave. *The Cult Explosion.* Irvine, Calif.: Harvest House, 1980. 270 pp.

852. Hunt, Everett N. "Moon Sun Myung and the Tong-il." In *Dynamic Religious Movements*, edited by David Hesselgrave, 103-27. Grand Rapids, Mich.: Baker Book House, 1978.

853. "Information about Mr. Sun Myung Moon." Seoul, Korea: Church of the Nazarene, Korea Mission, n.d. 1 p.

854. Inglehart, Glenn A. *Church Members and Nontraditional Religious Groups.* Nashville: Broadman, 1985. 154 pp.

855. "An Interview about Dr. Sun Myung Moon." *Your Church* 23 (January-February 1977): 11, 49-55.

856. Irving, Joy. "Cults and Pluralism." *The Christian Century* 99 (April 14, 1982): 450-51.

857. Jaeger, Henry J. "By the Light of a Masterly Moon." *Christianity Today* 20 (December 19, 1975): 13-16.

858. Jeffrey, Paul. "By the Light of the Reverend Moon: Unification Church Members at PSR." *Evangelion* [A Publication of the Community Association, Pacific School of Religion, Berkeley, Calif.] 20 (January 18, 1980): 3-7.

859. Jennings, Ray. "Moonies: A Movement in Search of a Theology." *The American Baptist* 180 (January 1982): 11-13.

860. Johnson, Gerry. "The Korean Messiah." *Faith for the Family* 3 (May-June 1975): 9-10.

861. Johnson, Rose, as told to Don Ratzlaff. *As Angels of Light.* Hillsboro, Kans.: Kindred Press, 1980. 141 pp.

862. "Judge Upholds Parents in 'Moonie' Dispute." *Report from the Capital* 37 (July 1982): 13-.

863. Kang, Wi Jo. "The Influence of the Unification Church in the United States of America." *Missiology, An International Review* 3 (July 1975): 357-68.

864. _____. "The Unification Church: Christian Church or Political Movement?" *Japanese Religions* 9 (July 1976): 19-32.

865. Karcz, Lorraine. "Members of Rev. Moon's Church Enroll at HDS. *Harvard Divinity Bulletin* 9 (February-March 1979): 6-7.

866. Keifer, Everett W. "Shining Sun and Moon." *Christian Standard* 111 (April 4, 1976): 7-9.

867. Kemperman, Steve. *Lord of the Second Advent.* Ventura, Calif.: Regal, 1982. 175 pp.

868. Keylock, Leslie R. "To Combat Charges That They Are Anti-Semitic, Moonies Alter Their Doctrine." *Christianity Today* 28 (December 14, 1984): 56-57.

869. Kim, Hyun Chil. "Sun Myung Moon and His Unification Church." *Capital Baptist*, March 7, 1974, 3,6.

870. Kirban, Salem. "The Unification Church." In *Satan's Angels Exposed,* 282-85. Huntington Valley, Pa.: Salem Kirban, 1980.

871. Kolbe, Edward H. "The Cults--Counterfeit Hope for the Aimless." *The Disciple* 6 (May 20, 1979): 4-6.

872. Koranda, Tom. *The Moon Cult.* Collingswood, N.J.: The Bible for Today, 1976.

873. "The Korean Christ." *Christianity Today* 18 (October 12, 1973): 67.

874. "Korean Churches Denounce Rev. Moon." *The Alliance Witness* 114 (November 28, 1979): 13.

875. "Korea's Christian Churches Call Moon Unchristian." *The Presbyterian Outlook* 161 (October 8, 1979): 5.

876. "Korea's Christian Churches call Rev. Moon un-Christian." *The Church Herald*, October 19, 1979.

877. Lane, Beldon C. "Brainwashing and Conversion." *The Reformed Journal* 29 (April 1979): 9-12.

878. Langford, Harris. *Traps: A Probe of Those Strange New Cults.* Montgomery, Ala.: Presbyterian Church in America, 1977. 191 pp.

879. Larsen, David L. "The World Unification Church of Sun Myung Moon." *The Discerner*, April-June 1975, 7 pp.

880. Larson, Bob. "Rev. Sun Myung Moon (Unification Church)." Chap. 38 in *Larson's Book of Cults*, 224-33. Wheaton, Ill.: Tyndale, 1982.

881. Lenz, Doug. "Twenty-two Months as a Moonie." *LCA Patterns: The Magazine For Professional Leaders of the Lutheran Church in America*, February 1982, 12-15.

882. Lestarjette, Steve. "A Moonie Finds God." *Christ for the Nations,* September 1978, 10-12.

883. Levitt, Zola. *The Spirit of Sun Myung Moon.* Irvine, Calif.: Harvest House, 1976. 127 pp.

884. Lewis, James N., Jr. "The Unification Church of Sun Myung Moon." *The California Southern Baptist*, November 5, 1974, 8-9.

885. ———. "The Unification Church of Sun Myung Moon." In *The Christian Confronting the Cults.* N.p.: The Sunday School Board of the Southern Baptist Convention, 1979. 64 pp.

886. Lewis, Warren. "Is The Rev. Moon a Christian." *Mission* 12 (December 1978): 7-9.

887. Lochhass, Philip. "The New Messiahs." *The Lutheran Witness* 96 (April 10, 1977): 8-9.

888. ———. "The Unification Church." Chap. 3 in *How to Respond to... the New Christian Religions*, 20-23. St. Louis: Concordia, 1979.

889. Loucks, Celeste. "Contempo Interview: Chris Elkins." *Contempo* 9 (January 1979): 1-.

890. Lowen, A. Wayne. "A Bright Light on Moon." *The Lookout*, April 2, 1978, 8-9.

891. Luidens, Donald. "Lessons from a Summer Wedding." *The Church Herald* 39 (November 5, 1982): 6-9.

892. Lyles, Jean Caffey. "Letting Go: Everybody Has the Right to Be Wrong; Deprogramming Issue." *The Christian Century* 94 (May 11, 1977): 451-53.

893. _____. "The Religious Rights of the Unlovely." *The Christian Century* 99 (June 2, 1982): 652-53.

894. McBeth, Leon. "The Unification Church: The Korean Christ, Sun Myung Moon." Chap. 1 in *Strange New Religions*, 7-27. Nashville: Broadman, 1977.

895. MacCollam, Joel A. *Carnival of Souls: Religious Cults and Young People.* New York: Seabury, 1979. 188 pp.

896. _____. Joel A. "Cults and Their Victims: The Case for Deprogramming." *The Living Church* 175 (July 24, 1977): 9-11.

897. _____. "The Unification Church." *The Living Church* 173 (December 12, 1976): 8-9.

898. _____. *The Weekend that Never Ends.* New York: Seabury Professional Services, 1977. 37 pp.

899. McDowell, Josh, and Don Stewart. "The Unification Church/'Moonies.' " In *Understanding the Cults: Handbook of Today's Religions,* 133-40. San Bernadino, Calif.: Here's Life, 1982.

900. McManus, Una, and John Cooper. *Dealing with Destructive Cults.* Grand Rapids, Mich.: Zondervan, 1984. 159 pp.

901. "Many Shall Come in My Name." *Christianity Today* 19 (November 8, 1974): 28-29.

902. Martin, Dan. "From Moon Back to Christ." *World Mission Journal* 49 (March 1978): 4-5.

903. _____. "God Never Let Me Go." *Home Missions Notebook* 49 (April 1978): 12-13.

904. _____. "To Moon and Back." *Probe* 9 (June 1979): 2-5.

905. Martin, Walter. "The Unification Church." In *Walter Martin's Cults Reference Bible,* 57-62. Santa Ana, Calif.: Vision House, 1981.

906. Marty, Martin E. "American Religion: Its Stocks in the 70's." *The Christian Century* 96 (December 5, 1979): 1206-10.

907. _____. "I Dreamed I Went to Seminary in Its Maiden-term. Rah!" *The Christian Century* 92 (October 15, 1975): 911.

908. _____. "Religious Cause, Religious Cure." *The Christian Century* 96 (February 28, 1979): 210-15.

909. _____. "Say It Ain't So, Roger!" *The Christian Century* 92 (June 25, 1975): 647.

910. Matthews, Arthur, and Edward E. Plowman. "Meeting Moon at the Monument." *Christianity Today* 21 (October 8, 1976): 59-62.

911. Maust, John. "Cleaver: Gazing at a Different Moon." *Christianity Today* 23 (December 7, 1979): 49-50.

912. _____. "The Moonies Cross Wits with Cult-watching Critics." *Christianity Today* 23 (July 20, 1979): 38-40.

913. Means, Pat. "Sun Myung Moon: The Militant Messiah." Chap. 9 in *The Mystical Maze*, 183-95. Arrowhead Springs, Calif.: Campus Crusade, 1976.

914. Melton, J. Gordon. "What Is Moon Up To?" *Christianity Today* 22 (April 7, 1978): 47-50.

915. _____. "What's behind the Moonie Mass Marriages." *Christianity Today* 27 (December 16, 1983): 28-31.

916. Melton, J. Gordon, and Robert L. Moore. *The Cult Experience: Responding to the New Religious Pluralism.* New York: Pilgrim Press, 1982. 180 pp.

917. Messer, Donald E. "Rescuing the Cult Member." *The Christian Century* 99 (February 24, 1982): 213-15.

918. "Mr. Moon Comes on Strong and Rather Strange." *Eternity* 25 (December 4, 1974): 12.

919. Mojzes, Paul. "New ERA Conference on Unification Theology." *Journal of Ecumenical Studies* 19 (Fall 1982): 864-65.

920. Mook, Jane Day. "The Unification Church." *A.D.* 3 (May 1974): 30-36.

921. "Moon Called unChristian." *The Christian Century* 96 (October 10, 1979): 969.

922. "Moon Church Loses Libel Suit." *The Christian Century* 98 (April 22, 1981): 440-41.

923. "Moon Held Guilty of Tax Fraud." *Christianity Today* 26 (June 18, 1982): 59.

924. "Moon Performs Mass Matching." *The Alliance Witness* 114 (July 11, 1979): 13.

925. "Moon Pleads Not Guilty in Tax Case, Cites Discrimination." *Christianity Today* 25 (November 20, 1981): 75.

926. "Moon Sect 'Non-Christian.' " *The Christian Century* 102 (December 4, 1985): 1112.

927. "Moon Sentenced." *The Christian Century* 99 (August 4, 1982): 816-17.

928. "Moon Trek; Many Enterprises." *Christianity Today* 22 (October 21, 1977): 43.

929. "Moon Wins Two, Loses One." *The Christian Century* 99 (June 2, 1982): 656.

930. "Moonie Tactics in New York ... and Minnesota." *The Christian Century* 96 (February 28, 1979): 209.

931. "The Moonies Almost Got Me." In *Escape from Darkness*, edited by James R. Adair and Ted Miller, 80-85. Wheaton Ill.: Victor Books, 1982.

932. "Moonies Arrested." *The Christian Century* 98 (April 29, 1981): 472-73.

933. "Moonies Buy Bank." *The Christian Century* 100 (April 13, 1983): 336.

934. "Moon's Credibility Game." *The Christian Century* 92 (September 24, 1975): 812-13.

935. "Moon's Marriages." *Christianity Today* 19 (February 28, 1975): 42.

936. Morgan, Mary Neal. "Meet the Missionary Chris Elkins-Sharing the Truth about the Unification Church." *Royal Service* 73 (August 1978): 10-11.

937. _____. "Responding to a Moon Disciple; Chris Elkins Speaks from Experience." *Royal Service* 73 (August 1978): 12.

938. ———. Zen and the Unification Church." *Royal Service* 73 (August 1978): 2-5.

939. "NAC Personality ... Chris Elkins." *Accent* 9 (April 1979): 10-.

940. Newport, John P. "The Unification Church." In *Christ and the New Consciousness*, 119-39. Nashville: Broadman, 1978.

941. "The New Right Disagrees over Taking Donations from Sun Myung Moon (Sun Myung Moon's Unification Church)." *Christianity Today* 28 (October 19, 1984): 42-43.

942. Noebel, David A. *World Unification Church: New Christianity or Old Paganism? The "Gospel" According to the Reverend Sun Myung Moon.* 3d ed. Tulsa: American Christian College Publishers, 1974. 14 pp.

943. "$1 Million Due in Back Taxes." *Eternity* 34 (May 1983): 8-9.

944. *An Open Letter to the Unified Family of Sun Myung Moon.* Berkeley, Calif.: Spiritual Counterfeits, n.d. 6 pp.

945. Osborne, Grant R. "Countering the Cultic Curse." *Christianity Today* 23 (June 29, 1979): 22-24.

946. "Our Son Joined the Moonies." *The Mennonite* 94 (July 10, 1979): 450-51.

947. Owen, R.J. *The Moonies: A Critical Look at a Contemporary Group.* London, England: Wardlock Educational, 1982. 63 pp.

948. Pakkala, Lorainne J. "God's Word Breaks the Piper's Spell." *Good News Broadcaster* 35 (December 1977): 17-19.

949. "Pardon for Moon?" *The Christian Century* 102 (August 28-September 4, 1985): 762-63.

950. Park, Young-Kwan. *Unification Church.* Seoul, Korea: Christian Literature Crusade, 1980. 105 pp.

951. Passantino, Robert, and Gretchen Passantino. "Answers to the Moonies." Chap. 5 in *Answers to the Cultist at Your Door*, 122-38. Eugene, Ore.: Harvest House, 1978.

952. Peerman, Dan. "Korean Moonshine." The *Christian Century* 91 (December 4, 1974): 1139-41.

953. Pennel, Joe E., Jr. "Prophets-True and False." *Accent-On Youth* 10 (August 1978): 14-17.

954. Peterson, William J. "Sun Myung Moon and the Unification Church." Chap. 14 in *Those Curious New Cults in the Eighties*, 163-77. New Canaan, Conn.: Keats, 1982.

955. Plowman, Edward E. "Deprogramming: A Right to Rescue?" *Christianity Today* 20 (May 7, 1976): 38-39.

956. _____. "Help Us Get Our Children Back." *Christianity Today* 20 (March 12, 1976): 45-46.

957. Pritchett, Ballard. "Religious Cults." *The Chaplain* 34 (3rd quarter 1977): 43-55.

958. Proctor, William. "False Prophets and the Cults ... Sun Myung Moon and the Unification Church." *The New Logos* (March-April 1979).

959. _____. "Moon Eclipse." *Christianity Today* 19 (October 11, 1974): 49-50.

960. Quebedeaux, Richard. "Korean Missionaries to America." *New Conversations* 6 (Spring 1982): 6-15.

961. "Religion on the Right in South Korea: Moon, Sun Myung, Etc.; An ICUIS Selected Bibliography." In *An ICUIS Country Profile: South Korea*, 28-34. Chicago: The Institute on the Church in Urban-Industrial Society, 1976.

962. "Religion Not Primary; Moonies Lose Exemption." *Report from the Capital* 36 (July 1981): 9-.

963. "Reverend Moon Wins and Loses." *Eternity* 33 (July 1982): 8-9.

964. Robbins, Mary Ann. "Not by Works." *Accent* 10 (May 1980): 30-.

965. Robertson, Irvine. "Sun Myung Moon's Unification Church." Chap. 3 in *What the Cults Believe*, 2d ed. 62-74. Chicago: Moody Press, 1979.

966. Ross, Alan Dean. "The Moonies; A Quest for an Objective View." *Mission* 12 (December 1978): 3-6.

967. Salladay, Tim. "Wise Moonie Management?" *Student* 63 (April 1984): 46.

968. Sandon, Leo, Jr. "Korean Moon: Waxing or Waning?" *Theology Today* 35 (July 1978): 159-67.

969. _____. *True Family: Korean Communitarianism and American Loneliness.* Communications Office Monograph #3. New York: United Ministries in Higher Education, 1978. 13 pp.

970. Sawatsky, Rodney. "Dialogue with the Moonies." *Theology Today*
     35 (April 1978): 88-89.

971. "Seminary Denounced." *The Christian Century* 102 (August 28-
     September 4, 1985): 102.

972. Schipper, Earl. "First Unification Church." In *Cults in North
     America*, 127-48. Grand Rapids, Mich.: Baker Book House,
     1982.

973. Seaman, Lee. "The Unification Church--Blessing or Monster?" *Japan
     Christian Activity News* nos. 470, 472, 474-75 (March 14-May 23,
     1975).

974. "Seminary Honors Moon." *The Christian Century* (June 19, 1985):
     609.

975. Sheridan, George. "The 'New' Religions." *Home Missions* 48
     (November 1977): 26-35.

976. _____. "Unification Church." *Missions USA* 55 (September 1984):
     87-.

977. Short, Shirl. "The Menace of the New Cults." *Moody Monthly* 77
     (July-August 1977): 26-31.

978. "Should Christians Help Defend Moonie Leader?" *Chrisma* 10 (August
     1984): 97-98.

979. Sire, James W. *Scripture Twisting (20 Ways the Cults Misread the
     Bible)*. Downers Grove, Ill.: Intervarsity, 1980. 177 pp.

980. Sontag, Fredrick. "Issues for the 1980s: Two Meditations." *The
     Drew Gateway* 51 (Spring 1981): 45-52.

981. _____. "Marriage and the Family in Unification Theology." *New
     Religious Movements Up-Date* 6 (September 1982).

982. _____. "New Minority Religions as Heresies." *New Religious
     Movements Up-Date* 7 (June 1983): 18-26.

983. _____. "New Moon Sophistry." *Religion in Life* 46 (Fall 1977): 269-
     77.

984. _____. "Religion and Violence." *The Circuit Rider* 3 (October 1979):
     8-9.

985. _____. *Sun Myung Moon and the Unification Church*. Nashville:
     Abingdon, 1977. 224 pp.

986. *The Son Will Never Set on This Moon.* Holbrook, N.Y.: Narrow Way Ministries, n.d. 7 pp.

987. Sovik, Anne. "A Selected and Annotated Bibliography." *International Review of Mission* 67 (October, 1978): 474-78.

988. Sparks, Jack. "The Unification Church of Sun Myung Moon." In *The Mind Benders,* 121-53. Nashville: Thomas Nelson, 1977.

989. Spring, Beth. "Sun Myung Moon's Followers Recruit Christians to Assist in Battle against Communism." *Christianity Today* 29 (June 14, 1985) 55, 57-58.

990. _____. "With Their Leader in Prison, Moonies Pursue Legitimacy." *Christianity Today* 28 (September 7, 1984): 56-60.

991. Steinkuehler, Pearl. "Religionists, Witnessing to Us." *Royal Service* 76 (March 1982): 16-.

992. Stellway, Richard J. "The Four Steps to Cultic Conversion." *Christianity Today* 23 (June 29, 1979): 24-26.

993. Stenzel, James. "Rev. Moon and His Bicentennial Blitz." *Christianity and Crisis* 36 (July 19, 1976): 173-75.

994. Streiker, Lowell. "The Unification Church of Sun Myung Moon." In *The Cults Are Coming!* 20-49. Nashville: Abingdon, 1978.

995. Studer, Carol. "The Heresies of Sun Myung Moon." *Theolog* 19 (December 8, 1976): 1.

996. "Sun Myung Moon." *The Herald of Freedom* 17 (July 19, 1974): 1.

997. "Sun Myung Moon Says Unification Church Will Accomplish Goal." *Newscope* 5 (September 23, 1977): 4.

998. Swope, George W. "What I Learned about Sun Myung Moon." 3-part series. *Christian Herald* 99 (July-October, 1976).

999. Thelle, Notto R. "The Unification Church: A New Religion." *Japanese Religions* 9 (July 1976): 2-13.

1000. Tingle, Donald S., and Richard A. Fordyce. *Phases and Faces of the Moon (A Critical Evaluation of the Unification Church and Its Principles).* Hicksville, N.Y.: Exposition Press, 1979. 90 pp.

1001. Toalston, Art. "The Unification Church Aims a Major Public Relations Effort at Christian Leaders." *Christianity Today* 29 (April 19, 1985): 50-51.

1002. Touchton, Judy. "Bayou Residents Protest 'Moonie' Industries." *Home Missions* 49 (October 1978): 16-.

1003. Turner, D. "What Is the Unification Church?" *Adult Leader* 10 (Winter 1977-78): 14-.

1004. Turner, J. "Current Religious Movements." *Junior Hi Ways* 4 (September 1978): 25-.

1005. Vander Werff, Lyle. "Moon and Christian Orthodoxy." *The Reformed Journal* 27 (August 1977): 6-10.

1006. "Vatican Takes Exception." *The Christian Century* 102 (January 2-9, 1985): 9-10.

1007. Verghese, C. Sam. "Unification Church (Moonies)." In *Confronting the Cults*, 49-55. Boston: Evangelistic Association of New England, 1979.

1008. Webb, Lawrence E. "Witness to Unification Church Members." *Royal Service* 74 (July 1979): 26-28.

1009. Weldon, John F. "A Sampling of the New Religions: Four Groups Described." *International Review of Mission* 67 (October 1978): 407-26.

1010. White, James W. "Unification Church's Anti-Communist Drive." *The Christian Century* 102 (August 28-September 4, 1985): 771-72.

1011. Winkler, Kathleen Knief. "Morning with the Moonies." *The Lutheran Witness* 99 (January 1980): 7-9.

1012. Won, Yong Ji. "World Mission Observer: Jesus or Moon." *Concordia Journal* 6 (May 1980): 88-89.

1013. Woodruff, Michael J. "Religious Freedom and the New Religions." *International Review of Mission* 67 (October 1978): 468-73.

1014. Worthing, Sharon. "Courts, 'Cults,' Conservators: A Constitutional Challenge." *Christianity and Crisis* 41 (March 16, 1981): 57-59.

1015. _____. "Deprogramming and Religious Freedom." *Church and State* 30 (May 1977): 10-15.

1016. Yamamoto, J. Isamu. *The Moon Doctrine*. Madison, Wis.: Intervarsity, 1976. 41 pp.

1017. _____. *The Puppet Master: An Inquiry into Sun Myung Moon and the Unification Church*. Downers Grove, Ill.: Intervarsity, 1977. 136 pp.

1018. _____. "Unification Church (Moonies)." In *A Guide to Cults & New Religions* (item 819), pp. 151-72.

B. THE CATHOLIC RESPONSE

Catholic responses to the UC range from the parochial to the progressive. Parochial responses, which predominate in mass-circulation and local diocesan periodicals, have reacted to alleged UC inroads into the American Catholic community. This thrust is evident in such titles as "My Nightmare Years as a Moonie" [1039], "35% of This Man's Followers Were Catholic" [1047], and "The Reverend Sun Myung Moon: Pied Piper of Tarrytown" [1060]. At the same time, resurgent conservatism within the Catholic hierarchy has resulted in some official opposition to the UC. In early 1985, for example, the Vatican opposed the Catholic University of La Plata, Argentina, granting an honorary degree to Rev. Moon. Later that year, Japanese bishops issued a statement saying that the UC "has nothing to do with Catholicism, not even with Christianity, and is not an object of ecumenism." These reactions were reported in the American religious press [926, 1006, 1038, 1057].

Progressive responses to the UC stem from Catholic reflection on their past minority status in the United States and from the climate of openness to other faiths evident within sectors of Catholicism since Vatican II. Alleged encroachments on the UC's civil and religious liberties have elicited a number of responses in progressive Catholic publications. Though, on the whole, supportive of UC claims, these treatments have stressed broader questions of U.S. constitutional guarantees, continuing American intolerance of new religions and modern secularism. These larger concerns are apparent in several articles defending the UC aginst charges of "brainwashing" its members. Herbert Richardson, for example, in "The Psychiatric State" [1050], argued that "attacks against the Unification Church are directed against all religion." Further, as a Protestant theologian writing in a Catholic journal, Richardson reminded his readers "what we Protestants knew about Catholics in pre-Vatican II days." Similarly, Richard Walsh, in "Moonies--Religious Converts or Psychic Victims?" [1058] suggested that complaints against UC religious indoctrination "should have an ominous ring to American Catholics" (440). Also, Peter Steinfels, in "A Setback for What?" [1056] asserted that in ordering temporary conservatorships for UC members the issue is "not whether Reverend Moon's Unification Church suffers a 'setback,' but whether freedom of religion suffered a setback" (232). In addition to opposing deprogramming, progressive Catholic publications have supported UC solicitation rights [1035] and criticized what was perceived as legal harassment of Rev. Moon [1028]. Catholic support of the UC on libertarian grounds, however, has not been automatic. In "Dr. Moon and Church Property" [1029], the Jesuit weekly *America* analysed concerns expressed over the Supreme Court's decision not to review Rev. Moon's conviction on tax evasion charges and argued, "Government is not being oppressive when it puts the burden on church leaders to distinguish clearly between private and church property in accordance with well-settled rules" (409).

Ecumenical as opposed to libertarian approaches to the UC derive, as suggested, from the climate of openness to other faiths prevailing in progressive sectors of the Catholic Church since Vatican II. According to Joseph Fichter [1033], ecumenical treatments can be distinguished from descriptive accounts by the "positive effort" not only to understand from the other's perspective but also "to seek out the truth in any religious cult" (19). At the same time, ecumenical should not be confused with "uncritical" or with the minimizing of religious differences. These latter dimensions are well illustrated in Richard A. Blake's "The Attraction of the Moonies" [1022] and Edward J. Cripps' "Listening to Those Who Search" [1024], both of which criticize the UC for "uneasiness ... in the face of mystery" (Blake: 84). Tom Holahan, however, wrote of "Learning from Reverend Moon" [1037].

The most thoroughgoing Catholic ecumenical response to the UC has been that of noted "Catholic sociologist" Joseph Fichter in *The Holy Family of Father Moon* [1033] and "Marriage, Family, and Sun Myung Moon" [1034]. The earlier of these, a controversial cover article in *America*, credits the UC with having "come upon a family program that works" (228). The latter treatment combines "a sociological analysis of the main structural features of the Unification Church" with "a deep desire to promote ecumenical outreach" (3, 4). In this respect, Fichter's approach is an example of what might be termed "academic" ecumenism. Other ecumenical responses include Thomas McGowan's "The Unification Church" [1041], Noel Dermot O'Donoghue's "The Community in Question--Reflections on the Cult Phenomemon" [1048], and John Saliba's "The New Religious Movements: Some Theological Reflections" [1054].

Ecumenical Catholic journals also have published articles on the UC by non-Catholics, frequently academics with long-standing research interests in the UC or with particular expertise. Examples are Eileen Barker's discussion of conversion in "Free to Choose? Some Thoughts on the Unification Church and Other Religious Movements" [1021] and Thomas Robbins and Dick Anthony's "The Unification Church" [1051], an analysis of the UC's political orientation. Even more striking was Regnery Gateway's decision to publish Unification Church in America President Mose Durst's autobiographical *To Bigotry No Sanction: Reverend Sun Myung Moon and the Unification Church* [1031]. In this work, Dr. Durst ranges over a variety of topics including his personal background, conversion and beliefs as well as his views on Rev. Moon, UC community life, social service, religious conflict, UC mistakes and the UC "vision of the future." Neither Dr. Durst nor his editors indicate, however, why he sought out a Catholic publisher or why Regnery Gateway agreed to publish his volume.

1019. Ackerman, Todd. "In Moon's Case, Fundamental Issues Are at Stake." *National Catholic Register* 60 (May 27, 1984): 1-.

1020. Anthony, C. "In Moon's Church: One Woman's Story." *Our Sunday Visitor* 66 (August 7, 1977): 3-4.

1021. Barker, Eileen. "Free to Choose? Some Thoughts on the Unification Church and Other Religious Movements." 2 parts. *The Clergy Review* 65 (October-November 1980): 365-68; 392-98.

1022. Blake, Richard A. "The Attraction of the Moonies." *America* 142 (February 2, 1980): 83-85.

1023. Carmen, Topia, Maria de. "What Opus Dei Has Done for the Church ... and for the Sake of Its Reputation." Interview by Mark R. Day. *National Catholic Reporter* 19 (May 27, 1983): 12-13.

1024. Cripps, Edward J. "Listening to Those Who Search." *America* 135 (September 18, 1976): 147-49.

1025. Day, Mark R. "Moonies Release Irish Woman after Protests." *National Catholic Reporter* 17 (October 2, 1981): 23.

*   Deedy, John. "The Church in the World: The Unification Church and the City of Gloucester." Cited above as item 802.

1026. _____. "Dangerous Cults." *Tablet* 236 (September 11, 1982): 906-8.

1027. Desiderio, Frank. "Rev. Sun Moon: Prophet or Promoter?" *Paulist Institute for Religious Research*, Summer 1978, 19 pp.

1028. "Dr. Moon and the Courts." *America* 146 (June 12, 1982): 452.

1029. "Dr. Moon and Church Property." *America* 150 (June 2, 1984): 409.

1030. Drinan, Robert Francis. "Sun Myung Moon's Conviction on Tax Fraud, Even if Justified, Is Incongruous." *National Catholic Reporter* 20 (May 25, 1984): 8.

1031. Durst, Mose. *To Bigotry No Sanction: Reverend Sun Myung Moon and the Unification Church.* Chicago: Regnery Gateway, 1984. 181 pp.

1032. Fichter, Joseph H. "Hammering the Heretics: Religion vs. Cults." *The Witness* 66 (January 1983): 4-6.

1033. _____. *The Holy Family of Father Moon.* Kansas City, Mo.: Leaven Press, 1985. 155 pp.

1034. _____. "Marriage, Family and Sun Myung Moon." *America* 141 (October 27, 1979): 226-28.

1035. "Freedom and the Unification Church." *America* 146 (May 8, 1982): 352.

1036. Garvey, John. "Are the Cults a Judgement on the Churches?" *Katallagete* 6 (Fall 1977): 21-26.

1037. Holahan, Tom. "Learning from Rev. Moon." *Paulist Institute for Religious Research*, Summer 1978, 19-20.

1038. "Japanese Warned about Moon's Unification Church." *National Catholic Register* 61 (July 28, 1985): 3.

1039. Kemperman, Steve. "My Nightmare Years as a Moonie." *Catholic Digest* 44 (June 1980) 88-98.

1040. _____. My 3 1/2 Years with the Moonies." *Sign* 59 (December 1979): 44-51.

1041. McGowan, Thomas. "The Unification Church." *Ecumenist* 17 (January 8, 1979): 21-25.

1042. Marchland, Roger. "Mr. Moon and the Unification Church." *Ligourian* 66 (June 1978): 34-39.

1043. "Moon Beams." *America* 151 (December 15, 1984): 395.

*   "Moon Sect 'Non-Christian.' " Cited above as item 926.

1044. "Moon's Church Launches PR Campaign." *National Catholic Register* 61 (April 14, 1985): 12.

1045. Moran, Gabriel. "Movies." *Sign* 61 (February 1982): 38-39.

1046. O'Conner, Liz. "The Moonies: An Exercise in Manipulation." *Saint Anthony Messenger* 84 (May 1977): 28-34.

1047. _____. "35% of This Man's Followers Were Catholic." *Catholic Digest* 41 (September 1977): 64-73.

1048. O'Donoghue, Noel Dermot. "The Community in Question: Reflections on the Cult Phenomenon." *Furrow* 34 (September 1983): 543-56.

1049. "Rev. Moon Waxes and Wanes." *America* 131 (October 5, 1974): 162.

1050. Richardson, Herbert W. "The Psychiatric State; Attacks on the Unification Church of Sun Myung Moon." *Ecumenist* 15 (November-December 1976): 11-13.

1051. Robbins, Thomas, and Dick Anthony. "The Unification Church." *Ecumenist* 22 (September-October 1984): 88-92.

1052. Ross, Barbara. "Despite Korea Clouds, the Moon Also Rises."
      National Catholic Reporter 13 (September 9, 1977): 16.

1053. Sadler, A. "Moon over Miami." *Horizons* 4 (Fall 1977): 227-28.

1054. Saliba, John A. "The New Religious Movements: Some Theological
      Reflections." *Horizons* 6 (Spring 1979): 113-18.

1055. _____. *Religious Cults Today.* Liguori, Mo.: Liguori Publications,
      1983. 48 pp.

1056. Steinfels, Peter. "Setback for What? Deprogramming Issue."
      Commonweal 104 (April 15, 1977): 232, 255.

1057. Swyngedouw, Jan. "Partners for Dialogue, the Search for
      Discriminating Norms: The Case of Japan." *East Asian Pastoral
      Review* 22 (No. 4, 1985): 239-45.

*   "Vatican Takes Exception." Cited above as item 1006.

1058. Walsh, Richard A. "Moonies--Religious Converts or Psychic
      Victims?" *America* 136 (May 14, 1977): 438-40.

1059. Whalen, William. "The Moonies." Chap. 7 in Strange Gods, 47-61.
      Huntington, Ind.: *Our Sunday Visitor,* 1981.

1060. _____. "The Rev. Sun Myung Moon: Pied Piper of Tarrytown."
      U.S. Catholic 41 (October 1976): 29-33.

1061. Wojeiki, Ed. "Rev. Moon's Appeal Rejection Seen as Religious
      Threat." *Our Sunday Visitor* 73 (May 24, 1984): 3

C. THE JEWISH RESPONSE

Jewish responses to the UC have been almost uniformly negative. This is in part due to longstanding Jewish opposition to evangelism in general and to a more recently expressed hostility toward "cults" in particular. Nonetheless, criticism of the UC has been especially pronounced as a result of its alleged deceptive recruitment practices and anti-semitism. At the same time, Jewish leaders, more so than leaders of other religious groups, have agonized over factors contributing to what has been perceived to be a disproportionate number of former Jews in the UC. These frequently critical self-appraisals add a note of ambiguity and complexity to what otherwise would be a stark portrayal of the UC as an unmitigated menace.

Of those Jewish commentators attacking the UC on the basis of its recruitment practices, Maurice Davis has been the most vehement. A Reformed rabbi from White Plains, New York, Davis became aware of the UC when two members of his congregation joined, and he quickly became a leading Church critic. Further, as founder and leader of C.E.R.F. (Citizens Engaged in Re-Uniting Families), Davis [1071] claims to have "suceeded in rescuing 174 kids" (11). His position is advanced in such articles as "In Defense of Deprogramming" [1070], "Lonely Homes, 'Loving' Cults" [1071], "Moon for the Misbegotten" [1072], and "The Moon People and Our Children" [1073]. Overall, these articles move from exposure of the UC as "evil and dangerous" to a defense of his own methods ("no force, no restraint, no threatening, no lying, no frightening") to an analysis of why youth, and Jewish youth in particular, are "vulnerable." Other accounts sounding similar alarms are "Dangerous Brainwashing" [1068], Lottie Robins' "Heavenly Deception" [1087], and Elsa A. Solender's "The Making and Unmaking of a Jewish Moonie" [1093]. For treatments of the UC within the context of opposition toward cults in general, see the Jewish Community Relations Committee of Greater Philadelphia's *The Challenge of the Cults* [1079], Jack Nusen Porter's *Jews and the Cults: A Bibliography* [1084], and Marcia R. Rudin's "The New Religious Cults and the Jewish Community" [1091]. Although not sympathetic, Earl Rabb's "Reverend Moon and the Jews: The San Francisco Experience" [1086] and David Silverberg's "Heavenly Deception: Reverend Moon's Hard Sell" [1092] reflect more interaction with UC members. Rabb recounts his experience with "Judaism in Service to the World," a short-lived organization sponsored by the UC's San Francisco Bay Area branch and attempts to explain how a given UC adherent "can be a Jew and a Christian at the same time" (9). Silverberg sought out partisans pro and con including "Jewish" members of the UC. These treatments should be read in tandem with American UC President Mose Durst's *To Bigotry No Sanction: Reverend Sun Myung Moon and the Unification Church* [1031], which recounts his pilgrimage from Judaism to the Unification Church.

Of those Jewish leaders attacking the UC for its alleged anti-semitism, Rabbi A. James Rudin has been the most outspoken. Formerly Assistant Director and currently Director of the American Jewish Committee Interreligious Affairs Department, Rudin charged in an official report, *Jews and Judaism in Reverend Moon's Divine Principle* [1088], that the UC's primary text "reveals an orientation of almost unrelieved hostility toward the Jewish people" (1). Citing specific references, Rudin asserted, "Whether he is discussing the Israelites of the Hebrew Bible or the 'Jews' of the New Testament period, Reverend Moon portrays their behavior as reprobate, their intentions as evil (often diabolical), and their religious mission as eclipsed" (1). Rudin's report, which influenced the National Council of Churches later theological critique [798], elicited two important responses from the UC. The first was Rev. Moon's "Statement on Jews and Israel" [359] which repudiated anti-semitism and pledged support for the state of Israel. Subsequently, Andrew M. Wilson drew up "A Unification Position on the Jewish People" [1098]. A convert to the UC from Judaism, Wilson acknowledged mutual grievances but argued that UC doctrine rejects notions of Jewish guilt and affirms their continued election (192-201; see also item 1491). Further, Wilson noted that the UC "has published new texts which have excised most of the offending statements" (201). Although these alterations were reported elsewhere [868], they have not been acknowledged by the American Jewish Committee.

1062. "Blue Moon." *Moment* 2 (February-March 1977): 6.

1063. Brickner, Balfour. *Information Kit on the Activities of Sun Myung Moon.* New York: Union of American Hebrew Congregations, 1976.

1064. Burstein, Patricia. "Rabbi Maurice Davis." *People* 6 (December 13, 1976): 44-45.

1065. "Can Religion Include Politics?" *Congressional Monthly* 49 (January 1982): 25.

1066. Commission on Law, Social Action and Urban Affairs. *The Cults and the Law.* New York: American Jewish Congress, 1978.

1067. "Confronting the Moonies." *United Synagogue Review Quarterly* 30 (Summer 1977): 3.

1068. "Dangerous Brainwashing." *Reconstructionist* 42 (April 1976): 5-6.

1069. Daum, Annette. "The Unification Church." In *Missionary and Cult Movements: A Mini-Course for the Upper Grades in Religious Schools.* Lessons 13-14. New York: Union of American Hebrew Congregations, 1977, 1979.

1070. Davis, Maurice. "In Defense of Deprogramming." In *All Our Sons and Daughters* (item 1202), pp. 26-43.

1071. ———. "Lonely Homes, 'Loving' Cults." *Reform Judaism* 11 (Winter 1983): 11-.

1072. ———. "Moon for the Misbegotten." *Reform Judaism*, November 1974.

1073. ———. "The Moon People and Our Children." *Jewish Community Center Bulletin* [White Plains, N.Y.] 20 (July 10, 1974): 1-2.

1074. ———. "Update on Moon." *Brotherhood*, March-April 1977.

* Durst, Mose. *To Bigotry No Sanction: Reverend Sun Myung Moon and the Unification Church.* Cited above as item 1031.

1075. Fisch, Dov Aharoni. "The Unification Church: Worshipping the Sun-Moon." Chap. 2 in *Jews for Nothing*, 72-96. New York: Feldheim, 1984.

1076. Fishman, Samuel Z. *Comments on the Campus: The Moonies and the Response of the American Jewish Community.* Washington, D.C.: B'nai Brith/Hillel Foundations, 1977.

1077. Harmgaal, Ya'AGov. "Dangerous Deprogramming: A Critical View." *American Zionist* 68 (1977): 16-19.

1078. Hecht, Shea, with Chaim Clorfene. "Glenn and the Moonies." Chap. 3 in *Confessions of a Jewish Cultbuster,* 33-46. New York: Tosefos Media, 1985.

1079. Jewish Community Relations Committee of Greater Philadelphia. *The Challenge of the Cults: An Examination of the Cult Phenomenon and Its Implications for the Jewish Community. A Report of the Special Committee on Exotic Cults.* 2nd ed. Philadelphia: Jewish Community Relations Committee of Greater Philadelphia, 1979.

* Moon, Sun Myung. "Statement on Jews and Israel." Cited above as item 359.

1080. Myers, Kenneth A. "The Doctrine of Sun Myung Moon." *Tenth* 9 (April 1979): 9-21.

1081. Pearlstein, Ira. "Jews and Reverend Moon." *Women's American Ort Reporter*, March-April 1977, 3.

1082. ———. "The Rev. Moon Phenomenon." *Jewish Digest* 21 (June 1976): 55-59.

1083. Pollock, I. "'God' of the Moonies." *Jewish Spectator* 47 (September 1982): 61.

1084. Porter, Jack Nusen. *Jews and the Cults: A Bibliography.* Fresh Meadows, N.Y.: Biblio Press, 1981. 49 pp.

1085. _____. "Many Jewish Professors at Moon's Conference in Boston." *The Jewish Advocate,* December 1, 1978.

1086. Rabb, Earl. "Reverend Moon and the Jews--The San Francisco Experience." *Congress Monthly* 43 (December 1976): 8-12.

1087. Robins, Lottie. "Heavenly Deception: One Family's Encounter with the Moonies." *Moment* 7 (June 1982): 35-38.

1088. Rudin, A. James. *Jews and Judaism in Rev. Moon's Divine Principle.* New York: The American Jewish Committee, December 1976. 7 pp.

1089. _____. "The Peril of Rev. Moon." *Jewish Digest* 22 (June 1977): 74-78.

1090. Rudin, A. James, and Marcia R. Rudin. "The Unification Church." *In Prison or Paradise: The New Religious Cults,* 31-45. Philadelphia: Fortress, 1980.

1091. Rudin, Marcia R. "The New Religious Cults and the Jewish Community." *Religious Education* 73 (May-June 1978): 350-60.

1092. Silverberg, David. "Heavenly Deception: Rev. Moon's Hard Sell." *Present Tense* 4 (Autumn 1976): 49-56.

1093. Solender, Elsa A. "The Making and Un-making of A Jewish Moonie." *Jewish Digest* 24 (April 1979): 18-24.

1094. Spero, M.H. "Cults: Some Theoretical and Practical Perspectives." *Journal of Jewish Communal Service* 53 (Summer 1977): 330-38.

1095. Spiro, Solomon J. "Probing the Cults." *Jewish Spectator* 45 (Winter 1980): 31-36.

1096. Supreme Rabbinic Court of America--Commission on Cults and Missionaries. *Unification Church Master File.* Silver Spring, Md.: Supreme Rabbinic Court of America, n.d.

1097. Sweet, Larry. "Why I Left the Moonies." *Jewish Digest* 23 (September 1977): 67-70.

1098. Wilson, Andrew M. "A Unification Position on the Jewish People." *Journal of Ecumenical Studies* 20 (Spring 1983): 191-208.

D. THE SPIRITUALIST-SECTARIAN RESPONSE

Responses to the UC in religious groups outside the Protestant-Catholic-Jewish mainstream--primarily "new age" or spiritualist fellowships and the major sects--are a study in contrasts. New age and spiritualist groups, for example, are ideologically permissive but wary of UC organizational intensity. Sectarian groups, by way of contrast, have few problems with the UC on organizational grounds but substantial difficulties with divergence from their own understandings of revealed truth. Thus, while new age groups interacted with the UC during the early phases of its development in the United States, they became more distant as the UC gained organizational potency. Conversely, despite initial antagonism or indifference, sectarian groups have begun to recognize continuities with the UC on historical, political, moral and even doctrinal grounds.

Of those "new age" leaders interacting with the UC, the most important was Anthony Brooke. A quixotic figure born into a line of 'white' rajahs ruling Sarawak (part of current Malaysia) from 1841-1946 when it became a British colony, Brooke was a tireless ambassador of global consciousness and, after 1961, of the British-based "Universal Link Revelation." Encountering a UC adherent in Los Angeles and traveling to Korea in 1964, Brooke [1103] became convinced that "Sun Myung Moon was in a particular sense the 'earth form of Limitless Love'" (90-91). Subsequently conceiving his mission to be that of "co-ordinating revelations," Brooke referred to Sun Myung Moon in his *Revelation for the New Age* [1103] and *Towards Human Unity* [1104]. More significant, however, were the "links" he established between the UC and several spiritual groups and their leaders. The most important of these was the Spiritual Frontiers Fellowship (SFF) and its principal founder, Arthur Ford. Ford, a well-known American trance-medium, conducted two seances for UC adherents in 1964 and 1965. Edited transcripts were later published as "The Sun Myung Moon Sittings" in Ford's *Unknown But Known* [1106]. While some assert this material supports UC claims, others place the sessions within the period of Ford's decline as a medium [1122]. For a balanced discussion of the entire episode, see J. Gordon Melton's "Spiritual Frontiers Fellowship, The New Age Groups, and the Unification Church" [1111]. With the emergence of the UC as an increasingly well-defined and controversial movement during the seventies, new age and spiritualist publications generally ignored or criticized the Church. A good example of the latter thrust is Bob Banner's "In Search of Certitude: An Inside View of Sun Myung Moon's Booneville, California, Community" [1100]. For an exception to this overall trend, see Elaine Margolis' "Methodists, Moonies and Mormons: All Are Welcome in the Berkeley Area Interfaith Council" [1109].

Of the major sects, the most significant response to the UC has come from Mormonism. Although stiff opposition is apparent within conservative quarters, some liberal LDS scholars have identified common traits of both groups. Phillip L. Barlow, in "On Moonists and Mormonites" [1101] listed a number of these. Included are broad misrepresentations of both in the popular press, belief in the presence of a living prophet and new and continuous revelation, the formation of new scripture, "phenomenal" growth, active proselyting and special appeal to the young and idealistic, common views of themselves as "Christianity restored" and of the various stages in the world's history as divinely-inspired preparation for their own vital work, anti-communism, unpaid ministries, a "disproportionate" emphasis on the import of marriage and the family structure, "extraordinary" care within their ecclesiastical structures to the development of leadership and "unusual" stress on education (38-40). Barlow, however, also ennumerated "fundamental contrasts" in the area of doctrine. For a critique of Barlow's reading of the UC, see David J. Cannon's "Response to Moonists and Mormonites" [1105]. LDS ambivalence also is evident in Marvin R. Rytting's "Mormons Meet the Moonies" [1117]. One of eight Mormon scholars invited to meet with students at the Unification Theological Seminary, Rytting noted, "Our trip of a few hours ... at times seemed like a trip of 140 years to a community on the banks of the Mississippi ... not an exact mirror image of life in the Mormon cult of the 1840s, but a reflection nonetheless" (7). At the same time, he acknowledged, "A different group of Mormons might not have seen the same thing ... The Moonies ... had to find some Mormons who were not inclined to ask permission before attending conferences" (7).

1099. Bach, Marcus. "Togetherness." In *Strangers at the Door*, 129-55. Nashville: Abington, 1971.

1100. Banner, Bob. "In Search of Certitude: An Inside View of Sun Myung Moon's Booneville, California, Community." *New Age Journal* 11 (April 1976): 8.

1101. Barlow, Phillip L. "On Moonists and Mormonites." *Sunstone* 4 (January-February 1979): 37-41.

1102. Benton, E. "Teaching the Town Fathers." *Columbia Union Visitor* 83 (October 19, 1978): 12.

1103. Brooke, Anthony. *Revelation for the New Age*. London: Regency Press, 1967. 92 pp.

1104. ———. *Towards Human Unity*. London: Mitre Press, 1976. 133 pp.

1105. Cannon, David J. "Response to Moonists and Mormonites." *Sunstone* 4 (July-August 1979): 2-3.

1106. Ford, Arthur. "The Sun Myung Moon Sittings." In *Unknown But Known: My Adventures into the Meditative Dimension*, 106-28. New York: Harper and Row, 1968.

1107. "Former Sarawak Ruler Visits Korean Church." *Korea Report,* February-March 1964, 20.

1108. McFarland, K. "Sun Moon's Dark Star Rises." *Insight* 8 (January 4, 1977): 12-16.

1109. Magalis, Elaine. "Methodists, Moonies and Mormons; All are Welcome in the Berkeley Area Interfaith Council." *New World Outlook,* May 1979, 16-20.

1110. Martin, C.M. "Deprogramming Defended." *Liberty* 73 (May-June 1978): 16-21.

1111. Melton, J. Gordon. "Spiritual Frontiers Fellowship, the New Age Groups and the Unification Church." *Spiritual Frontiers* 12 (Spring 1980): 76-86.

1112. "Moon Convicted on Tax Evasion Charges." *These Times* 91 (December 1982): 6.

1113. "Moonie Update." *New Age* 4 (March 1979): 14.

1114. "Moon's Unification Church--What Does It Believe?" *Awake!* 63 (September 8, 1982): 10-15.

1115. Nixon, R.W. "Equal Treatment for Churches." *Liberty* 77 (September-October 1982): 28.

1116. _____. "What is a Church?" *Liberty* 28 (September-October 1982): 28.

1117. Rytting, Marvin R. "Mormons Meet the Moonies." *The Sunstone Review* 3 (July-August 1983): 7.

1118. Schurch, M. "The Three Times I Saw John." *Review [Adventist Herald and Sabbath Herald]* 153 (December 9, 1976): 13-14.

1119. Sensaki, T. "Pastor Rescues Six." *Far Eastern Division Outlook,* December 1978, 7.

1120. Skousen, W. Cleon. "Who is the Real Reverend Sun Myung Moon." *Freeman Digest,* September 1984, 7-12.

1121. "Spiritual Revolutionaries vs. U.S." *The Coptic Scroll*, July 1984, 1, 4.

1122. Spraggett, Allen, with William V. Raucher. *Arthur Ford: The Man Who Talked with the Dead.* New York: New America Library, 1973.

1123. "When Is a Religion Not a Religion: The IRS Cracks Down on 'Reverend' Moon." *New Age* 7 (June 1982): 13.

1124. Wiers, Walter. "Moon's Children." *Search Magazine* 136 (Fall 1978): 7-11.

1125. Winterbottom, Neil A. "A New Age Prophet from Korea, Sun Myung Moon." *Psychic Observer* 31 (June 1970): 42-45.

1126. Worthing, Sharon. "Deprogramming." *Liberty* 72 (September 1977): 8-12.

1127. _____. "A Nation of Laws or Rape of the Mind?" *Liberty* 73 (May-June 1978): 19-21.

IV.

RESPONSES TO THE CHURCH: SECULAR

Secular responses to the Church, unlike responses in religious publications, do not fall into clear-cut institutional categories but rather into opposing camps in what has been a wide-ranging public debate less over the merits or faults of the UC (relatively few treatments depict the Church in favorable terms) than over the Church's right to exist and propagate its beliefs. In this respect, a fundamental distinction has emerged between the UC's opposition critics and its libertarian defenders. These two camps further subdivide into several subgroupings. Opposition critics, for example, include deprogrammed apostates, interventionists, resisters and debunkers. Libertarian defenders include demythologizers, politicizers, civil libertarians and apologists. In addition, a residual category of more neutralist commentaries and general reportage exists.

OPPOSITION CRITICS

As suggested, UC critics subdivide into several distinct subgroupings. The most important of these, in that they have supplied the raw data on which other critics have drawn, is made up of deprogrammed apostates. Although uneven in quality, their reports differ from apostate accounts in religious publications in that little credence is attached to conversion, or at least to conversion within the UC. Instead, alterations in attitude and conduct are understood to derive from psychological coercion or "brainwashing." Interventionists, who include relatives of Church members, deprogrammers and an assortment of journalists, psychiatrists and jurists, have used apostate materials to reinforce their efforts to extricate individuals from the UC. Resisters, by way of contrast, have not emphasized intervention in UC internal affairs but have sought to discourage outsiders, especially imminent scholars, from interacting with the Church. Debunkers, unlike other critics, have depicted the UC as a passing phenomenon unworthy of serious attention. Taken together, these positions have been mutually reinforcing and comprise what some have termed the "anti-cult movement" (ACM) or what UC officials characterize as the "anti-religion movement."

Apostate accounts in secular publications fall along a spectrum ranging from the sensational to the sensitive. In general, accounts of ex-members who were in the Church only a matter of months (and, in some cases, weeks) are sensationalized with stress placed on their "rescue" and on stark contrasts between life in the Church and on the outside. Accounts of ex-members in the Church for several years, however, though frequently severely critical, note progressive disillusionment and areas of overlap between life within and without. Examples of sensationalized accounts are Claudia Dreifus' "Rita Ashdale vs. The Reverend Sun Myung Moon" [1185], Janice Harayda's "I Was a Robot for Sun Myung Moon" [1214], and Charles and Bonnie Remsberg's "Why I Quit the Moon Cult" [1317], all of which appeared in popular womens' magazines. More sustained treatments of the sensational variety include Christopher Edwards' *Crazy for God* [1191] and Susan Swatland's *Escape From the Moonies* [1371]. Although these are book-length treatments, since Edwards and Swatland were in the Church for only seven and eight-and-one-half months respectively, their accounts focus almost exclusively on their recruitment and deprogramming. More substantive treatments, written from the standpoint of several years' membership, are Barbara and Betty Underwood's *Hostage to Heaven* [1374] and Allen Tate Wood's *Moonstruck* [1389]. The Underwoods' volume, generally regarded as the best of the genre, is well documented and, at points, surprisingly balanced. Betty Underwood wrote, "To Barb the four years had not been just one grand loss but had meant a deep and estatic religious experience and commitment, had made of her a religious person, and had given her a closeness with peers never before experienced" (272).

Interventionists, though dependent on apostate accounts, also helped shape those accounts in that they supplied the conceptual categories by which deprogrammed ex-members have understood their experience. Apostate accounts, in fact, often mirror the perceptions of interventionists. In general, these perceptions derive from three interrelated assertions. First, the UC is asserted to be not a "true" religion but a pseudo-religion or "cult" utilizing manipulative tactics to induce sudden personality changes. Although interventionists differ as to the complexity of these tactics--some arguing in favor of a brainwashing hypothesis, others for on-the-spot hypnosis--they are in agreement about their impact which is said to be the complete loss of an individual's free will. Thus, a second major assertion follows: once in, an individual is powerless to leave. Further, the effects of membership are said to be cumulative and beyond a certain point, irreversible. A third key assertion of interventionists is that families who have lost offspring to the UC should not expect understanding or help from established authorities. For this reason, interventionists have sought recourse outside existing institutional networks through vigilante-style abductions, novel interpretations of guardianship laws and efforts in favor of legislation designed to block UC recruitment.

Interventionist treatments, overall, divide into two major types. The first includes triumphalist accounts of relatives, friends and deprogrammers who have forcibly removed individuals from the Church. Examples include William Adler's "Rescuing David From the Moonies" [1130], Charles Edwards' "How I Rescued My Son From the Moonies" [1189], and Josh Freed's *Moonwebs: Journey into the Mind of a Cult* [1199]. Freed's volume, the most comprehensive of these, is an expansion of a series of articles written for the *Montreal Star* (see Bart Testa's "Making Crime Seem Natural: The Press and Deprogramming" [1638] for a critique of the original series). The major work by a deprogrammer is Ted Patrick's *Let Our Children Go!* [1300]. Although Patrick treated a number of new movements, he emphasized, "Sun Myung Moon is public enemy number one as far as the cults are concerned" (224). The second type of interventionist treatment includes writings of psychiatrists, lawyers, government officials and journalists who share interventionist assumptions. Two important works of this type which treat the UC are Robert Boettcher's *Gifts of Deceit* [1146] and Flo Conway and Jim Siegelman's *Snapping* [1165]. Boettcher's volume, though departing from other accounts by emphasizing the UC's political rather than its psychosocial machinations, nonetheless articulates an interventionist line by calling on federal agencies to pool information and resources to combat the Church (346-347). Conway and Siegelman's work, which characterizes adherence to the UC and other new groups as a form of "information disease," was the single most influential treatment popularizing the interventionist perspective. Additional articles on the UC from an interventionist perspective frequently appear in periodicals published by "anti-cult" organizations. The most important of these are *The Advisor* [1395], its successor *The Cult Observer* [1398], the *Citizen's Freedom Foundation News* [1397], and *Ex-Moon* [1399].

Resisters, as distinguished from interventionists, have not advocated interference in internal UC affairs and do not necessarily share interventionist assumptions. For example, Irving Louis Horowitz [1226], Distinguished Professor of Sociology and Political Science at Rutgers University and the leading proponent of the resister position, asserted, "The question of whether any particular grouping like the Unification Church represents a cult, as its critics claim, or an authentic religion, as the Moon personnel claim, is fundamentally irrelevant" (365). What is relevant and to be resisted, according to Horowitz, were UC incursions into secular areas of society. In opposition to this, resisters have organized letter-writing campaigns, discouraged participation in UC-sponsored academic conferences, refused to advertise in UC-funded newspapers, advocated strict enforcement of existing statutes and ignored the UC in hopes that it would settle down or go away. Horowitz developed conceptual rationales for these postures in several articles including "Religion and the Rise of Reverend Moon" [1226] and "Science, Sin and Sponsorship" [1227; see also items 1562-67]. In these articles, Horowitz criticized UC sponsorship of its annual International Conference on the Unity of the Sciences (ICUS) as well as the Church's "civil religious character," and suggested the UC represents "a categorical denial of the Lockean-Jeffersonian principle of the separation of church and state."

Debunkers differ from other UC opponents in that they do not take the Church seriously. Instead, the UC is depicted as being hopelessly deviant. Some of these treatments, accompanied by ludicrous photographs or illustrations, tend toward ridicule and mockery. Examples include William Claiborne's "Now-Rev. Moon's Free Ad Service" [1157], Morton Kondrake's "Nixon's New Defenders and Their Strange Pasts" [1240], Mark C. Miller's "The Manichean in Moon" [1269], *People* magazine's "Obedience to the Law of Diminishing Returns May Cost This Little King 18 Months Away from His Counting House" [1290], and Michael Pousner's "Who's Afraid of Sun Myung Moon?" [1304]. A second type of debunking treatment consists of more informed, often detailed accounts that, nonetheless, characterize the Church as a passing phenomenon. The best examples are Mark Rasmussen's "How Sun Myung Moon Lures America's Children" [1310] and Chris Welles' "The Eclipse of Sun Myung Moon" [1383]. Rasmussen, who termed the UC "by far the most successful of the religious cults," nonetheless, wondered "where these pleasant, wounded kids will turn when the movement, as in five or ten years it must, falls apart" (102, 175). Welles asserted that the only real success of the Church has been financial and questioned "whether Moon ever had power and influence even remotely resembling that which has been widely attributed to him" (32).

LIBERTARIAN DEFENDERS

Defenders of the Church on libertarian grounds also include several subgroupings. Most important are demythologizers, frequently academics, who as a result of interaction with or study of the UC, criticize opposition portrayals and suggest alternative interpretations. This subgrouping also includes UC adherents who have escaped from or resisted deprogramming. Based on these accounts, politicizers have pointed out underlying biases and vested interests of Church opponents. Civil libertarians have articulated the broader implications of attacks on the UC. Finally, apologists have discerned positive features of the Church.

Demythologizers have attempted to demystify the activities and arguments of UC opponents. They have done so on two fronts. First, survivors of deprogramming have depicted that process in terms just as sensational as apostate accounts of recruitment into the Church. Coercive deprogrammings have been portrayed as brutal affairs characterized by violent kidnapping, forced incarceration, verbal harassment, sleep deprivation and sexual enticement. For the single most complete compendium of these testimonies, see *Deprogramming: Documenting the Issue* [1325]. Second, some academics have questioned the assumptions of Church opponents. They argued that recruitment techniques utilized by the UC are comparable to those employed by other religious groups and that charges of individuals being unable to leave of their own free will are belied by high voluntary defection rates. Further, they accused Church critics of imprecision, obscurantism and intellectual laziness in their usage of "cult" and "brainwashing" terminology as well as in their minimization of distinctions between the UC and other new groups. The single most useful demythologizing treatment is David G. Bromley and Anson D. Shupe, Jr.'s *Strange Gods: The Great American Cult Scare* [1150]. Written, in part, "to correct the impression that the so-called cults are mysterious, or that very little information is known about them, or that only their critics really understand them," Bromley and Shupe insisted, "Much of the controversy ... is a hoax, a 'scare' in the truest sense of the word." They argued:

> There is no avalanche of rapidly growing cults. In fact, there are probably no more such groups existing today than there has been at any other time in our recent history. Furthermore, the size of these groups has been grossly exaggerated and almost all have long since passed their peak periods of growth. Much of the 'cult explosion'

has been pure media hype. There is no mysterious brainwashing process used to trap and enslave millions of young Americans. Few young adults have found these new religions attractive enough even to experiment with membership, and the vast majority of those who have tried them have walked away after only a brief stay (3-4).

Of those who remain as members, Bromley and Shupe maintained, "most ultimately settle down into stable, if unconventional (by outside standards) life-styles and pursue alternative, sometimes prestigious careers within the movement" (91).

If the UC, as demythologizers suggest, does not pose a grave threat to the U.S. or to its adherents, it still is necessary to account for the social conflict that has accompanied its emergence. Politicizers have done so in one of two ways. More partisan treatments impugn the motives of Church opponents. Deprogrammers are portrayed as mercenaries, parents as well-meaning but deceived, and apostates as seeking a face-saving way of explaining their involvement [1236, 1341]. Stephen Chapman's "Cult-mongering" [1154] is a variation on this *ad hominem* line as it depicts Robert Dole's *ad hoc* 1979 hearing on the UC and other groups as a ploy "to get his incipient presidential campaign off the ground" (11). Prejudice against Asians and conversion of offspring from the well-to-do also have been cited as sources of strain. Bromley and Shupe [1150], however, acknowledged legitimate grounds of conflict and grievances in that the UC and other new religious movements "are at odds with the values, lifestyles and aspiration of the majority of contemporary Americans" (4). While these differences, according to Bromley and Shupe, have been a source of irritation or embarassment but not a serious threat to the government and other Churches, they have been devastating to families suffering the "loss" of a son or daughter. For this reason, "relatives posess a greater interest in combatting cults and a willingness to take more extreme measures" (77).

Civil libertarians, as distinguished from politicizers, focus less on reasons for assaults on the UC and more on the broader implications of those assaults. In general, these are depicted as having a negative impact on religious freedom and on freedom of association. Some libertarians have pointed to attempted deprogrammings of persons belonging to long-standing religious associations or to radical political organizations [1236]. Others have questioned legal precedents implied in proposed legislation restricting recruitment and solicitation by the UC and other groups. These issues were well articulated by Thomas Robbins in a series of articles including "'Brainwashing'and Religious Freedom" [1326], "Cults and the Theraputic State" [1327], "Even a Moonie Has Civil Rights" [1328], and with Dick Anthony, "Cult Phobia: A Witch-Hunt In the Making?" [1329]. According to Robbins and Anthony [1329], "If persecution of deviant religions on obscurantist grounds of 'mind control' is institutionalized, its application to political dissidents may be inevitable. The Left has a stake in the liberties of Moonies ..." (241). Other commentators have defended their freedom to associate with the UC. Roy Wallis, for example, in "Should Academics Attend Moonie Conferences?" [1379] asserted, "hostility towards and isolation of ideologically deviant groups are at least as likely to lead to the escalation of deviance and mutual distrust ... I regard the counsel to isolate the Moonies and deny them contact with respectable academics as potentially dangerous" (6-7). See also Geering [1203] and Kurti [1243] for defenses of their associations.

Apologists differ from the UC's other defenders in that they discern positive features in the Church. While stopping short of endorsing UC theological claims, apologists' accounts typically discuss the Church in functionalist terms. That is, they credit the UC for revitalizing the religious impulse or for resocializing alienated youth. Leo Sandon, for example, in "The Moonie Family: Do We Have a Stake in Being Fair to the Far Out?" [1342] posited the UC "experience of religious community" as an alternative "to that pervasive tendency in American culture that is radically individualistic in its understanding of human existence." Bromley and Shupe [1150] suggested that by recruiting countercultural youth, the UC has functioned as "a bridge back to more conventional lives" (208). Based on his observations of the UC and other movements, Dean Kelley, as quoted by Bromley and Shupe [1150], argued:

> ...a vigorous, dynamic religious movement can not only attract and hold some very impressive and gifted people, but ... it can and does attract a great many more people who are not visibly impressive or gifted and install or bring out in them abilities they did not know they had ... because new religious movements make higher demands upon their members than your average church or synogogue, and obtain fuller commitment and investment of self in return, they are able to accomplish far more with even less promising material (209).

COMMENTARIES AND REPORTAGE

In addition to opposition critiques and libertarian defenses, responses to the UC in secular publications include commentaries and reportage. Commentaries, which reflect both sides of controversies surrounding the UC, differ from partisan treatments in that while contributing to the public debate, their authors refrain from making policy recommendations. General reportage is primarily informational and includes overviews of UC activities as well as coverage of specific events.

Commentaries, to the extent they reflect both sides of the debate over the UC, are frequently ambivalent. This is evident in the titles of such treatments as "Moon Madness: Greed or Creed?" [1138], "Reverend Moon: Satan or Savior?" [1241], "Rev. Moon--A Messiah or a Menace?" [1307], and *All God's Children: The Cult Experience--Salvation or Slavery?* [1361]. Of these, the last work, written by Carroll Stoner and Jo Anne Parke, is the most complete and even-handed. Their treatment is particularly useful in that it quotes extensively from interviews conducted with current and former UC members. For a study similar to Stoner and Parke's but which focuses on a single Church adherent, see Barbara Grizzuti Harrison's "The Helanders and the Moonies: A Family Story" [1216]. Other commentary pieces include

Peter Collier's "Bringing Home the Moonies: The Brain Snatch" [1163], Berkeley Rice's "Messiah from Korea: Honor Thy Father Moon" [1323] and Kenneth Woodward's, *et al*'s, "Life With Father Moon" [1393]. Moira Johnston's "Showdown in the Valley of the Moonies" [1233] is a perceptive assessment of a Northern California county's attempt to block the opening of a UC-related weekend seminar site. Political commentators also have expressed ambivalence toward the UC. Liberals, for example, have criticized the Church's anti-communism and civil religiosity but refrain from advocating suppression of the UC as antithetical to libertarian values. Conservatives, the would-be recipients of Church support, have been put off by UC references to 'God-centered socialism', one-worldism, and reports of UC internal authoritarianism. See Dinesh D'Souza's "Moon's Planet" [1186] for the best statement of this conservative dilemma.

General reportage in secular publications has focused less on the UC *per se* that on its interaction with American society. In particular, reports have dealt with recruitment controversies, Church businesses and UC-sponsored conferences but in ways that are more descriptive than interpretive. Examples of reports on controversies over UC recruitment practices are "Cult Wars on Capitol Hill" [1174], "Fighting For Minds" [1196], "Parents v. Moonies" [1197] and "Mad about Moon" [1260]. With regard to Church businesses, interest has centered on UC-funded fishing enterprises and newspapers. Representative pieces on aspects of UC maritime industry include Scott Cramer's "Why Moonies Catch More Tuna" [1170], Geoffrey Moorhouse's "Moonies Invade Gloucester" [1278], and Calvin Trillin's "U.S. Journal--Bayou La Batre, Ala." [1373]. Accounts of UC media initiatives include Bryan Abas' "Inside the Paper God Wanted" [1128] and Karen Rothmeyer's "Mapping Out Moon's Media Empire" [1338]. Coverage of sponsored conferences has focused on the UC's annual International Conference on the Unity of the Sciences (ICUS). In addition to recruitment, businesses and conferences, UC mass marriages have stimulated some public interest. See Jennifer Allen's "Marriage a la Moon" [1131] and Ann Fadiman's "A Moon-Made Match" [1195].

1128. Abas, Bryan. "Inside the Paper God Wanted (Sun Myung Moon's Paper)." *Columbia Journalism Review* 23 (May-June 1984): 46-49.

1129. Adasiak, Allan. "Moonrise in Kodiak: The Unification Church Goes Fishing." *Alaska Journal* 10 (1980): 66-72.

1130. Adler, Warren. "Rescuing David from the Moonies." *Esquire* 89 (June 6, 1978): 23-30.

1131. Allen, Jennifer. "Marriage a la Moon." *New York Magazine* 15 (September 27, 1982): 11-13.

1132. Allen, Steve. "Rev. Moon and the Unification Church." In *Beloved Son*, 169-78. Indianapolis: Bobbs-Merrill, 1982.

1133. Anthony, Dick, Thomas Robbins, and Jim McCarthy. "Legitimating Repression." *Society* 17 (March-April 1980): 39-42.

1134. Appel, Willa. *Cults in America: Program for Paradise.* New York: Holt, Rinehart and Winston, 1983. 204 pp.

1135. Barber, Steven. "Foreign Devils in Reverse." *Far Eastern Economic Review* 96 (May 27, 1977): 25-26.

1136. Barnes, Fred. "The Washington Times, A Critical Look at News Coverage by Washington's 'Alternative Newspaper.' " *Washington Journalism Review* 4 (October 1982): 39-40.

1137. Bastil, Dennis. "Who's Who In Gurus." *Harper's* 267 (November 1983): 50-56.

1138. Bateson, C. Daniel. "Moon Madness: Greed or Creed?" *APA Monitor* 7 (June 1976): 32-35.

1139. "Battening Down." *Time* 116 (July 14, 1980): 23.

1140. Beck, Melinda, and Susan Fraker, with Elaine Shannon, and Jeff B. Copeland. "The World of Cults." *Newsweek* 92 (December 4, 1978): 78-81.

1141. Belford, Lee A. "Sun Myung Moon and the Unification Church." *Intellect* 105 (April 1977): 336-37.

1142. Bergman, David. "Some See 'Inchon' Contest as Moonie Recruitment Drive." *Variety* 308 (September 29, 1982): 3.

1143. Biemiller, L. "On Campus for the Rev. Moon: Recollections of a Former Unification Church Recruiter." *Chronicle of Higher Education* 26 (April 6, 1983): 6-7.

1144. Blasdale, Jean. "The Strange Cult of the Reverend Moon." *The Review of the News* 12 (June 9, 1976): 35-46.

1145. Bock, Gordon M. "Learning to Live Together Is Tough Moonies in Gloucester)." *U.S. News & World Report* 93 (July 5, 1982): 37-39.

1146. Boettcher, Robert. *Gifts of Deceit.* New York: Holt, Rinehart and Winston, 1980. 402 pp.

1147. Boyjak, G.J., and G.A. Macy. "The Fall of Sun Myung Moon and the Unification Church in America." *USA Today* 114 (November 1985): 62-65.

1148. "Brainwashing Moonies; Conservatorship Strategy." *Time* 109 (April 4, 1977): 73.

1149. Brandon, George. "Rev. Moon-owned Daily Debuts in Nation's Capital [Washington Times]." *Editor & Publisher* 115 (May 22, 1982): 15-.

1150. Bromley, David G., and Anson D. Shupe, Jr. *Strange Gods: The Great American Cult Scare.* Boston: Beacon Press, 1981. 249 pp.

1151. Brookshier, Richard. "One Big Family." *National Review* 28 (July 9, 1976): 728.

1152. Butterworth, John. "The Moonies." In *Cults and New Faiths*, 28-31. Elgin, Ill.: David C. Cook, 1981.

1153. Carroll, Jerry, and Bernard Baure, "Suicide Training in the Moon Cult." *New West* 4 (January 29, 1979): 62-63.

1154. Chapman, Stephen. "Cult-mongering." *The New Republic* 180 (February 17, 1979): 11-13.

1155. "Charity Begins at Westminister; Moonies." *Economist* 279 (April 11-17, 1981): 64.

1156. Chesnoff, R.Z., and A. Nagorski. "The Living God is with Me: Excerpt from Interview." *Newsweek* 87 (June 14, 1976): 62.

1157. Claiborne, William. "Now-Rev. Moon's Free Ad Service." *American Atheist*, May 1977.

1158. Cohen, Daniel. "The Unification Church." In *The New Belivers*, 42-53. New York: M. Evans, 1975.

1159. Cohen, Robert. "The Unification Church and the Reverend Moon." *Current Contents* no. 3 (January 17, 1977): 6-12.

1160. Cohen, S.E. "Washington Times: Not a Me Too Effort." *Advertizing Age* 53 (July 19, 1982): sec. 2, M34-M35.

1161. Coleman, Kate. "Souled Out." *New West* 5 (May 19, 1980): 17-27.

1162. Colford, Steven W. "Washington Times Develops New 'Insight.' " *Advertising Age* 56 (September 2, 1985): 47.

1163. Collier, Peter. "Bringing Home the Moonies: The Brain Snatch." *New Times* 8 (June 10, 1977): 25-28, 36-40.

1164. Collins, Denis. "Ex-Cultists Need Not Apply." *Across the Board* 21 (December 1984): 59-64.

1165. Conway, Flo, and James Siegelman. *Snapping: America's Epidemic of Sudden Personality Change.* Philadelphia: J.B. Lippincott, 1978. 254 pp.

1166. _____. "Snapping: Welcome to the Eighties." *Playboy*, March 1979, 217-19.

1167. Cornell, George W. "Those 'Guru' Cults--Religion or Exploitation?" *Readers Digest* 108 (February 1976): 96-100.

1168. Cowley, Susan Cheever. "Moon Rising." *Newsweek* 85 (May 26, 1975): 63.

1169. Cowley, Susan Cheever, and Tae Hoon Shim. "Many Moons." *Newsweek* 87 (April 26, 1976): 94-95.

1170. Cramer, Scott. "Why 'Moonies' Catch More Tuna." *Yankee* 44 (November 1980): 127-33, 246-49.

1171. Crittenden, Ann. "The Incredible Story of Ann Gordon and Reverend Sun Myung Moon." *Good Housekeeping* 183 (October 1976): 86, 90-100.

1172. _____. "Moon Sect Pushes Pro-Seoul Activities." In *Science, Sin, and Sponsorship: The Politics of Reverend Moon and the Unification Church* (item 1567), pp. 176-91.

1173. "Crusade That Pays." *Atlas World Press Review* 23 (September 1976): 31.

1174. "Cult Wars on Capitol Hill." *Time* 113 (February 19, 1979): 54.

1175. "Dark Side of Mr. Moon." *Science Digest* 80 (September 1976): 18.

1176. "The Darker Side of Sun Moon." *Time* 107 (June 14, 1976): 48-50.

1177. David, P. "British Academics Attend Moonie Conference." *Times Educational Supplement* 3467 (December 10, 1982): 13.

1178. "D.C. Times Accepts Ads." *Advertizing Age* 53 (August 30, 1982): 51.

1179. Delgado, Richard. "Limits to Proselytizing." *Society* 17 (March-April 1980): 25-33.

1180. "Dole Holds Hearing on 'Cults.' " *Church and State* 32 (March 1979): 17-19.

1181. Dominic, Michael. "A Compendium of Cults." In *All Our Sons and Daughters* (item 1207), pp. 6-23.

1182. Donohoe, Tony. "Weekend with the Moonies." *Intellect* 105 (April 1, 1977): 338-39.

1183. Donovan, Hedley. "Up front." *People*, October 20, 1975.

1184. Doress, Irvin, and Jack Nusan Porter. "Kids in Cults." *Society* 15 (May-June 1978): 69-71.

1185. Dreifus, Claudia. "Rita Ashdale vs. the Reverend Sun Myung Moon." *Mademoiselle* 88 (April 1983): 130-.

1186. D'Sousa, Dinesh. "Moon's Planet: The Politics and Theology of the Unification Church." *Policy Review* 32 (September 1985): 28-34.

1187. "Eclipsed Moon." *Time* 118 (July 6, 1981): 37.

1188. Edsall, J.T., and E.P. Wigner. "Unification Church." *Physics Today* 33 (October 1980): 15, 88.

1189. Edwards, Charles H. "How I Rescued My Son from the Moonies." *Medical Economics* 53 (November 1, 1976): 72-80.

1190. _____. "Rescue from a Fanatic Cult." *Reader's Digest* 110 (April 1977): 129-33.

1191. Edwards, Christopher. *Crazy for God: The Nightmare of Cult Life by an Ex-Moon Disciple.* Englewood Cliffs, N.J.: Prentice-Hall, 1979. 233 pp.

1192. Edwards, Morrison. "Moon's Tuna Fleet." *National Fisherman,* December 1984.

1193. "Eleventh Child Born to Mother and Father." *Newsweek* 94 (October 8, 1979): 57.

1194. "Equal Rights for Moonies (Supreme Court Rules on Minnesota Reporting Law)." *Time* 119 (May 3, 1982): 60.

1195. Fadiman, Anne. "A Moon-Made Match." *Life* 5 (August 1982): 91-95.

1196. "Fighting for Minds." *Economist* 263 (April 9, 1977): 34.

1197. Footlick, Jerold K., with Peter S. Greenberg. "Parents v. Moonies." *Newsweek* 89 (April 25, 1977): 83.

1198. Fraker, Susan, and Anthony Marro. "Washington's Korea Lobby." *Newsweek* 88 (November 22, 1976) 37-39.

1199. Freed, Josh. *Moonwebs: Journey into the Mind of a Cult.* Toronto, Canada: Dorset, 1980. 216 pp.

1200. Friedman, R. "Cults: Are Teens Being Brainwashed? Case of Barbara Anna Larson." *Seventeen* 38 (May 1979): 178-79, 200-202.

1201. Gann, L.H. "The Fatal Assumptions of Social Therapy." *Worldview* 21 (April 1978): 23-27, 35.

1202. Garvey, John, ed. *All Our Sons and Daughters.* Springfield, Ill.: Templegate, 1977. 131 pp.

   Contains items 1070, 1181, 1282.

1203. Geering, Lloyd. "Moonies and the Search for Truth." *NZ Listener,* May 17, 1980, 56-57.

1204. Gillis, John W. "Rev. Sun Myung Moon: 'Heavenly Deception.' " *Trial* 12 (August 1976): 22-25.

1205. Gittings, James. "Korean Sect Wins Japanese Support." *An Asia Notebook,* January-February 1968, 3 pp.

1206. Gordon, James S. "The Kids and the Cults." *Children Today* 6 (July-August 1977): 24-27, 36.

1207. Gosney, Dana. "Did Christ Start This Way?" *American Atheist,* May 1977.

1208. Greenberg, Daniel S. "Korean Evangelist's Role Upsets 'Unity of Sciences.' " *The Chronicle of Higher Education* 11 (October 14, 1975): 3.

1209. _____. "Rev. Moon's Unity Conference." *Science Digest* 78 (November 1975): 83-84.

1210. _____. "Scientific Elite Flocks to Rev. Moon's Conference." *Science & Government Report* 5 (August 1, 1975): 1-3.

1211. "Guilty Father." *Time* 119 (May 31, 1982): 23.

1212. Gunther, Max. "Brainwashing: Persuasion by Propoganda." *Today's Health* 54 (February 1976): 15-17, 54.

1213. Hanson, Lauren. "Moonie Mom at Cult Hearing." *New York* 12 (February 19, 1979): 11.

1214. Harayda, Janice. "I Was a Robot for Sun Myung Moon." *Glamour,* April 1976, 216, 256, 261-.

1215. Hargrove, Barbara. "Evil Eyes and Religious Choices." *Society* 17 (March-April 1980): 20-24.

1216. Harrison, Barbara Grizzuti. "The Helanders and the Moonies: A Family Story." In *Off Center*, 221-61. New York: Dial Press, 1980.

1217. _____. "The Struggle for Wendy Helander." *McCall's* 107 (October 1979): 87-94.

1218. Heftmann, Erica. *The Dark Side of the Moonies.* Hammondsworth, Middlesex, England: Penguin, 1982. 292 pp.

1219. Heller, R.K. *Deprogramming for Do-It-Yourselfers (A Cure for the Common Cult).* Medina, Ohio: Gentle Press, 1982. 145 pp.

1220. Hentoff, Nat. "Kidnapping and the Free Exercise of Religion." *Inquiry* 2 (March 19, 1979): 4-6.

1221. Hershell, Marie, and Ben Hershell. "Our Involvement with a Cult." In *Cults and the Family* (item 1569), 131-40.

1222. Hitchens, Christopher. "Minority Report." *Nation* 236 (January 22, 1983): 70.

1223. Holden, Constance. "Moon's Annual Science Meeting Is Becoming a Tradition." *Science* 194 (December 17, 1976): 1254.

1224. _____. "Science and Values Discussed at Moon-sponsored Parley." *Science* 190 (December 12, 1975): 1073.

1225. "Honest, There's No Moon in that Muffin." *Newsweek* 98 (November 23, 1981): 92.

1226. Horowitz, Irving. "Religion and the Rise of the Rev. Moon." *The Nation* 228 (April 7, 1979): 365-67.

1227. _____. "Science, Sin and Sponsorship." *Atlantic* 239 (March 1977): 98-102.

1228. Hyde, Margaret O. "Mind Control and the Religious Cults." In *Brainwashing & Other Forms of Mind Control*, 109-24. New York: McGraw-Hill, 1977.

1229. Isikoff, M. "New Moon." *The New Republic* 193 (August 6, 1985): 14-16.

1230. Jensen, Ros. "Watergate's Elmer Gantry." *Progressive* 38 (April 1974): 6-7.

1231. Jervey, G. "Entenmann's Fight Moonie Link." *Advertizing Age* 52 (November 23, 1981): 33.

1232. Johnson, Joan. *The Cult Movement.* New York: Franklin Watts, 1984. 106 pp.

1233. Johnston, Moira. "Showdown in the Valley of the Moonies." *New West* 5 (February 11, 1980): 116-19.

1234. Keeler, Scott. "A California Teenager Goes Undercover to Investigate Life among the Moonies." *People* 10 (July 24, 1978): 20-24.

1235. Keerdoja, E., and J. Foote. "Gone Fishing: Moonies in the Fishing Business." *Newsweek* 92 (September 11, 1978): 10-11.

1236. Kelly, Dean. "Deprogramming and Religious Liberty." *The Civil Liberties Review* 4 (July-August 1977): 23-33.

1237. "Kidnapping of a Moonie (Bo Hi Pak)." *Time* 124 (December 10, 1984): 40.

1238. Kirk, Donald. "Dirty Tricks Korean Style." *Saturday Review* 4 (January 8, 1977): 8, 66-67.

1239. Kirschner Associates, with the Institute for the Study of American Religion. "Holy Spirit Association for the Unification of World Christianity." In *Religious Requirements and Practices of Certain Selected Groups: A Handbook for Chaplains.* Washington, D.C.: Department of the Army, 1978. I41-I46.

1240. Kondrake, Morton. "Nixon's New Defenders and Their Strange Pasts." *Rolling Stone Magazine,* August 29, 1974, 10-14.

1241. Kurlansky, Mark J. "Reverend Moon: Satan or Savior?" *San Francisco* 18 (July 1976): 36-41, 94-96.

1242. _____. "Rev. Moon's Daily Counts 10,000 Paid Circulation." *Editor & Publisher* 110 (February 12, 1977): 14.

1243. Kurti, Nicholas. "Should Scientists Attend the ICUS?" *Nature* 276 (November 16, 1978): 206-207.

1244. Lacy, A. "Irving Horowitz on Journalism and Theory." *Chronicle of Higher Education* 17 (October 16, 1978): R11.

1245. Lande, Nathaniel. "Reverend Sun Myung Moon/The Unification Church." In *Mindstyles-Lifestyles: A Comprehensive Overview of*

Today's Life-Changing Philosophies, 265-66. Los Angeles: Price/Stern/Sloan, 1976.

1246. Landes, Marie-Gisele. "Making of a Moonie." *Atlas World Press Review* 23 (September 1976): 29-32.

1247. Lanier, Linda K. "America's Cults: Gaining Ground Again." *U.S. News & World Report* 93 (July 5, 1982): 37-40.

1248. Lenz, Doug. "The Moonie Life and How One Left It." *U.S. News & World Report* 93 (July 5, 1982): 41.

1249. Lester, Marianne. "The Moon Movement: An Air Force Family Struggles over Sun Myung Moon." Part 1. *The Times Magazine* 77 (July 11, 1977): 6-10, 12-14.

1250. _____. "Profits, Politics, and Power: The Heart of the Controversy." Part 2. *The Times Magazine* 77 (July 25, 1977): 13-16.

1251. Levy, Art. "CARP's Quest for Legitimacy." *Columns*, Spring 1980.

1252. Lopez, Anthony. *The Second Coming*. London, England: New English Library, 1975. 128 pp.

1253. McClaughry, John. "The Uneasy Case against Reverend Moon." *National Review* 35 (December 23, 1983): 1611-12.

1254. McCue, Marion. "Dark Side of the Moon." *Sevendays Preview* edition no. 8 (May 17, 1976): 20-22.

1255. McKenzie, Bill, Kim Ruberg, and Jim Leach. "Theocracy from the Right: The Reverend Sun Myung Moon and the American Political Process." *Ripon Forum* 19 (January 1983): 8-14.

1256. McNamara, Steve, and Joanne Williams. "The Moon Battle." *Pacific Sun*, week of May 13-19, 1977, 5-10.

1257. MacRobert, Alan M. "The Dark Side of the Moon." *The Real Paper* 6 (March 5, 1977).

1258. _____. "Frontlines: Moonies in Reagandom." *Mother Jones* 6 (May 1981): 12-.

1259. _____. "Uncovering the Cult Conspiracy." *Mother Jones* 4 (February-March 1979): 8.

1260. "Mad about Moon." *Time* 106 (November 10, 1975): 44.

1261. Mano, D. Keith. "Moon Madness." *National Review* 26 (November 8, 1974): 1301-2.

1262. Marbuch, William D., with Frank Gibney, Jr. "Honest, There's No Moon in That Muffin." *Newsweek* 98 (November 23, 1981): 92.

1263. Marks, John D. "From Korea with Love." *The Washington Monthly* 5 (February 1974): 55-61.

1264. Marshall, Jonathan. "Korean Evangelism." *Pacific Research and World Empire Telegram* 5 (September-October 1974): 1-4.

1265. Mathews, T., and D. Camper. "Clouded Moon." *Newsweek* 92 (November 13, 1978): 69.

1266. Medved, Harry, and Michael Medved. "Delusions of Grandeur: Heaven's Gate and Inchon." In *Hollywood's Hall of Shame: The Most Expensive Flops in Movie History,* pp. 186-99. New York: Putnam, 1984.

1267. Middleton, L. "Moon Group's Seminar Stirs Dispute." *Chronicle of Higher Education* 19 (November 13, 1979): 6.

1268. _____. "Unit of Moon's Church Sues to Force M.I.T. Press to Withdraw Book." *Chronicle of Higher Education* 18 (July 2, 1979): 4.

1269. Miller, Mark C. "The Manichean in Moon." *The Village Voice* 19 (September 12, 1974): 5, 88.

1270. Montagno, Margaret, "Is Deprogramming Legal?" *Newsweek* 89 (February 21, 1977): 44.

1271. "Moon Backed 'Inchon' Ballyhoo at Cannes, Oliver as MacArthur." *Variety,* May 12, 1982.

1272. "Moon Landing in Manhattan." *Time* 104 (September 30, 1974): 68-69.

1273. "Moon over the Pacific." *Attenzione,* May 1980, 33-34.

1274. "Moon Recruiter's Day in Harvard Square." *Chronicle of Higher Education* 19 (November 13, 1979): 6.

1275. "Moonies May Start Up 8 Newspapers." *Editor & Publisher* 115 (September 11, 1982): 31.

1276. "Moon-Struck." *Time* 102 (October 15, 1973): 129-30.

1277. "Moonstruck." *Economist* 258 (February 7, 1976): 39.

1278. Moorhouse, Geoffrey. "Moonies Invade Gloucester." *Harper's* 262 (January 1981): 46-52.

1279. Moose, Anne. "Carol Nevin" and "Paul Foreman." In *Berkeley USA*, 12-19 and 131-35. Berkeley, Calif.: Alternative Press, 1981.

1280. Moses, Paul. "Rematch Promised: Moonies Thwarted in West New York Showdown." *New Jersey Monthly* 3 (November 1978): 11.

1281. Mwensongole, Mbole Aram. "Moonies over Africa." *Africa Now,* April 1983, 9.

1282. Neier, Aryeh. "Deprogramming and Civil Liberties." In *All Our Sons and Daughters* (item 1207), pp. 46-64.

1283. Nelson, Ann. "Church Political: God, Man and the Reverend Moon." *The Nation* 228 (March 31, 1979): 325-28.

1284. "A New National Paper." *Newsweek* 103 (March 19, 1984): 92.

1285. "New Record: Moon Matches and Marries 4,150." *U.S. News & World Report* 93 (July 12, 1982): 10.

1286. "New York City Daily Bows on Schedule [News World]." *Editor & Publisher* 110 (January 8, 1977): 10-.

1287. Noah, Timothy. "Paper Moon." *The New Republic* 187 (July 19-26, 1982): 16-18.

1288. Nussbaum, Bruce. "Diplomat National Bank Control by Moon Scrutinized." *American Banker* 151 (June 14, 1976): 1, 22.

1289. _____. "Probing the Dark Side of the Moon." *Far Eastern Economic Review* 92 (June 18, 1976): 42, 45-46.

1290. "Obedience to the Law of Diminishing Returns May Cost This Little King 18 Months Away from His Counting House." [The Twenty-five Most Intriguing People of 1982] *People* 18 (December 27, 1982-January 2, 1983): 92.

1291. "Of Moon and Mammon." *Time* 118 (October 26, 1981): 24.

1292. O'Hara, Jane. "Taxing Times for the Reverend." *MacLeans* 95 (April 5, 1982): 32.

1293. "Oh What a Lively Year." *Life,* January 1983, 36.

1294. "One Big, Happy Family." *Newsweek* 82 (October 15, 1973): 54.

1295. Ostling, Richard N. "Sun Myung Moon's Goodwill Blitz." *Time* 125 (April 22, 1985): 60.

1296. Papayannopaulos, Takis E. *Religions in Korea and the Movement of Unification.* Athens, Greece: the Author, 1979. 45 pp.

1297. "Paper Moon." *Economist* 283 (May 22-28, 1982): 34.

1298. "Paper Trenches." *The Nation* 222 (January 24, 1976): 68.

1299. Parsons, Arthur S. "The Moonies: The Triumph of a Family." *Smith Alumni Quarterly*, Summer 1984, 8-13.

1300. Patrick, Ted, with Tom Dulack. *Let Our Children Go!* New York: Ballantine, 1976. 276 pp.

1301. Pavlos, Andrew J. *The Cult Experience.* Westport, Conn.: Greenwood, 1982. 209 pp.

1302. "The Playboy Enemies List (List of People Playboy Considers Enemies Such as Moon, Founder of the Unification Church)." *Playboy* 24 (October 1977): 155-.

1303. Poole, Fredrick King. "Moonset in Brazil." *Psychology Today* 17 (April 1983): 86.

1304. Pousner, Michael. "Who's Afraid of Sun Myung Moon?" *Penthouse*, June 1976.

1305. "Pressure to Crack Down on Cults." *U.S. News & World Report* 85 (December 11, 1978): 26.

1306. "Proctor and Gamble is Clean." *Newsweek* 95 (April 7, 1980): 64.

1307. Putney, Michael. "Rev. Moon--A Messiah--or a Menace?" *National Observer* 15 (June 12, 1976): 1, 19.

1308. Ramsey, Paul. "Korean Creeds and the Rejection of Old Heresies." *Worldview* 20 (November 1977): 27-28.

1309. Randi, James. "Moon May Be the Son (Some of Rev. Moon's More Startling Statements at Court Trial)." *Skeptical Inquirer* 7 (Winter 1982): 15-.

1310. Rasmussen, Mark. "How Sun Myung Moon Lures America's Children." *McCall's* 103 (September 1976): 102-15, 175.

1311. _____. "The Moon Testament." *Harper's Weekly* 44 (December 1, 1975): 3-4.

1312. ———. "Promising People the Moon: A View from the Inside." *State and Mind*, November-December 1977, 11-15.

1313. Reed, Rex. "Shooting Stars." *Gentleman's Quarterly*, December 1980, 43-46.

1314. "Religious Cults: Is the Wild Fling Over?" *U.S. News & World Report* 84 (March 27, 1978): 44-45.

1315. "Religious Cults: Newest Magnet for Youth." *U.S. News & World Report* 80 (June 14, 1976): 52-54.

1316. "Religious Martyr or Tax Cheat?" *U.S. News & World Report* 96 (May 28, 1984): 14.

1317. Remsberg, Charles, and Bonnie Remsberg, eds. "Why I Quit the Moon Cult." *Seventeen* 35 (July 1976): 106-7, 117-27.

1318. "Rendering unto Caesar." *National Review* 34 (May 28, 1982): 603.

1319. Reuter, Madalynne. "Moon Church Files Libel Suit against H. and R., Author." *Publishers Weekly* 213 (May 1, 1978): 29-30.

1320. ———. "Moon Church Sues MIT Press over Speech Copyright." *Publishers Weekly* 215 (June 18, 1975): 26, 30.

1321. "Reverend Moon to Host Media Conferences; Free Trips for Newspeople." *Editor & Publisher* 115 (July 10, 1982): 27.

1322. "The Rev. Sun Myung Moon: A Furor over Brainwashing Hits a Korean Pied Piper." *People* 4 (October 20, 1975): 7-9.

1323. Rice, Berkeley. "Messiah from Korea: Honor Thy Father Moon." *Psychology Today* 9 (January 1976): 36-47.

1324. ———. "The Pull of Sun Moon." In *Science, Sin, and Sponsorship: The Politics of Reverend Moon and the Unification Church* (item 1567), pp. 226-41.

1325. Richardson, Herbert, comp. *Deprogramming: Documenting the Issue*. New York: Edwin Mellen, 1977.

1326. Robbins, Thomas. "Brainwashing and Religious Freedom." *The Nation* 224 (April 30, 1977): 518.

1327. ———. "Cults and the Theraputic State." *Social Policy* 10 (May-June 1979): 42-46.

1328. ———. "Even a Moonie Has Civil Rights." *The Nation* 224 (February 26, 1977): 238-42.

1329. Robbins, Thomas, and Dick Anthony. "Cult Phobia: A Witch Hunt in the Making?" *Inquiry* 2 (January 8, 1979).

1330. ———. "New Religions, Families and 'Brainwashing.'" *Society* 15 (May-June 1978): 77-83.

1331. Roberts, John. "Happiness Ginseng from Earth-conquering Moonies." *Far Eastern Economic Review* 100 (June 23, 1978): 57-.

1332. Robins, Lottie. "Our Son's New 'Heavenly Father.'" *The Saturday Evening Post* 251 (September 1976): 37-38, 117, 180.

1333. Roeder, Bill. "Sun Myung Moon University." *Newsweek* 93 (April 16, 1979): 21.

1334. Roiphe, Anne. "Why Kids Follow the Rev. Sun Myung Moon? Are We Too 'Open' Now?" *Vogue*, November 1976.

1335. Roper, James E. "Capital Dailies' Feud Goes Public." *Editor & Publisher* 117 (October 13, 1984): 12-13.

1336. ———. "Editor Raps Coverage of Washington Times." *Editor & Publisher* 116 (May 28, 1983): 42.

1337. ———. "Upheaval at the Washington Times: Ousted Editor James Whelan Says Moonies Are Taking Over." *Editor & Publisher* 117 (July 21, 1984): 9-11.

1338. Rothmeyer, Karen. "Mapping Out Moon's Media Empire." *Columbia Journalism Review* 23 (November-December 1984): 23-31.

1339. Rupp, Carla Marie. "News World Publisher Says Rev. Moon Is the Messiah." *Editor & Publisher* 115 (April 21, 1982): 10-.

1340. ———. "Unification Church May Start a Daily in NYC." *Editor & Publisher* 109 (December 4, 1976): 8.

1341. Sage, Wayne. "The War on the Cults." *Human Behavior* 5 (October 1976): 40-49.

1342. Sandon, Leo, Jr. "The Moonie Family: Do We Have a Stake in Being Fair to the Far-Out? *Worldview* 21 (October 1978): 7-11.

1343. Scharff, Gary. "Autobiography of a Former Moonie." *The Center Magazine* 15 (March-April 1982): 14-17.

1344. "S.E.C. and Moon Church Settle Dispute." *Church and State* 32 (September 1979): 21.

1345. "Secret Sayings of Master Moon; Excerpts from Speeches." *Time* 107 (June 14, 1976): 49.

1346. Serrill, Michael S. "A Prophet's Unlikely Defender." *Time* 123 (January 23, 1984): 34.

1347. Shim, Jae Hoon. "Christianity and Controversy; Interview with Pak, Bo Hi." *Far Eastern Economic Review* 114 (November 20-26, 1981): 38-40.

1348. _____. "Treasures upon Earth--and Invisible Big Hands." *Far Eastern Economic Review* 114 (November 20-26, 1981): 40.

1349. Shim, Jae Hoon, and Nancy Langston. "Moon's Time of Trial." *Far Eastern Economic Review* 114 (November 20-26, 1981): 36-39.

1350. Shupe, Anson D., and David G. Bromley. "Witches, Moonies and Evil." *Society* 15 (May-June 1978): 75-76.

1351. Shupe, Anson D., Roger Spielman, and Sam Stigall. "Cults of Anti-Cultism." *Society* 17 (March-April 1980): 43-46.

1352. "Side of the Moon Hidden from Seoul." *Far Eastern Economic Review* 92 (June 25, 1976): 31-32.

1353. Sidney, Hugh. "A Summer Week in Washington." *Time* 104 (August 5, 1974): 27.

1354. Sklar, Dusty. *Gods and Beasts: The Nazis and the Occult.* New York: Thomas Y. Crowell, 1977. 180 pp.

1355. Srodes, James. "Testing Time for the Asian Lobby." *Far Eastern Economic Review* 92 (April 16, 1976): 21-22.

1356. _____. "Tracing the Links with Seoul." *Far Eastern Economic Review* 93 (July 23, 1976): 22.

1357. Srouji, Jaculine. "Watching Sun Myung Moon." *The Tennessee Register* 44 (Decemeber 14, 1981).

1358. Stanford, Phil. "The Quiet War on the Cults." *Inquiry* 2 (October 15, 1979): 6-7.

1359. Stein, Jeff. "Moon's Latest Phase." *Progressive* 46 (July 1982): 20.

1360. Stein, M.L. "Wining and Dining the Media (Journalists Attend All Expense Paid Unification Church Sponsored World Media Conference in Tokyo)." *Editor & Publisher* 117 (December 29, 1984): 13-.

1361. Stoner, Carroll, and Jo Anne Parke. *All God's Children: The Cult Experience, Salvation or Slavery?* New York: Penguin Books, 1977. 479 pp.

1362. Sullivan, Tim. "Florida Based Fish Trader Loses Shirt in Deals with Moon Firm." *National Fisherman* (December 1980): 34-36.

1363. _____. "'Moonie' Fishing Operations Regroup in Alabama amid Two Federal Probes." *National Fisherman,* September 1979, 14, 54.

1364. _____. "'Moonies' Fishing Ventures Show Little or No Profit." *National Fisherman,* September 1981, 2, 25, 103.

1365. _____. "Moon's Hopes for Tuna Fishery May Not Prove Financially Viable." *National Fisherman,* September 1981, 25-26, 52.

1366. _____. "UCI Funds Back Fishing Ventures despite Charter." *National Fisherman,* September 1979, 15-16.

1367. "Sun Myung Moon." *Current Biography* 44 (March 1983): 30-33.

1368. "Sun Myung Moon and the Law." *Church and State* 32 (January 1979): 9-12.

1369. "Sun Myung Moon--Troubles Build Up for the Mysterious Leader of the Unification Church." *People* 6 (January 3, 1977): 35.

1370. "Supreme Court Allows Deprogramming Suits." *Church & State* 35 (March 1982): 14.

1371. Swatland, Susan. *Escape From the Moonies.* London: New English Library, 1982. 159 pp.

1372. "They Call Him the Negative Messiah" [Interview with Steve Hassan]. *Real Paper,* August 28, 1980, 7-8.

1373. Trillin, Calvin. "U.S. Journal--Bayou La Batre, Ala." *New Yorker* 54 (March 27, 1978): 99-104.

1374. Underwood, Barbara, and Betty Underwood. *Hostage to Heaven.* New York: Clarkson N. Potter, 1979. 304 pp.

1375. "Unification Church Founds Paragon House." *Publishers Weekly* 225 (April 20, 1984): 18-19.

1376. "Unification Church Planning Washington, D.C. Newspaper [Washington Times]." *Editor & Publisher* 115 (March 20, 1982): 40b.

1377. "The Ups and Downs of the Reverend Moon." *U.S. News & World Report* 92 (May 31, 1982) 13.

1378. Waggoner, D. "Ex-believers Gary Scharff and Barbara Underwood Battle the Dark Side of the Reverend Moon." *People* 13 (January 28, 1980): 65-.

1379. Wallis, Roy. "Open Mind about Moonies." *Times Higher Education Supplement* 517 (October 1, 1982): 15.

1380. Walsh, John. "Meeting on the Unity of the Sciences: Reflections on the Rev. Moon." *Science* 189 (September 19, 1975): 975-76.

1381. Waters, Craig. "Bringing Home the Moonies: The Body Snatch." *New Times*, June 10, 1977, 30-34.

1382. Weiss, Fred. "Welcome to Britain." *The New Statesman* 93 (June 24, 1977): 853.

1383. Welles, Chris. "The Eclipse of Sun Myung Moon." *New York Magazine* 9 (September 27, 1976): 33-38.

1384. Whang, Roy. "Messiah with a Deft Political Touch." *Far Eastern Economic Review* 87 (February 21, 1975): 12-13.

1385. Wiener, Tom. "Newsreel: Cult Movie (U.C. behind Movie 'Inchon')." *American Film* 6 (September 1981): 13.

1386. Williams, Carson. "How Cults Bilk All of Us." *Reader's Digest* 115 (November 1979): 237-44.

1387. Wills, Garry. "Piety in the Bunker." *Harper's* 249 (October, 1979): 18-22.

1388. Wolmuth, Roger. "His Mass-Matched Bride Long Gone, Rick La Martina Finds Deliverance from the Moonies." *People* 19 (March 14, 1983): 125-.

1389. Wood, Allen Tate, with Jack Vitek. *Moonstruck: A Memoir of My Life in a Cult.* New York: William Morrow, 1979. 189 pp.

1390. Woodward, Kenneth, with Patrice Johnson. "Rev. Moon's New Friends." *Newsweek* 99 (May 3, 1982): 88.

1391. Woodward, Kenneth, and E. Woodward. "Why Are Teens Turning to Religion? Eastern and Traditional Religions." *Seventeen* 34 (July 1975): 96-97.

1392. Woodward, Kenneth, with Mary Hager, Janet Huck, Michael Reece, Rachel Mark, and William B. Marbuch. "How They Bend Minds." *Newsweek* 92 (December 4, 1978): 72-77.

1393. Woodward, Kenneth, with Henry McGee, William J. Cook and Sylvester Monroe. "Life with Father Moon." *Newsweek* 87 (June 14, 1976): 60-66.

1394. "Word from Reverend Moon (The Korean 'Billy Graham' Makes Four Month Save Richard Nixon Crusade). *Rolling Stone* 155 (February 14, 1974): 9.

Periodicals

1395. *The Advisor.* Lexington, Mass.: American Family Foundation. Bimonthly. 1979-82.

1396. *Alliance for the Preservation of Religious Liberty* [newsletter]. San Francisco: Alliance for the Preservation of Religious Liberty. Irregular. 1979-81. Continued as Americans Preserving Religious Liberty, 1982.

1397. *Citizen's Freedom Foundation News.* Chula Vista, Calif.: Citizen's Freedom Foundation. Monthly. 1974-83. Continued as Cult Awareness Network News, 1984-.

1398. *The Cult Observer.* Weston, Mass.: American Family Foundation. Monthly. 1984-.

1399. *Ex-Moon* [newsletter]. Brookline, Mass., Washington, D.C. and Santa Cruz, Calif.: Ex-Members against Moon. Monthly. 1979-81.

1400. *International Foundation for Individual Freedom Newsletter.* 1978-80. Chapter newsletters, Philadelphia and Berkeley, Calif.

1401. *Love Our Children, Inc.* [newsletter]. Omaha, Neb.: Love Our Children. Monthly. 1976-81.

V.

SCHOLARLY TREATMENTS

A. THEOLOGICAL ASSESSMENTS

Theological assessments of the UC are to a degree unprecedented among new religious movements both in their quantity and in that they have been solicited by the Church. Due in part to the establishment of the Unification Theological Seminary in 1975 and to the launching in 1977 of a series of UC-financed dialogues between its seminarians and interested scholars, there has emerged a substantial body of scholarship on Unification theology and thought. A number of these studies take the form of conference proceedings and include both articles and discussion. Most but not all have been published under Church auspices and edited by outside scholars. Some include contributions from UC seminary graduates as they have interacted with professional theologians. In this sense, sponsorship of ecumenical dialogues has furthered UC apologetic, educational and theological purposes. Published material includes theological overviews, analyses of specific doctrines and evaluations of the Church's social teaching and practices.

Theological overviews elaborate the cultural and institutional contexts, sources, core elements, significance and internal coherence of UC theological texts and teachings. Generally sympathetic, some treatments hail Unification theology as holding forth the promise of fresh departures in longstanding theological debates or of a coming synthesis of Eastern and Western thought. Others contrast underlying potentialities in UC teachings with shortcomings in their present articulation. A number of treatments eschew final conclusions and simply explore continuities and discontinuities between Unification theology and other traditions. Some do so in explicitly comparative terms.

The single most useful theological overview of UC teachings is Lonnie Kliever's "Unification Thought and Modern Theology" [1457]. Kliever, who includes a helpful bibliographical survey, characterizes the UC as a "messianic revitalization movement" which, at the same time, "is highly self-conscious about communication theory, group dynamics and theological apologetics." Further, he argues, "The unavoidable clash between the two-- messianic revitalization and self-conscious modernization is the source of 'Unification Mystique' for committed insiders and interested outsiders alike" (214-15). Noting that this "collision of consciousness" is at the heart of modern theological development, Kliever concludes:

> Through a glass darkly, we see the distinctive ethos and pathos of modern theology mirrored in Unification thought. The need,

therefore, to take account of these theological materials goes beyond theological defensiveness or theological charity. A careful study of Unification theology is a valuable exercise in self-discovery and self-criticism (221).

Other important theological overviews are Thomas Boslooper's "Unificationism and Biblical Studies" [1409]; Frank K. Flinn's "The Hermeneutics of Completed Testaments" [1429]; Warren Lewis' "Is the Rev. Sun Myung Moon a Heretic? Locating Unification Theology on the Map of Church History" [1464]; Hae Soo Pyun's "*Divine Principle* and Oriental Philosophy" [1478]; Herbert Richardson's "A Brief Outline of Unification Theology" [1480]; and Richard L. Rubenstein's "Radical Secularization, the Modern Age and the New Religions" [1484].

Analyses of specific doctrines are more detailed and sharply focused than theological overviews. At the same time, while overviews take into account a broad range of cultural, religious and institutional influences, treatments of specific doctrines tend to be preoccupied with the question of whether or not and in what ways UC tenets are identifiably "Christian." This concern derives primarily from the fact that UC theological texts follow the traditional divisions of God and Creation, Human Nature and the Fall, Christology, History and Eschatology. Analyses of these doctrines include general expositions, comparative studies, critical reflections and constructive restatements.

The most comprehensive expositions of UC doctrines are Young Oon Kim's *Unification Theology* [509], an updated and expanded version of her earlier *Unification Theology and Christian Thought* [711-12] and Sebastian A. Matczak's *Unificationism: A New Philosophy and Worldview* [1471]. Kim's work "compares the basic teaching of the *Divine Principle* ... with that found in theological writings published by mainline denominations" and argues "how often this new Korean theology is confirmed by professional theologians in the West" (iii-iv). Matczak supplements Kim's treatment by treating philosophical and social aspects of UC doctrines. Terming Unificationism "a theistic and Christian worldview," he emphasizes its relationship and reconcilability to "the traditional Christian position." See Clark [1419], Eby [1424], Wells [1497], and Wilson [1501] for expositions of specific doctrines. Key comparative and critical reflections as opposed to general expositions include M. Darrol Bryant's "Unification Eschatology and American Millennial Traditions" [1411], Durwood Foster's "Unification and Traditional Christology: An Unresolved Relationship" [1435], Gary E. Kessler's "Indemnity: Does It Make Sense?" [1449], and Fredrick Sontag's "The God of Principle: A Critical Evaluation" [1488]. Rather than emphasizing theological convergence, these treatments as often highlight a vigorous diversity of interpretation at work within Unification teachings reflective of diversity within the Christian tradition. This more pluralistic view has led to further development of UC positions, particularly as related to issues of evil, suffering and human freedom.

Evaluations of UC social teachings and practices differ from overviews and analyses of specific doctrines in that the cleavage between sympathetic and critical readings is more pronounced. Sympathetic treatments describe UC social theory and practice as continuous with, mediating between or as an alternative to contemporary ethical systems. Critiques fault the UC for theoretical imprecision and implicit authoritarianism. Other studies are more descriptive or balance critique with recognition of positive features in the Church's social vision and praxis.

The most ambitious applications of UC doctrine to society are San Hun Lee's *The End of Communism* [637], an updated version of his earlier *Communism: A Critique and Counterproposal* [578], and *Explaining Unification Thought* [638], an updated version of his earlier *Unification Thought* [639]. Although presented in lecture form and cognizant of scholarly limitations and gaps in formulation, Lee extrapolates an unambiguous social agenda from UC doctrinal texts: the eradication of communism and final synthesis of all sciences and philosophies under Unification Thought as the basis for a new world order. More provisional, though still appreciative readings depict UC social theory as an alternative to Western social contract and Oriental hierarchial paradigms [1423] or to the modern liberal conception of marriage as a purely contractural agreement [1430]. Others have detected resonance with liberation theology [1427] and the Catholic natural law tradition [1477]. The most representative statement of objections to UC social teachings is David F. Kelly's "Religion and Society in Unificationism" [1448]. Besides alleging contradictions in its vision of the ultimate society, Kelly chides the UC for a tendency "too quickly to identify the heavenly side and the satanic side," for an "emphasis on the family apt ... to lead to the relative disvaluing of other modes of human generativity and creativity," and for "sexism" (360-62). See Heinz [1440], James [1442] and Kliever [1456] for related critiques. It may be, however, that ambiguities and unresolved tensions in UC social theory serve to undercut a perceived authoritarianism. This has been the implicit conclusion of several feminist critiques [1418, 1436, 1503].

1402. Anderson, Gordon L. "God Is Parent: Rich and Poor Nations Are Siblings." In God and Global Justice: Religion and Poverty in an Unequal World (item 704), pp. 120-35.

1403. _____. "Indemnity for World Peace." In *Restoring the Kingdom* (item 703), pp. 45-55.

1404. _____. "The Unification Vision of the Kingdom of God on Earth." In *The Coming Kingdom: Essays in American Millennialism and Eschatology* (item 695), pp. 209-21.

1405. Aslid, Dagfinn. "The Future God." *In Hermeneutics and Horizons: The Shape of the Future* (item 706), pp. 399-407.

1406. _____. "Unification Theology as History." In *Hermeneutics and Horizons: The Shape of the Future* (item 706), pp. 251-59.

1407. _____. "Spiritual Discipline as Actualization of the Heart of God." In *Ultimate Reality and Spiritual Discipline* (item 701), pp. 139-51.

1408. Boslooper, Thomas. "Critique of Divine Principle's Reading of the New Testament." In *Hermeneutics and Horizons: The Shape of the Future* (item 706), pp. 103-13.

1409. _____. "Unification and Biblical Studies." In *Unity in Diversity: Essays in Religion by Faculty Members of the Unification Theological Seminary* (item 728), pp. 297-323.

1410. Bryant, M. Darrol. "Critical Reflections on Unification Eschatology." In *Exploring Unification Theology* (item 697), pp. 147-56.

1411. _____. "Unification Eschatology and American Millennial Traditions." In *A Time for Consideration: A Scholarly Appraisal of the Unification Church* (item 1412), pp. 261-74.

* Bryant, M. Darrol, and Susan Hodges, eds. *Exploring Unification Theology.* Cited above as item 697.

1412. Bryant, M. Darrol, and Herbert W. Richardson. *A Time for Consideration: A Scholarly Appraisal of the Unification Church.* New York: Edwin Mellen 1978. 317 pp.

Contains items 1411, 1432, 1463-64, 1468, 1480, 1482, 1485, 1638, 1650.

1413. Campbell, Debra. "Indulgences and Indemnity in the Life of the Believer: A Modern Catholic Perspective." In *Restoring the Kingdom* (item 703), pp. 165-74.

1414. Chang, Byung Kil. "A Study of the Unification Principle from the Perspective of Religious Studies." In *Research on the Unification Principle: Seminar of Korean Scholars on Unification Theology* (item 723), pp. 149-62.

1415. Chang, Ki Kin. "The Unification Principle and Oriental Thought." In *Research on the Unification Principle: Seminar of Korean Scholars on Unification Theology* (item 723), pp. 63-77.

1416. Choi, Dong Hee. "Unification Doctrine--Its Philosophical Nature and Significance." In *Research on the Unification Principle: Seminar of Korean Scholars on Unification Theology* (item 723), pp. 37-47.

1417. Choi, Min Hong. "The Unification Principle and Korean Thought (Centering on the 'Oneness in Buddha' Concept of Wonhyo)." In *Research on the Unification Principle: Seminar of Korean Scholars on Unification Theology* (item 723), pp. 95-108.

1418. Clark, Elizabeth. "Women in the Theology of the Unification Church." In *Exploring Unification Theology* (item 697), pp. 109-21.

1419. Clark, Francis. "The Fall of Man in Divine Principle." In *Ten Theologians Respond to the Unification Church* (item 724), pp. 141-65.

1420. _____. "The Principle of Indemnity." In *Restoring the Kingdom* (item 703), pp. 17-31.

1421. Eby, Lloyd. "Is God Good and Can God Be Defended?" In *The Defense of God* (item 725), pp. 48-67.

1422. _____. "The Kingdom of Heaven." In *Unity in Diversity: Essays in Religion by Members of the Faculty of the Unification Theological Seminary* (item 728), pp. 149-61.

1423. _____. "Society and Ethics in Unificationism." In *Hermeneutics and Horizons: The Shape of the Future* (item 706), pp. 345-56.

1424. _____. "The Unification Understanding of God." In *Hermeneutics and Horizons: The Shape of the Future* (item 706), pp. 159-69.

1425. Edwards, Cliff. "Paul and Unificationism: Restoration through Grace or Indemnity?" In *Restoring the Kingdom* (item 703), pp. 141-51.

1426. Feige, Franz. "Salvation as Restoration in Unification Thought." In *Orthodox-Unification Dialogue* (item 730), pp. 115-23.

1427. Ferm, Deane William. "A Preference for the Poor: Where Liberation Theology and Unification Theology Might Converge." In *Restoring the Kingdom* (item 703), pp. 183-92.

1428. Fleming, James R. "Restoration through Indemnity and the Problem of Suffering." In *Restoring the Kingdom* (item 703), pp. 33-43.

1429. Flinn, Frank K. "The Hermeneutics of Completed Testaments." In *Hermeneutics and Horizons: The Shape of the Future* (item 706), pp. 115-29.

1430. _____. "Marriage as Eschatological Type in Unification Theology." In *The Family and the Unification Church* (item 709), pp. 235-53.

1431. _____. "The New Religions and the Second Naivete: Beyond Demystification and Demythologization." In *Ten Theologians Respond to the Unification Church* (item 724), pp. 41-59.

1432. ———. "Unification Hermeneutics and Christian Theology." In *A Time For Consideration: A Scholarly Appraisal of the Unification Church* (item 1412), pp. 141-66.

1433. Foster, Durwood. "The Fall in Divine Principle." In *Society and Original Sin: Ecumenical Essays on the Impact of the Fall* (item 707), pp. 73-85.

1434. ———. "Notes on Christology and Hermeneutics: Especially Regarding Dialogue with Unification Theology." In *Hermeneutics and Horizons: The Shape of the Future* (item 706), pp. 201-28.

1435. ———. "Unification and Traditional Christology: An Unresolved Relationship." In *Ten Theologians Respond to the Unification Church* (item 724), pp. 179-99.

1436. Getz, Lorine M. "Women and the Hermeneutics of the Future." In *Hermeneutics and Horizons: The Shape of the Future* (item 706), pp. 409-16.

1437. Guerra, Anthony J. "The Historical Jesus and Divine Principle." In *Hermeneutics and Horizons: The Shape of the Future* (item 706), 49-59.

1438. Hadden, Jeffrey K. "Indemnity Lost, Indulgences Regained: Theological Convergence in American Televangelism." In *Restoring the Kingdom* (item 703), pp. 211-13.

1439. Han, Tai Soo. "The Unity of Eastern and Western Civilizations through the Unification Principle." In *Research on the Unification Principle: Seminar of Korean Scholars on Unification Theology* (item 723), pp. 257-69.

1440. Heinz, Donald. "The Family: The New Christian Right's Symbol for a Lost Past, The Unification Movement's Hope for a Second Advent." In *The Family and the Unification Church* (item 709), pp. 67-85.

1441. Hendricks, Tyler. "Voluntary Association, Intermarriage and 'The World of the Heart.'" In *Unity in Diversity: Essays in Religion by Members of the Faculty of the Unification Theological Seminary* (item 728), pp. 413-23.

1442. James, Gene. "Family, Spiritual Values and World Government." In *The Family and the Unification Church* (item 709), pp. 255-68.

1443. ———. "The Unification Doctrine of the Fall and the Problem of Evil." In *Society and Original Sin: Ecumenical Essays on the Fall* (item 707), pp. 86-99.

1444. James, Theodore E. "Reason, Revelation, and Romans." In *Unity in Diversity: Essays in Religion by Members of the Faculty of the Unification Theological Seminary* (item 728), pp. 325-58.

1445. Johannesen, Stanley. "Historical Narration in *Divine Principle*: The Ideology of Religious Story." In *Hermeneutics and Horizons: The Shape of the Future* (item 706), pp. 281-314.

1446. Johnson, Kapp L. "Critique of *Divine Principle*'s Reading of the Old Testament." In *Hermeneutics and Horizons: The Shape of the Future* (item 706), pp. 93-101.

1447. Johnson, Kurt. "The Unification Principle and Science: Promise, Paradox, and Predicament." In *Unity in Diversity: Essays in Religion by Members of the Faculty of the Unification Theological Seminary* (item 728), pp. 395-412.

1448. Kelly, David F. "Religion and Society in Unificationism." In *Hermeneutics and Horizons: The Shape of the Future* (item 706), pp. 357-64.

1449. Kessler, Gary E. "Indemnity: Does It Make Sense?" In *Restoring the Kingdom* (item 703), pp. 59-70.

1450. Kim, David S.C. "Marxism and the Unification Alternative." In *Unity in Diversity: Essays in Religion by Members of the Faculty of the Unification Theological Seminary* (item 728), pp. 255-96.

1451. Kim, Tae Chang. "Modern Ideological Conflicts and Victory over Communism (VOC) Theory." In *Research on the Unification Principle: Seminar of Korean Scholars on Unification Theology* (item 723), pp. 283-91.

1452. Kim, Young Min. "A Comparative Study of the View of God in Divine Principle." In *Research on the Unification Principle: Seminar of Korean Scholars on Unification Theology* (item 723), pp. 17-24.

1453. Kim, Young Oon. "God Is Now Closer." In *God, the Contemporary Discussion* (item 726), pp. 313-31.

1454. _____. "Satan: Reality or Symbol?" In *Society and Original Sin: Essays on the Impact of the Fall* (item 707), pp. 21-36.

* _____. *Unification Theology*. Cited above as item 509.

* _____. *Unification Theology and Christian Thought*. Cited above as items 711-12.

1455. Kliever, Lonnie D. "The Unification Church as Metainstitution." In
      Ten Theologians Respond to the Unification Church (item 724),
      pp. 61-74.

1456. _____. "Unification Social Hermeneutic: Theocratic or Bureaucratic?"
      In *Hermeneutics and Horizons: The Shape of the Future* (item
      706), pp. 365-71.

1457. _____. "Unification Thought and Modern Theology." *Religious
      Studies Review* 8 (July 1982): 214-21.

1458. Kodera, T. James. "Toward an Asianization of Christianity: Demise
      or Metamorphosis?" In *Ten Theologians Respond to the
      Unification Church* (item 724), pp. 75-88.

1459. Kwak, Chung Hwan. "God and Creation in Unification Theology."
      In *God, the Contemporary Discussion* (item 726), pp. 85-94.

1460. Lee, Hang Nyong. "Sun Myung Moon--His Faith and Thought." In
      Sun Myung Moon: The Man and His Ideal (item 675), pp. 65-
      104.

1461. Lee, James Michael. "John Dewey and the Unification Church; Some
      Points of Contact." In *Unity in Diversity: Essays in Religion by
      Members of the Faculty of the Unification Theological Seminary*
      (item 728), pp. 371-93.

*   Lee, Sang Hun. *Communism: A Critique and Counterproposal.*
      Cited above as item 578.

*   _____. *The End of Communism.* Cited above as item 637.

*   _____. *Explaining Unification Thought.* Cited above as item 638.

*   _____. *Unification Thought.* Cited above as item 639.

1462. _____. "The Unification View of God." In *God in Contemporary
      Thought: A Philosophical Perspective,* edited by Sebastian
      Matzcak, 727-49. New York: Learned Publications, 1977.

1463. Lewis, Warren. "Hero with the Thousand-and-First-Face." In *A
      Time for Consideration: A Scholarly Appraisal of the Unification
      Church* (item 1412), pp. 275-89.

1464. _____. "Is the Reverend Sun Myung Moon a Heretic? Locating
      Unification Theology on the Map of Church History." In *A Time
      for Consideration: A Scholarly Appraisal of the Unification
      Church* (item 1412), pp. 167-219.

1465. Lindner, Klaus M. "The Periods of Christian History in Unification Theology." In *Hermeneutics and Horizons: The Shape of the Future* (item 706), pp. 261-69.

1466. McGowan, Thomas. "Horace Bushnell and the Unification Movement: A Comparison of Theologies." In *Ten Theologians Respond to the Unification Church* (item 724), pp. 19-39.

1467. Masefield, Peter. "The Muni and the Moonies." *Religion* 15 (April 1985): 143-60.

1468. Matczak, Sebastian. "God in Unification Philosophy and Christian Tradition." In *A Time For Consideration: A Scholarly Appraisal of the Unification Church* (item 1412), pp. 220-57.

1469. _____. "Human Nature in the Unification View and in the Christian Tradition." In *Orthodox-Unification Dialogue* (item 730), pp. 21-33.

1470. _____. "The Role of Jesus in Man's Salvation According to Unification Thought and Christian Tradition." In *Orthodox-Unification Dialogue* (item 730), pp. 75-88.

1471. _____. *Unificationism: A New Philosophy and Worldview.* New York: Learned Publications, 1982. 493 pp.

1472. Mavrodes, George I. "Indemnity: An Essay in Clarification." In *Restoring the Kingdom* (item 703), pp. 71-85.

1473. Meagher, John C. "Two Cheers for Indemnity." In *Restoring the Kingdom* (item 703), pp. 87-99.

1474. Miller, Timothy. "Families within a Family: Spiritual Values of Hutterites and Unificationists." In *The Family and the Unification Church* (item 709), pp. 53-65.

1475. O'Sullivan, Michael. "Blood, Sweat, and Tears: Suffering for the Kingdom." In *Restoring the Kingdom* (item 703), pp. 101-11.

1476. Phan, Peter C. "The Doctrine of Reparation in *Divine Principle* and Anselm's Cur Deus Homo." In *Restoring the Kingdom* (item 703), pp. 153-63.

1477. Post, Steven. "Divine Principle and Natural Law." In *Hermeneutics and Horizons: The Shape of the Future* (item 706), pp. 337-43.

1478. Pyun, Hae Soo. "*Divine Principle* and Oriental Philosophy." In *Unity in Diversity: Essays in Religion by Members of the Faculty of the Unification Theological Seminary* (item 728), pp. 359-70.

1479. Quitsland, Sonya A. "A Christian Feminist Critique of the Doctrine of Indemnity." In *Restoring the Kingdom* (item 703), pp. 123-38.

1480. Richardson, Herbert. "A Brief Outline of Unification Theology." In *A Time for Consideration: A Scholarly Appraisal of the Unification Church* (item 1412), pp. 133-40.

1481. _____. "Freedom and the Will: A Unification Theory." In *Ten Theologians Respond to the Unification Church* (item 724), pp. 167-78.

1482. _____. "A Lecture to Students at the Unification Theological Seminary in Barrytown, New York." In *A Time for Consideration: A Scholarly Appraisal of the Unification Church* (item 1412), pp. 290-317.

1483. Roberts, James Deotis. "Hermeneutics: History and Providence." In *Hermeneutics and Horizons: The Shape of the Future* (item 706), pp. 315-26.

1484. Rubenstein, Richard L. "Radical Secularization, the Modern Age and the New Religions." In *Ten Theologians Respond to the Unification Church* (item 724), pp. 89-105.

1485. Sawatsky, Rodney. "Moonies, Mormons and Mennonites: Christian Heresy and Religious Toleration." In *A Time for Consideration: A Scholarly Appraisal of the Unification Church* (item 1412), pp. 20-40.

1486. Sonneborn, John Andrew. "God, Suffering and Hope: A Unification View." In *Unity in Diversity: Essays in Religion by Faculty Members of the Unification Theological Seminary* (item 728), pp. 163-239.

1487. _____. "Unification Theology, Ecumenicity, and 'The God of Principle': A Response to F. Sontag's Essay." *Journal of Ecumenical Studies* 22 (Fall 1985): 754-63.

1488. Sontag, Fredrick. "The God of Principle: A Critical Evaluation." In *Ten Theologians Respond to the Unification Church* (item 724), pp. 107-39. Reprinted (abridged) in *Journal of Ecumenical Studies* 22 (Fall 1985): 741-53.

1489. _____. "Marriage and Family in Unification Theology." In *The Family and the Unification Church* (item 709), pp. 217-34.

1490. _____. "The Principle of the Future." In *Hermeneutics and Horizons: The Shape of the Future* (item 706), pp. 417-21.

1491. Thompson, Henry O. "A Study in Anti-Semitism: Israels in Divine Principle." In *Unity in Diversity: Essays in Religion by Members of the Faculty of the Unification Theological Seminary* (item 728), pp. 73-133.

1492. Tsirpanlis, Constantine N. "The Blessed Virgin's Place in God's Redemption According to the Church Fathers and Unification Thought." In *Orthodox-Unification Dialogue* (item 730), pp. 98-107.

1493. Vander Goot, Henry. "The Humanity of God and the Divinity of Man: Reflections on Unification's Theology of Creation." In *Exploring Unification Theology* (item 697), pp. 93-99.

1494. Walsh, Tom. "Celibacy, Virtue, and the Practice of True Family in the Unification Church." In *The Family and the Unification Church* (item 709), pp. 139-59.

1495. ———. "The Response to Suffering." In *Society and Original Sin: Ecumenical Essays on the Impact of the Fall* (item 707), pp. 119-32.

1496. Wells, Jonathan. "Some Reflections on the Unification Account of the Fall." In *Society and Original Sin: Ecumenical Essays on the Impact of the Fall* (item 707), pp. 62-72.

1497. ———. "Unification Christology." In *Unity in Diversity: Essays on Religion by Members of the Faculty of the Unification Theological Seminary* (item 728), pp. 135-47.

1498. ———. "Unification Hermeneutics and Christology." In *Hermeneutics and Horizons: The Shape of the Future* (item 706), pp. 185-200.

1499. Wentz, Richard E. "America: Mirror of the Faces of Restoration." In *Restoring the Kingdom* (item 703), pp. 193-210.

1500. Wilson, Andrew M. "Biblical Hermeneutics in Divine Principle: The Context of Confucianism." In *Hermeneutics and Horizons: The Shape of the Future* (item 706), pp. 3-23.

1501. ———. "The Unification Doctrine of Indemnity." In *Restoring the Kingdom* (item 703), pp. 3-15.

1502. Yoon, Se Won. "The Creation Doctrine and Contemporary Science." In *Research on the Unification Principle: Seminar of Korean Scholars on Unification Theology* (item 723), pp. 121-31.

1503. Zulkosky, Patricia. "Women: Guilt, Spirituality and Family." In *The Family and the Unification Church* (item 709), pp. 175-93.

B. SOCIOLOGICAL ANALYSES

Sociological analyses of the UC, for the most part, have been neither solicited by nor published under the auspices of the Church. That is, sociologists of religion, more so than theologians, have sought out the UC and have been able to publish their findings in both commercial and academic presses. Interest in the UC within this field has been stimulated to a certain extent by the emergence of new religious movements (NRMs) as a major research topic during the seventies. The best-known sociological analysis of the UC, however, was published before that emergence, and interest in the UC among sociologists of religion is still lively despite a waning of interest in NRMs during the eighties. In addition, sociologists, more so than practicioners of other disciplines, have exercised themselves over a variety of methodological and ethical considerations ranging from covert v. overt research postures to the propriety or impropriety of attending UC-funded conferences.

The earliest and still the best-known sociological analysis of the UC is John Lofland's *Doomsday Cult: A Study of Conversion, Proselytization, and Maintenance of Faith* [1579]. Employing pseudonyms and originally presented as a doctoral dissertation at the University of California, Berkeley, in 1964, Lofland's study was based on nearly a year's participant-observation of the original UC community in the San Francisco Bay Area. The book is well known for its model of conversion, a theory which Lofland and colleague Rodney Stark first published in the *American Sociological Review* [1585]. The Lofland-Stark or "world-saver" model, which became the most widely cited conversion model in the literature of sociology, elaborates "the conditions under which one may expect persons to take up a deviant role." According to Lofland [1579], conversion to the UC required that a person:

1. experience enduring, acutely felt tensions;
2. within a religious, problem-solving perspective;
3. which lead to defining himself as a religious seeker;
4. encountering the cult at a turning point in his life;
5. wherein an affective bond to adherents is formed (or pre-exists);
6. where extra-cult attachments are low or neutralized;
7. and where, to become a "deployable agent," exposure to interaction is accomplished (7-8).

In a 1977 epilogue to his original treatment, Lofland [1580] attempted to explain how "an obscure end-of-the-world religion ... went on to become nationally and internationally famous in the 1970s." He, however, placed this development within a "boom and bust" pattern and predicted the UC will "join the ranks of the many 'has been' movements that linger on in America" (v, 280).

After Lofland, the next significant treatment of the UC in social scientific literature consisted of several articles by Thomas Robbins and Dick Anthony. These include "The Last Civil Religion: Reverend Moon and the Unification Church" [1613], "The Effect of Detente on the Growth of New Religions: Reverend Moon and the Unification Church" [1506] and "Spiritual Innovation and the Crisis of American Civil Religion" [1507], all of which depict the UC as a "civil religion sect." That is, though acknowledging, "The growth of the Unification Church ... demonstrates the continued existence of a widespread hunger for religion with a pronounced civil dimension," Robbins et al. [1613] characterize the UC's reconstruction of "declining theistic and anti-communist patriotic values" as authoritarian and totalistic (124). Barbara Hargrove [1559], however, criticized Anthony and Robbins' work for "dealing primarily with the stated ideology" and only marginally with "the full nature of the Unification Church or its meaning to the rank and file membership" (212).

The work of sociologists Anson D. Shupe, Jr. and David G. Bromley has been more broad-ranging. In some twenty articles and two monographs published between 1977-82, they established themselves as authorities on the Church and, in a sense, as sucessors to Lofland. At the same time, there are important differences between their and Lofland's approach. The major one is that while Lofland utilized a close descriptive analysis to generate theory, Bromley and Shupe employed existing theories to facilitate their descriptive analysis of the Church. Terming the UC and its constellation of related organizations a "world-transforming social movement, i.e., one that seeks total, permanent, structural change of societies across all institutions," Bromley and Shupe used a "resource mobilization" approach to assess the UC's ideology, leadership, recruitment-socialization and public identity. This is most explicit in their monograph, *Moonies in America: Cult, Church, and Crusade* [1540]. Significantly, however, they noted, "those internal strategies most effective for the UM [Unification Movement] in mobilizing resources were also the ones that evoked the most outrage and social reaction" (224). The implications of this dilemma are explored in their companion volume, *The New Vigilantes: Deprogrammers, Anti-Cultists and the New Religions* [1624].

Along with Lofland, Bromley, and Shupe, the other major sociological interpreter of the UC has been Eileen Barker. Based in England, she did substantial research in the United States and published numerous articles on the Church as well as a monograph, *The Making of a Moonie: Choice or Brainwashing?* [1512]. As its title suggests, the primary topic of this volume is recruitment. Barker's other research interest, of which "Doing Love: Tensions in the Ideal Family" [1510] and "Living the *Divine Principle*" [1511] are good examples, related to questions of lifestyle. Her work, particularly on recruitment, differs from studies already cited in that it is heavily empirical. That is, she supplements participant-observation with in-depth interviewing and computer-coded questionaires. In addition, the British UC granted her access to complete membership lists and more than a thousand applications for workshop attendance in the London area during 1979. As a result, Barker was able to establish convincing membership profiles as well as rates of recruitment and defection. More important, her research on the Church signals a move beyond the NRM model to the kind of sociological studies characteristic of more established religious bodies.

As stated, sociologists more so than practitioners of other disciplines have exercised themselves over a variety of methodological issues related to the UC. At one level, questions of data collection, analysis and confidentiality have been complicated by delicate and not always successful negotiations with the Church. Lofland [1579], for example, recounted how he "was defined as a positive threat" and denied access to the group (274-75). Bromley and Shupe [1540], though not forced to terminate their study prematurely and having gained leverage by studying the UC in tandem with "anti-cultists," nonetheless, faced "uneasiness that we had seen so much and yet remained unconvinced" (201). Barker [1512], although more successful in forging an ongoing research relationship with the UC, still referred to "intellectual loneliness" and methodological schizophrenia (21, 262).

While these ambiguities and tensions are relatively standard in field research, they became increasingly "politicized" as the UC began sponsoring conferences not only for scientists and theologians but also for sociologists of religion. As a result, questions of funding, sponsorship and professional ethics emerged with some vehemence and prompted a symposium in a major sociological journal. These issues were first raised by Irving Louis Horowitz in a collection of essays and reprints entitled *Science, Sin and Sponsorship: The Politics of Reverend Moon and the Unification Church* [1567]. Criticizing the UC and, in particular, sponsorship of its annual International Conference on the Unity of the Sciences (ICUS), Horowitz called attention to what he termed, "the failure of nerve of one professional association after another and the failure of one esteemed scientist after another to inquire about the larger meanings of his research and what such activities signify" (280). Horowitz, however, was charged with undue intellectual bias by John Lofland in a review that sparked an acrimonious exchange between the two in *The Canadian Journal of Sociology* [1565, 1581]. See also Leo Sandon's critique of Horowitz in *Soundings* [1615, 1562].

The terms of this debate were enlarged after the UC sponsored an international conference on "The Social Impact of New Religious Movements." British sociologist Bryan Wilson [732], who edited a volume of essays from that meeting, directly challenged Horowitz by asserting, "scholars more involved with the new religions in their academic work than he is himself, are not to be stampeded by condemnations--all to McCarthy-like in tone--into abandoning their legitimate concerns" (xiii). Similarly, Barbara Hargrove, in a review article, "On Studying the Moonies as a 'Political' Act" [1559], complained that "pressures from scholars like Horowitz have made it most difficult to treat the Unification Church or other new religions in the balanced way that Lofland achieved in the early years of that movement" (212). Continued agitation over this issue led *Sociological Analysis* to sponsor a symposium on "Scholarship and Sponsorship" featuring several principals in the debate. Horowitz [1566], in the lead article, again questioned, "what compels otherwise highly refined scientific and social scientific imaginations to become representatives, spokespersons, even apologists for governmental or theological special interests?" (179).

James Beckford [1527] raised the spectre of specialists "split into two camps." One, he said, "may meet regularly at the Moonies' expense in order to plan its sponsored publications; the other may patronize the regular meetings of long-established professional associations in order to subject their work to the critical scrutiny of fellow scientists" (194).

On the other side, Barker [1515], Wallis [1640] and Wilson [1642] defended the academic integrity of individual scholars, argued that work, not personal connections, of researchers should be judged, and disputed specific claims about the UC.

Thomas Robbins [1597], in attempting to contextualize the discussion, speculated that a twenty-five year post-WW II period of "detente" between religion and social science had ended. He further argued that the reemergence of "controversial" religion "is contributing to what will surely be a period of enhanced theoretical, epistemological and political ferment in the sociology of religion" (211).

1504. Ambrose, Kenneth P. "Function of the Family in the Process of Commitment within the Unification Movement." In *The Family and the Unification Church* (item 709), pp. 23-33.

1505. Anthony, Dick, and Thomas Robbins. "Contemporary Religious Ferment and Moral Ambiguity." In *New Religious Movements: A Perspective for Understanding Society* (item 1519), pp. 243-63.

1506. _____. "The Effect of Detente on the Growth of New Religions: Reverend Moon and the Unification Church." In *Understanding the New Religions* (item 1590), pp. 80-100.

1507. _____. "Spiritual Innovation and the Crisis of American Civil Religion." *Daedalus* 3 (Winter 1982): 215-34.

1508. Austin, Roy. "Empirical Adequacy of Lofland's Conversion Model." *Review of Religious Research* 18 (1977): 282-87.

1509. Barker, Eileen. "Confessions of a Methodological Schizophrenic: Problems Encountered in the Study of Sun Myung Moon's Unification Church." *Institute for the Study of Worship and Religious Architecture Research Bulletin* (1978): 70-89.

1510. _____. "Doing Love: Tensions in the Ideal Family." In *The Family and the Unification Church* (item 709), pp. 35-52.

1511. _____. "Living the *Divine Principle*: Inside the Reverend Sun Myung Moon's Unification Church in Britain." *Archives de Sciences Sociales des Religions* 45 (1978): 75-93.

1512. _____. *The Making of a Moonie: Choice or Brainwashing?* Oxford: Basil Blackwell, 1984. 305 pp.

1513. _____. "The Ones Who Got Away: People Who Attend Unification Church Workshops and Do Not Become Moonies." In *Of Gods and Men: New Religious Movements in the West* (item 1520), pp. 309-36.

1514. _____. "Sun Myung Moon and the Scientists." The *Teilhard Review* 14 (Spring 1979): 35-37.

1515. _____. "Supping with the Devil: How Long a Spoon Does the Sociologist Need?" *Sociological Analysis* 44 (Fall 1983): 197-206.

1516. _____. "Who'd Be a Moonie? A Comparative Study of Those Who Join the Unification Church in Britain." In *The Social Impact of New Religious Movements* (item 732), pp. 59-96.

1517. _____. "Whose Service is a Perfect Freedom: The Concept of Spiritual Well-Being in Relation to the Reverend Moon's Unification Church in Britain." In *Spiritual Well-Being*, edited by David O. Moberg, 153-71. Washington, D.C.: University Press of America, 1979.

1518. _____. "With Enemies Like That ...: Some Functions of Deprogramming as an Aid to Sectarian Membership." In *The Brainwashing/Deprogramming Controversy: Sociological, Psychological, Legal and Historical Perspectives* (item 1536), pp. 329-44.

1519. _____, ed. *New Religious Movements: A Perspective for Understanding Society.* New York: Edwin Mellen, 1982. 398 pp.

Contains items 1505, 1522, 1542, 1557, 1576.

1520. _____. *Of Gods and Men: New Religious Movements in the West.* Macon, Ga.: Mercer University, 1983.

Contains items 1513, 1525, 1594, 1665.

1521. Beckford, James. "Accounting for Conversion." *British Journal of Sociology* 29 (1978): 249-62.

1522. _____. "Beyond the Pale: Cults, Culture and Conflict." In *New Religious Movements: A Perspective for Understanding Society* (item 1519), pp. 284-301.

1523. _____. "'Brainwashing' and 'Deprogramming' in Britain: The Social Sources of Anti-Cult Sentiment." In *The Brainwashing/*

Deprogramming Controversy: Sociological, Psychological, Legal and Historical Perspectives (item 1536), pp. 122-38.

1524. _____. *Cult Controversies: The Societal Response to New Religious Movements.* London: Tavistock, 1985. 327 pp.

1525. _____. "The 'Cult Problem' in Five Countries: The Social Construction of Religious Controversy." In *Of Gods and Men: New Religious Movements in the West* (item 1520), pp. 195-214.

1526. _____. "A Korean Evangelist Movement in the West." In *The Contemporary Metamorphosis of Religion?* Acts of the 12th International Conference on Sociology of Religion, 319-35, The Hague, 1973.

1527. _____. "Some Questions about the Relationship between Scholars and the New Religious Movements." *Sociological Analysis* 44 (Fall 1983): 189-96.

1528. _____. "Through the Looking Glass and Out the Other Side: Withdrawal from Rev. Moon's Unification Church." *Archives des Sciences Sociales Des Religions* 45 (January-March 1978): 95-116.

1529. _____. "Two Contrasting Types of Sectarian Organization." In *Sectarianism,* edited by Roy Wallis, 70-85. New York: Wiley, 1975.

1530. _____. "A Typology of Family Responses to a New Religious Movement." In *Cults and the Family* (item 1569), pp. 41-55.

1531. Beckford, James A., and James T. Richardson. "A Bibliography of of Social Scientific Studies of New Religious Movements." *Social Forces* 30 (1983): 11-35.

1532. Bedell, George C., Leo Sandon, Jr. and Charles T. Wellborn. "The Restoration of True Family." In *Religion in America.* 2nd ed., 511-16. New York: Macmillan, 1982.

1533. Berger, Alan I. "Hasidism And Moonism: Charisma in the Counterculture." *Sociological Analysis* 41 (Winter 1980): 375-90.

1534. Bird, Fredrick B., and Frances Westley. "The Economic Strategies of New Religious Movements." *Sociological Analysis* 46 (Summer 1985): 157-70.

1535. Bromley, David G. "Financing the Millennium: The Economic Structure of the Unificationist Movement." *Journal for the Scientific Study of Religion* 24 (September 1985): 253-74.

1536. Bromley, David G., and James T. Richardson. *The Brainwashing/Deprogramming Controversy: Sociological, Psychological, Legal and Historical Perspectives.* New York: Edwin Mellen, 1983. 367 pp.

Contains items 1518, 1523, 1546, 1631, 1636, 1643, 1685, 1718.

1537. Bromley, David G., and Anson D. Shupe, Jr. "Evolving Foci in Participant Observation: Research as an Emergent Process." In *The Social Experience of Fieldwork*, edited by W. Shaffir, A. Turowetz and R. Stebbins, 191-203. New York: St. Martin's, 1980.

1538. _____. "Financing the New Religions: A Research Mobilization Approach." *Journal for the Scientific Study of Religion* 19 (1980): 227-39.

1539. _____. "Just a Few Years Seems Like a Lifetime: A Role Theory Approach to Participation in Religious Movements." In *Research in Social Movements, Conflict and Change*, edited by Louis Kriesburg, 159-85. Greenwich, Conn.: JAI, 1979.

1540. _____. *Moonies in America: Cult, Church, and Crusade.* Beverly Hills, Calif.: Sage, 1979. 268 pp.

1541. _____. "Repression and the Decline of Social Movements: The Case of the New Religions." In *Social Movements in the Sixties and Seventies,* edited by Jo Freeman, 335-47. New York: Longman, 1983.

1542. Bromley, David G., Bruce C. Busching, and Anson D. Shupe, Jr. "The Unification Church and the American Family: Strain, Conflict and Control." In *New Religious Movements: A Perspective for Understanding Society* (item 1519), pp. 302-11.

1543. Bromley, David G., Anson D. Shupe, Jr., and Bruce C. Busching. "Repression of Religious Cults." In *Research in Social Movements, Conflict and Change,* edited by Louis Kriesberg, 25-45. Greenwich, Conn.: JAI, 1981.

1544. Bromley, David G., Anson D. Shupe, Jr., and Donna L. Oliver. "Perfect Families: Visions of the Future in a New Religious Movement." In *Cults and the Family* (item 1569), pp. 119-29.

1545. Bromley, David G., Anson D. Shupe, Jr., and Joseph C. Ventimiglia. "Atrocity Tales, the Unification Church and the Social Construction of Evil." *Journal of Communication* 29 (Summer 1979): 42-53.

1546. _____. "The Role of Anecdotal Atrocities in the Social Construction of Evil." In *The Brainwashing/Deprogramming Controversy: Sociological, Psychological, Legal and Historical Perspectives* (item 1536), pp. 139-60.

1547. Bryant, M. Darrol. "Media Ethics: The Elimimation of Perspective." In *New Religions and Mental Health: Understanding the Issues* (item 1678), pp. 69-73.

1548. Choi, Syn Duk. "Korea's Tong-Il Movement." *Transactions of the Royal Asiatic Society, Korea Branch* 43 (1967): 167-80.

1549. Cozin, Mark. "A Millenniarian Movement in Korea and Great Britian." In *A Sociological Yearbook of Religion in Great Britian*, no. 6, edited by Michael Hill, 100-121. London: S.C.M. Press, 1973.

1550. Dole, Arthur A., and Steve K. Dubrow-Eichel. "Moon over Academe." *Journal of Religion and Health* 20 (Spring 1981): 35-40.

1551. Ellwood, Robert S., Jr. "The Unified Family." In *Religious and Spiritual Groups in Modern America*, 291-95. Englewood Cliffs, N.J.: Prentice-Hall, 1973.

1552. Feige, Diana Muxworthy. "Relations in Progress: Paradigm for Education and the Family." In *The Family and the Unification Church* (item 709), pp. 195-215.

*   Fichter, Joseph. *The Holy Family of Father Moon.* Cited above as item 1033.

1553. _____. "Home Church: Alternative Parish." In *Alternatives to American Mainline Churches* (item 705), pp. 179-99.

*   _____, ed. *Alternatives to American Mainline Churches.* Cited above as item 705.

1554. Flinn, Jane Zeni. "Three Models of Family: Marriage Encounter, Parenting for Peace and Justice, Blessed Family." In *The Family and the Unification Church* (item 709), pp. 105-20.

*   Gallup, George, and Daniel Poling "The Yearnings of Youth." Chap. 1 in *The Search for America's Faith.* Cited above as item 824.

1555. Grace, James H. *Sex and Marriage in the Unification Movement: A Sociological Study.* New York: Edwin Mellen, 1985. 284 pp.

1556. Hampshire, A.P., and James A. Beckford. "Religious Sects and the Concept of Deviance: The Mormons and the Moonies." *British Journal of Sociology* 34 (June 1983): 208-29.

1557. Hardin, Bert L. and Guenter Kehrer. "Some Social Factors Affecting the Rejection of New Belief Systems." In *New Religious Movements: A Perspective for Understanding Society* (item 1519), pp. 267-83.

1558. Hargrove, Barbara. "New Religious Movements and the End of the Age." *The Iliff Review* 34 (Spring 1982): 41-52.

1559. ———. "On Studying the Moonies as a Political Act." *Religious Studies Review 8* (July 1982): 209-13.

1560. ———. "Some Thoughts about the Unification Movement and the Churches." In *Science, Sin and Sponsorship: The Politics of Reverend Moon and the Unification Church* (item 1567), pp. 86-100.

1561. Harper, Charles L. "Cults and Communities: The Community Interfaces of Three Marginal Religious Movements." *Journal for the Scientific Study of Religion* 21 (March 1982): 26-38.

1562. Horowitz, Irving. "The Politics of New Cults: Non-Prophetic Observations on Science, Sin and Sponsorship." *Soundings* 62 (Summer 1979): 209-19.

1563. ———. "A Reply to Critics and Crusaders." *Sociological Analysis* 44 (Fall 1983): 221-26.

1564. ———. "Sun Myung Moon: Missionary to Western Civilization." In *Science, Sin and Scholarship: The Politics of Reverend Moon and the Unification Church* (item 1567), pp. iv-viii.

1565. ———. "Topsy-turvy Preview: Response to John Lofland." *Canadian Journal of Sociology* 5 (1980): 163-64.

1566. ———. "Universal Standards, Not Uniform Beliefs: Further Reflections on Scientific Method and Religious Sponsors." *Sociological Analysis* 44 (Fall 1983): 179-82.

1567. ———, ed. *Science, Sin, and Scholarship: The Politics of Reverend Moon and the Unification Church.* Cambridge: MIT Press, 1978. 290 pp.

Contains items 1172, 1324, 1560, 1564, 1709, 1812.

1568. Judah, J. Stillson. "Belief and Behavior: Some Thoughts on the Dynamics of New Religious Movements Like the Unification

Church." In *Lifestyle: Conversations with Members of the Unification Church* (item 721), pp. 185-96.

1569. Kaslow, Florence, and Marvin Sussman. "Cults and the Family." New York: Haworth, 1982. Reprinted from *Marriage and Family Review* 4 (Fall-Winter 1981).

Contains items 1221, 1530, 1544, 1617, 1653.

1570. Kilbourne, Brock K. "The Conway and Siegelman Claims against Religious Cults: An Assessment of Their Data." *Journal for the Scientific Study of Religion* 22 (1983): 380-85.

1571. _____, ed. *Scientific Research and New Religions.* San Francisco: Pacific Division of the American Association for the Advancement of Science, 1985. 180 pp.

1572. Kilbourne, Brock K., and James T. Richardson. "Psychotherapy and New Religions in a Pluralistic Society." *American Psychologist* 39 (March 1984): 237-51.

1573. Kim, Byong-Suh. "Ideology, Conversion and Faith Maintenance in a Korean Sect: The Case of the Unified Family of Rev. Sun Myung Moon." *Korean Christian Scholars Review* 2 (Spring 1977): 8-59.

1574. _____. "Religious Deprogramming and Subjective Reality." *Sociological Analysis* 40 (Fall 1979): 197-207.

1575. Kim, Chong Sun. *Rev. Sun Myung Moon.* Washington, D.C.: University Press, 1978. 156 pp.

1576. Lewis, Warren. "Coming Again: How Society Functions through Its New Religions." In *New Religious Movements: A Perspective for Understanding Society* (item 1519), pp. 191-215.

1577. Lofland, John. "'Becoming a World-Saver' Revisted." *American Behavioral Scientist* 20 (July-August 1977): 805-18.

1578. _____. "Divine Principles." In *Man, Myths and Magic.* vol. 5, edited by Richard Cavendish, 661-63. New York: Marshall Cavendish Corporation, 1970.

1579. _____. *Doomsday Cult: A Study of Conversion, Proselytization, and Maintenance of Faith.* Englewood Cliffs, N.J.: Prentice-Hall, 1966. 276 pp.

1580. _____. *Doomsday Cult: A Study of Conversion, Proselytization, and Maintenance of Faith.* Enlarged ed. New York: Irvington, 1977, 1981. 362 pp.

1581. _____. "The Larger Challenge." *Canadian Journal of Sociology* 5 (1980): 165-68.

1582. _____. *Protest: Studies of Collective Bahavior and Social Movements.* New Brunswick, N.J.: Transaction, 1985. 349 pp.

1583. _____. "White-hot Mobilization: Strategies of a Millennarian Movement." In *The Dynamics of Social Movements,* edited by Mayer N. Zald and John D. McCarthy, 157-66. Cambridge, Mass.: Winthrop, 1979.

1584. Lofland, John, and Norman Skonovd. "Conversion Motifs." *Journal for the Scientific Study of Religion* 20 (December 1981): 373-85.

1585. Lofland, John, and Rodney Stark. "Becoming a World-Saver." *American Sociological Review* 30 (December 1965): 862-74.

1586. Long, Theodore E., and Jeffrey K. Hadden. "Religious Conversion and the Concept of Socialization: Integrating the Brainwashing and Drift Models." *Journal for the Scientific Study of Religion* 22 (March 1983): 1-14.

1587. Lynch, F.R. "Field Research and Future History: Problems Posed for Ethnographic Sociologists by the 'Doomsday Cult' Making Good." *American Sociologist* 12 (May 1977): 80-88.

1588. Melton, J. Gordon. "The Holy Spirit Association for the Unification of World Christianity." In *The Encyclopedia of American Religions,* 225-27. Wilmington, N.C.: McGrath, 1978.

1589. Mickler, Michael L. "Crisis of Single Adults: An Alternative Approach." In *The Family and the Unification Church* (item 709), pp. 161-73.

1590. Needleman, Jacob, and George Baker, eds. *Understanding the New Religions.* New York: Seabury, 1978. 314 pp.

Contains items 1506, 1701.

1591. Paik, Chull. "Sun Myung Moon--The Man and His Cultural and Artistic Genius." In *Sun Myung Moon: The Man and His Ideal* (item 675), pp. 11-63.

1592. Richardson, James T. "A Comparison between Jonestown and Other Cults." In *Violence and Religious Commitment,* edited by Ken Levi, 21-34. University Park, Pa.: University of Pennsylvania Press, 1982.

1593. ———. "Financing the New Religions." *Journal for the Scientific Study of Religion 21* (September 1982): 255-68.

1594. ———. "Financing the New Religions: A Broader View." In *Of Gods and Men: New Religious Movements in the West* (item 1520), pp. 65-88.

1595. ———. "New Religious Movements in the United States: A Review." *Social Compass* 30 (1983): 85-110.

1596. ———. "Psychological and Psychiatric Studies of New Religions." In *Advances in Psychology of Religion*, edited by Lawrence Brown. New York: Pergmon, 1985.

1597. Robbins, Thomas. "The Beach is Washing Away: Controversial Religion and the Sociology of Religion." *Sociological Analysis* 44 (Fall 1983): 207-14.

1598. ———. *Civil Liberties, "Brainwashing" and "Cults": A Select Annotated Bibliography*. Berkeley, Calif.: Center for the Study of New Religious Movements, Graduate Theological Union, 1981. 32 pp.

1599. ———. "Constructing Cultist 'Mind Control.' " *Sociological Analysis* 45 (1984): 241-56.

1600. ———. "Government Regulatory Powers and Church Autonomy: Deviant Groups as Test Cases." *Journal for the Scientific Study of Religion* 24 (September 1985): 237-52.

1601. ———. "New Religious Movements on the Frontier of Church and State." In *Cults, Culture and the Law* (item 1612), pp. 3-27.

1602. ———. "Nuts, Sluts and Converts: Studying Religious Groups as Social Problems: A Comment." *Sociological Analysis* 46 (Summer 1985): 171-78.

1603. ———. "Sociological Studies of New Religious Movements: A Selective Review." *Religious Studies Review* 9 (1983): 233-39.

1604. Robbins, Thomas, and Dick Anthony. "Brainwashing and the Persecution of 'Cults.' " *Journal of Religion and Health* 19 (Spring 1980): 66-69.

1605. ———. " 'Cults,' 'Brainwashing,' and Counter-Subversion." *The Annals of the American Academy of Political and Social Science* 446 (November 1979): 78-90.

1606. _____. "'Cults' vs. 'Shrinks': Psychiatry and the Control of Religious Movements." In *New Religions and Mental Health: Understanding the Issues* (item 1678), pp. 48-68.

1607. _____. "Deprogramming, Brainwashing and the Medicalization of Deviant Religious Groups." *Social Problems* 29 (February 1982): 283-97.

1608. _____. "The Limits of Coercive Persuasion as an Explanation for Conversion to Authoritarian Sects." *Political Psychology* 2 (1980): 27-37.

1609. _____. "The Sociology of Contemporary Religious Movements." *Annual Review of Sociology* 5 (1979): 75-89.

1610. _____, eds. *In Gods We Trust: New Patterns of Religious Pluralism in America.* New Brunswick, N.J.: Transaction, 1981. 338 pp.

Contains items 1628, 1684.

1611. Robbins, Thomas, Dick Anthony, and James T. Richardson. "Theory and Research on Today's 'New Religions.' " *Sociological Analysis* 39 (1978): 95-122.

1612. Robbins, Thomas, William C. Shepherd, and James McBride. *Cults, Culture and the Law.* Chico, Calif.: Scholars Press, 1985. 238 pp.

Contains items 1601, 1671.

1613. Robbins, Thomas, Dick Anthony, Madeline Doucas, and Thomas Curtis. "The Last Civil Religion: Reverend Moon and the Unification Church." *Sociological Analysis* 37 (Summer 1976): 111-25.

1614. Robertson, Roland. "Scholarship, Partisanship, Sponsorship and 'The Moonie Problem': A Comment." *Sociological Analysis* 46 (Summer 1985): 179-84.

1615. Sandon, Leo, Jr. "Responding to the New Cult Politics." *Soundings* 62 (Fall 1979): 323-28.

1616. Sawatsky, Rodney. "The Unification Church: Some Preliminary Suggestions for Social and Scientific Analysis." In *Exploring Unification Theology* (item 697), pp. 131-37.

1617. Schwartz, Lita Linzer, and Florence W. Kaslow. "The Cult Phenomenon: Historical, Sociological and Familial Factors

Contributing to Their Development and Appeal." *In Cults and the Family* (item 1569), pp. 3-30.

1618. Sheen, Doh Sung. "Sun Myung Moon--His Philosophy and Leadership." In *Sun Myung Moon: The Man and His Ideal* (item 675), pp. 105-38.

1619. Shupe, Anson D., Jr. *Six Perspectives on New Religions: A Case Study Approach.* New York: Edwin Mellen, 1981. 235 pp.

1620. Shupe, Anson D., Jr, and David G. Bromley. "Apostates and Atrocity Stories: Some Parameters in the Dynamics of Deprogramming." *In The Social Impact of New Religious Movements* (item 732), pp. 179-215.

1621. ———. "The Archetypal Cult: Conflict and the Social Construction of Deviance." In *The Family and the Unification Church* (item 709), pp. 1-22.

1622. ———. *A Documentary History of the Anti-Cult Movement.* New York: Edwin Mellen, 1984.

1623. ———. "The Moonies and the Anti-Cultists: Movement and Countermovement in Conflict." *Sociological Analysis* 40 (Winter 1979): 325-34.

1624. ———. *The New Vigilantes: Deprogrammers, Anti-Cultists, and the New Religions.* Beverly Hills, Calif.: Sage, 1980. 267 pp.

1625. ———. "Reverse Missionizing: Sun Myung Moon's Unification Church in the United States." Free Inquiry in *Creative Sociology* 8 (November 1980): 197-203.

1626. ———. "Shaping the Public Response to Jonestown: People's Temple and the Anticult Movement." In *Violence and Religious Commitment,* edited by Ken Levi, 105-32. University Park, Pa.: University of Pennsylvania Press, 1982.

1627. ———. "Walking a Tightrope: Dilemmas of Participant Observation in Groups in Conflict." *Qualitative Sociology* 2 (January 1980): 3-21.

1628. ———. "Witches, Moonies and Accusations of Evil. In *In Gods We Trust: New Patterns of Religious Pluralism in America* (item 1610), pp. 247-61.

1629. Shupe, Anson D., Jr., David G. Bromley, and Donna L. Oliver. *The Anti-Cult Movement in America: A Bibliographic and Historical Survey.* New York: Garland, 1984. 169 pp.

1630. Shupe, Anson D. Jr., Roger Spielmann, and Sam Stigall. "Deprogramming: The New Exorcism." *American Behavioral Scientist* 20 (Summer 1977): 941-56.

1631. Skonovd, Norman. "Leaving the Cultic Religious Milieu." In *The Brainwashing/Deprogramming Controversy: Sociological, Psychological, Legal and Historical Perspectives* (item 1536), pp. 91-105.

1632. Spurgin, Hugh, and Nora Spurgin. "Blessed Marriage in the Unification Church: Sacramental Ideals and Their Application to Daily Marital Life." In *The Family and the Unification Church* (item 709), pp. 121-37.

1633. Stark, Rodney, and William Sims Bainbridge. *The Future of Religion: Secularization, Revival and Cult Formation.* Berkeley: University of California Press, 1985. 571 pp.

1634. Stewart, Therese, and Henry O. Thompson. "Unification Theological Seminary." In *Unity in Diversity: Essays in Religion by Members of the Faculty of the Unification Theological Seminary* (item 728), pp. 425-31.

1635. Taylor, David. "Becoming New People: The Recruitment of Young Americans into the Unification Church." In *Millennialism and Charisma,* edited by Roy Wallis, 177-230. Belfast, Ireland: The Queen's University, 1982.

1636. _____. "Thought Reform and the Unification Church." In *The Brainwashing/Deprogramming Controversy: Sociological, Psychological, Legal and Historical Perspectives* (item 1536), pp. 73-90.

1637. Testa, Bart. "It Would Have Been Nice To Hear from You....On fifth estate's 'Moonstruck.' " In *New Religions and Mental Health: Understanding the Issues* (item 1678), pp. 74-80.

1638. _____. "Making Crime Seem Natural: The Press and Deprogramming." In *A Time for Consideration: A Scholarly Appraisal of the Unification Church* (item 1412), pp. 41-81.

1639. Wallis, Roy. *The Elementary Forms of the New Religious Life.* London, England: Routledge and Kegan Paul, 1984. 156 pp.

1640. _____. "Religion, Reason and Responsibility: A Reply to Professor Horowitz." *Sociological Analysis* 44 (Fall 1983): 215-20.

1641. Weightman, Judith M. "A Sociological Perspective on the Doctrine of Indemnity." In *Restoring the Kingdom* (item 703), pp. 113-22.

1642. Wilson, Bryan R. "Sympathetic Detachment and Disinterested Involvement: A Note on Academic Integrity." *Sociological Analysis* 44 (Fall 1983): 183-88.

*   _____, ed. *The Social Impact of New Religious Movements.* Cited above as item 732.

1643. Wright, Stuart A. "Defection from New Religious Movements: A Test of Some Theoretical Propositions." In *The Brainwashing/Deprogramming Controversy: Sociological, Psychological, Legal and Historical Perspectives* (item 1536), pp. 106-21.

1644. Yoon, Se Won. "Sun Myung Moon--His Ideal and Practice." In *Sun Myung Moon: The Man and His Ideal* (item 675), pp. 139-83.

C. PSYCHOLOGICAL PERSPECTIVES

Scholars and others examining the UC from a psychological point of view divide into three major groupings. The first consists of a small but influential group of physicians and psychiatrists who have assumed an adversarial posture in relation to the UC and other new religious movements (NRMs). Basing their assessments primarily on individual or group therapy with former members, these mental health professionals have discerned a variety of "cult-related" pathologies. Further, they have charged that in recruitment, the UC and other NRMs utilize mind-control or "brainwashing" techniques. Some of these opponents have supported or advocated deprogramming and testified in legal proceedings against the UC. A second group, consisting mainly of sociologists of religion, has criticized the mental pathology model. These critics have sought to discredit brainwashing, expose value-laden and interest-laden premises of opposing psychiatrists, and attack "rescue" attempts as incompatible with U.S. constitutional guarantees. A third group, recognizing the paucity of data and acknowledging discrepancies in reports, has subjected UC members, recruits and ex-members to a battery of standardized tests. Overall, these researchers have found theraputic benefits associated with UC membership but also have pointed out ambiguities and tensions leading to disaffiliation from the Church.

Among those psychiatrists assuming an adversarial role in relation to the UC, the most prominent have been Margaret Singer and John Clark. Although they have addressed questions of "cultism" in general, both have served as "expert" witnesses in court proceedings against and government hearings on the UC. Singer, a research psychiatrist whose background included the study of coercive-persuasion ("brainwashing") techniques used on American POWs during the Korean War, applied that model to UC recruitment practices. Further, in group sessions with several hundred former "cultists" including former members of the UC, Singer [1681] identified such "cult-related" emotional problems as indecisiveness, slipping into altered states, blurring of mental acuity and uncritical passivity. Clark [1645], a clinical psychiatrist associated with Harvard Medical School, concurred in the diagnosis of "destructive cultism as a public health problem and sociopathic illness" (280). Although not psychiatrists, the work of "communication experts" Flo Conway and Jim Seigelman also has been influential. Based on a nationwide survey of 400 former "cult" members from forty-eight groups including the UC, Conway and Seigelman [1648] elaborate what they termed "information disease," a new form of mental illness involving severe disturbance in perception, memory and other information-processing capabilities. Reporting that their data "showed what appeared to be a direct relationship between the number of hours spent per week in cult ritual and indoctrination and the number of long-term effects," they argued, "deprogramming is indeed a vital first step in the road back from cultic mind control" (88, 92). Some recent treatments have linked "cult" vulnerability to family pathology [1664, 1679, 1738].

As stated, a second group consisting mainly of sociologists of religion has criticized the mental pathology model. Major contributors have been Thomas Robbins and Dick Anthony. In a series of articles including "Brainwashing and the Persecution of 'Cults' " [1604], " 'Cults' vs. 'Shrinks' " [1606], and "Deprogramming, Brainwashing, and the Medicalization of Deviant Religious Groups" [1607], Robbins and Anthony attempted to discredit brainwashing, expose underlying biases, and oppose counter-indoctrination. In so doing, they criticized adversarial treatments for relying solely on retrospective accounts of former members (many of whom had been deprogrammed), characterized brainwashing as "a mystifying and inherently subjective metaphor" and noted expanded vocational opportunities for mental health workers in "religious deprogramming and auxiliary services for the 'rehabilitation' of cultists and ex-cultists." In a separate article, Robbins [1599] asserted, "Arguments in this highly subjective area are too often mystifications which embellish values and biases with the aura of value-free science and clinical objectivity" (253). For related critiques, see Kilbourne and Richardson [1572], J. Richardson [1596], Shupe et al. [1630], and H. Richardson [1678].

Given the paucity of research data and conflicting arguments, some scholars began collecting more data and subjecting NRM adherents to standardized personality tests. The most widely cited studies on UC members, recruits and ex-members were conducted by Marc Galanter. In his earliest and most widely cited article, "The Moonies: A Psychological Study of Conversion and Membership in a Contemporary Religious Sect" [1660], Galanter and associates administered a 216-item coded questionaire to 237 native-born American Church members. They reported that while a sizeable percentage (39%) felt they had serious emotional problems in the past, "Affiliation with the Unification Church apparently provided considerable and sustained relief from neurotic distress" (168). However, these members' "general well-being scores were significantly below the mean for the age and sex-matched comparison group" (167). Galanter reported similar findings for new recruits [1656], and in a study of sixty-six former members, Galanter [1658] found that while twenty-three (37%) reported serious emotional problems after leaving, "After an average of 3.8 years the former members studied ... had apparently achieved a stable adjustment" with those not deprogrammed retaining "a notable fidelity to the sect and its beliefs" (984). Finally, in a separate study of 321 engaged members of the UC, Galanter [1655] reported, "the abrogation of contemporary norms for mate selection was not associated with increased psychological distress" (1197). See Galanter [1657] and Galanter *et al* [1659] for discussions of informal UC controls of alcohol and drug use.

Besides Galanter's work, there are a number of other important psychological studies. Alexander Deutsch and Michael J. Miller, in two reports, one a clinical study of four UC members [1651], the other an intensive case study of a single member [1652], attempted to identify "characteristics common to subjects that seemed to presuppose them to the life-style and doctrines of the Unification Church." Wolfgang Kuner [1665], in administering the Minnesota Multiphase Personality Inventory (MMPI) to 303 German UC members and to over 200 adherents of two other NRMs, reported "the members of these new movements achieved 'better' scores than the control group of students" (257). At the same time, Kuner noted the NRM samples "reveal narcissistic traits and a need for social appreciation." Stuart A. Wright [1689], in a study of forty-five voluntary defectors from the UC and two other NRMs reported "a finding which clearly emerges from the data is the disconfirmation of any support for brainwashing" (181). Consonant with this, in an earlier study of 100 former members of the UC, sixty-five of whom had been deprogrammed, Trudy Solomon [1684] concluded "Conceptualization of the Moonie experience was found to vary as a function of the method of exit and degree of contact with the anti-cult movement" (287). On the other hand, Solomon reported an "unexpected sex effect in the data--females were more negative about their experience as members than males" (289). For a discussion of alleged sexism in the UC and other groups, see Janet Jacob's "The Economy of Love: The Deconversion of Women from Non-Traditional Religious Movements" [1662].

1645. Clark, John G., Jr. "Cults." *Journal of the American Medical Association* 242 (July 20, 1979): 179-81.

1646. Clark, John G., Jr., Michael D. Langone, Robert E. Schecter, and Roger C.B. Daly. *Destructive Cult Conversion: Theory, Research and Treatment.* Weston, Mass.: American Family Foundation, 1981. 84 pp.

1647. Coleman, Lee. *Psychiatry: The Faith Breaker.* Sacramento, Calif.: Printing Dynamics, 1982. 40 pp.

1648. Conway, Flo, and Siegelman, Jim. "Information Disease: Have Cults Created a New Mental Illness?" *Science Digest* 90 (January 1982): 86-92.

1649. Dean, Roger Allen. "Youth: Moonies' Target Population." *Adolescence* 17 (Fall 1982): 567-74.

1650. DeMaria, Richard. "A Psycho-Social Analysis of Conversion." In *A Time for Consideration: A Scholarly Appraisal of the Unification Church* (item 1412), pp. 82-130.

1651. Deutsch, Alexander, and Michael J. Miller. "Clinical Study of Four Unification Church Members." *American Journal of Psychiatry* 140 (June 1983): 767-70.

1652. _____. "Conflict, Character and Conversion: Study of a 'New Religion' Member." In *Adolescent Psychology,* vol. 7, edited by

Sherman C. Feinstein and Peter L. Giovacchini, 258-68. Chicago: University of Chicago Press, 1979.

1653. Edwards, Christopher. "The Dynamics of Mass Conversion." In *Cults and the Family* (item 1569), pp. 31-40.

1654. Feinstein, Sherman C. "The Cult Phenomenon: Transition, Repression and Regression." In *Adolescent Psychiatry,* vol. 8, edited by Sherman C. Feinstein, Peter L. Giovacchini, John G. Looney, Allan Z. Schwartzberg and Arthur D. Sorosky, 113-22. Chicago: University of Chicago Press, 1980.

1655. Galanter, Marc. "Engaged Members of the Unification Church." *Archives of General Psychiatry* 40 (November 1983): 1197-1202.

1656. _____. "Psychological Induction into a Large Group: Findings from a Modern Religious Sect." *American Journal of Psychiatry* 137 (December 1980): 1574-79.

1657. _____. "Sociobiology and Informal Controls of Drinking: Findings from Two Charismatic Sects." *Journal of Studies on Alcohol* 42 (January 1981): 64-79.

1658. _____. "Unification Church (Moonie) Dropouts: Psychological Readjustment after Leaving a Charismatic Religious Group." *American Journal of Psychiatry* 140 (August 1983): 984-89.

1659. Galanter, Marc, Buckley, Peter, Alexander Deutsch, Richard Rabkin and Judith Rabkin. "Large Group Influence for Decreased Drug Use: Findings from Two Contemporary Religious Sects." *American Journal of Drug and Alcohol Abuse* 7 (1980): 291-304.

1660. Galanter, Marc, Richard Rabkin, Judith Rabkin, and Alexander Deutsch. "The Moonies: A Psychological Study of Conversion and Membership in a Contemporary Religious Sect." *American Journal of Psychiatry 136* (February 1979): 165-70.

1661. Galanti, Geri-Ann. "Brainwashing and the Moonies." *Cultic Studies Journal 1* (May 1984): 27-36.

1662. Jacobs, Janet. "The Economy of Love in Religious Commitment: The Deconversion of Women from Non-traditional Religious Movements." *Journal for the Scientific Study of Religion* 23 (June 1984): 155-71.

1663. Jeong, Han Tack. "A Psychological Study of Spiritual Consciousness." In *Research on the Unification Principle: Research of Korean Scholars on Unification Theology* (item 723), pp. 185-95.

1664. Kaslow, Florence, and Lita Linzer Schwartz. "Vulnerability and Invulnerability to the Cults: An Assessment of Family Dynamics, Functioning and Values." In *Marital and Family Therapy: New Perspectives in Theory, Reserach and Practice*, edited by Dennis A. Bagarozzi, Anthony P. Jurich, and Robert W. Jackson, 165-90. New York: Human Sciences, 1983.

*   Kilbourne, Brock K. "The Conway and Siegelman Claims against Religious Cults: An Assessment of Their Data." Cited above as item 1570.

*   ———, ed. *Scientific Research and New Religions.* Cited above as item 1571.

*   Kilbourne, Brock, and James T. Richardson. "Psychotherapy and New Religions in a Pluralistic Society." Cited above as item 1572.

1665. Kuner, Wolfgang. "New Religious Movements and Mental Health." In *Of Gods and Men: New Religious Movements in the West* (item 1520), pp. 255-63.

1666. Levine, Edward M. "Religious Cults: Their Implications for Society and the Democratic Process." *Political Psychology* (Fall-Winter 1981-82): 34-49.

1667. Levine, Saul V. "Cults and Mental Health: Clinical Conclusions." *Canadian Journal of Psychiatry* 26 (December 1981): 534-39.

1668. ———. "The Role of Psychiatry in the Phenomenon of Cults." In *Adolescent Psychiatry,* vol. 8, edited by Sherman C. Feinstein, Peter L. Giovacchini, John G. Looney, Allan Z. Schwartzberg and Arthur D. Sorosky, 123-37. Chicago: University of Chicago Press, 1980.

1669. ———. "Youth and Religious Cults: A Societal and Clinical Dilemma." In Adolescent Psychiatry, vol. 6, edited by Sherman C. Feinstein and Peter L. Giovacchini, 75-89. Chicago: University of Chicago Press, 1978.

1670. Levine, Saul V., and Nancy E. Salter. "Youth and Contemporary Religious Movements: Psychosocial Findings." *Canadian Psychiatric Association Journal* 21 (October 1976): 411-20.

1671. Lifton, Robert J. "Cult Processes, Religious Totalism, and Civil Liberties." In *Cults, Culture, and the Law* (item 1612), pp. 59-70.

1672. McGowan, Thomas. "Conversion and Human Development." In *New Religions & Mental Health: Understanding the Issues* (item 1678), pp. 127-73.

1673. Maher, Brendon A., and Michael D. Langone. "Kilbourne on Conway and Siegelman: A Statistical Critique." *Journal for the Scientific Study of Religion* 24 (September 1985): 325-26.

1674. Maleson, Franklin G. "Dilemmas in the Evaluation and Management of Religious Cultists." *American Journal of Psychiatry* 138 (1981): 925-29.

1675. Mosatche, Harriet S. *Searching: Practices and Beliefs of the Religious Cults and Human Potential Groups.* New York: Stravon Educational Press, 1984. 237 pp.

1676. Richardson, Herbert. "Critique of the Goelters Report." In *New Religions and Mental Health: Understanding the Issues* (item 1678), pp. 90-105.

1677. _____. "Mental Health, Conversion, and the Law." In *New Religions and Mental Health: Understanding the Issues* (item 1678), pp. ix-lv.

1678. _____, ed. *New Religions and Mental Health: Understanding the Issues.* New York: Edwin Mellen, 1980. 177 pp.

      Contains items 1547, 1606, 1637, 1672, 1676-77.

*   Richardson, James T. "Psychological and Psychiatric Studies of New Religions." Cited above as item 1596.

*   Robbins, Thomas. "Constructing Cultist 'Mind Control.' " Cited above as item 1599.

*   Robbins, Thomas, and Dick Anthony. "Brainwashing and the Persecution of 'Cults.' " Cited above as item 1604.

*   _____. "'Cults,' 'Brainwashing,' and Counter Subversion." Cited above as item 1605.

*   _____. "'Cults' vs. 'Shrinks': Psychiatry and the Control of Religious Movements." Cited above as item 1606.

*   _____. "Deprogramming, Brainwashing and the Medicalization of Deviant Religious Groups." Cited above as item 1607.

*   _____. "The Limits of Coercive Persuasion as an Explanation for Conversion to Authoritarian Sects." Cited above as item 1608.

*   Robbins, Thomas, Dick Anthony, and Jim McCarthy. "Legitimating Repression." Cited above as item 1133.

1679. Schwartz, Lita Linzer, and Florence W. Kaslow. "Religious Cults, the Individual, and the Family." *Journal of Marital and Family Therapy* 5 (1979): 15-26.

1680. Schwartz, Lita Linzer, and Jacqueline L. Zemel. "Religious Cults: Family Concerns and the Law." *Journal of Marital and Family Therapy* 6 (1980): 301-8

1681. Singer, Margaret. "Coming Out of the Cults." *Psychology Today* 12 (January 1979): 72-82.

1682. _____. "Therapy with Ex-Cult Members." *American Association of Private Psychological Hospitals Journal* 9 (Summer 1978): 14-18.

1683. Slade, Margot. "New Religious Groups: Membership and Legal Battles." *Psychology Today* 12 (January 1979): 81.

1684. Solomon, Trudy. "Integrating the Moonie Experience." In *In Gods We Trust: New Patterns of Religious Pluralism in America* (item 1610), pp. 275-94.

1685. _____. "Programming and Deprogramming the Moonies: Brainwashing Revisited." In *The Brainwashing/Deprogramming Controversy: Sociological, Psychological, Legal, and Historical Perspectives* (item 1536), pp. 163-82.

1686. Stewart, Therese. "Unification and the Middle Years." In *Unity in Diversity: Essays in Religion by Members of the Faculty of the Unification Theological Seminary* (item 728), pp. 241-54.

1687. Sunden, H. "Tong-il: Some Observations on a Central Problem in the Psychology of Religion." *Scriptu Instituti Donneriani Aboensis* 7 (1974): 175-88.

1688. Verdier, Paul A. *Brainwashing and the Cults.* North Hollywood, Calif.: Wilshire, 1977. 117 pp.

1689. Wright, Stuart. "Post-Involvement Attitudes of Voluntary Defectors from Controversial New Religious Movements." *Journal for the Scientific Study of Religion* 23 (June 1984): 172-82.

D. LEGAL STUDIES

Controversy over the UC and other new religious movements (NRMs) has spawned a whole series of legal issues ranging from tax exemption and public solicitation privileges to health and child-rearing practices, immigration rights and zoning ordinances. The most important and constitutionally significant of these issues, however, involved efforts of parents and their agents to remove adherents from various groups. In particular, legal scholars have reflected on the legality and constitutionality of extra-legal and state-sanctioned deprogrammings. The UC, because it has been a prime target of deprogrammers and because it sought relief through the courts, has been at the center of this controversy. In general, on the basis of free exercise and civil rights provisions of the United States Constitution, the weight of legal opinion has run against involuntary deprogramming. Proponents of the practice have attempted to override these provisions on the basis of "compelling state interest."

The most forceful proponent of legalized controls over the UC and other NRMs has been Richard Delgado. His basic position, developed in a major article, "Religious Totalism: Gentle and Ungentle Persuasion under the First Amendment" [1697], is based on the distinction between freedom of belief and freedom of action. Freedom of belief, Delgado asserted, is absolute, but freedom of action, in the nature of things, cannot be. Drawing on this belief/action dichotomy, Delgado argued that the state's interest in restricting religious activities derives from individual and social harms presented by religious practices. In the case of the UC and other NRMs, he described those harms as "serious enough to warrant serious judicial concern." At the same time, Delgado acknowledged that the U.S. legal system is reluctant to impose restraints on "self-regarding actions of competent adults." Thus, the crux of his discussion hinged on the question of voluntariness or informed consent which he saw as being undermined in the UC and other groups by coercion, deception and inducement of mental or physical debility. Further, in "drawing the line" between "those techniques of persuasion which are necessarily tolerated by society and those which are so harmful as to be unacceptable," Delgado stated, "There appear to be no insuperable constitutional, moral, or public policy obstacles in the way of state or federal action designed to curb the abuses of religious groups that utilize high-pressure, harmful and deceptive tactics in recruiting and indoctrinating young members" (98). Besides deprogramming (using "carefully defined guidelines"), Delgado proposed other remedies such as self-identification by recruiters, mandatory "cooling-off" periods, public education programs, proselytizing prohibitions and state liscensing as well as tort, civil and criminal actions against groups as necessary.

Legal scholars and others critical of these measures have criticized Delgado's formulation both in its depiction of NRMs and in its theory of religious freedom. Those criticizing Delgado's depiction of NRMs include scholars who have discerned an alternate "fact pattern." These commentators preferred to set the UC and other NRMs within a history of religions perspective and faulted Delgado for relying on adversarial psychiatric testimony, ex-member accounts and journalistic treatments at odds with more reputable scholarship. According to one critic [1690], "the cogency of Delgado's article breaks down once the selective nature of his citations is understood" (79). Further, as the *New York University Law Review* [1707] pointed out, "Despite the public ballyhoo over and concern about brainwashing activities, no court that has conducted an evidentiary hearing has found that any religious organization has subjected its adherents to mind control, coercive persuasion or brainwashing" (1281). Other scholars attacked Delgado's belief/action dichotomy as an outdated interpretation of religious freedom claims. William C. Shepherd, for example, in "The Prosecutor's Reach: Legal Issues Stemming From the New Religious Movements" [1719] and *To Secure the Blessings of Liberty: American Constitutional Law and the New Religious Movements* [1720], noted that by the 1960s the simple belief versus action distinction "could no longer be invoked by itself to solve hard cases of conflict involving genuinely free exercise claims against compelling state interests." Instead, as he pointed out, the courts have institutionalized a complex balancing procedure (the so-called *Sherbert-Yoder* test) consisting of the following five points:

1. Are the religious beliefs in question sincerely held?
2. Are the religious practices under review germane to the religious belief system?
3. Would carrying out the state's wishes constitute a substantial infringement on the religious practice?
4. Is the interest of the state compelling? Does the religious practice perpetuate some grave abuse of a statutory prohibition or obligation?
5. Are there alternative means of regulation by which the state's interest is served but the free exercise of religion is less burdened?

Based, then, on an alternate reading of the "facts" and a balancing formula "designed to accord the free exercise clause substantially greater weight than before," legal scholars have opposed Delgado's remedies, particularly deprogramming.

Extra-legal or "self-help" deprogramming involving abduction, physical restraint and counter-indoctrination proliferated during the seventies for two major reasons. First, parents and deprogrammers usually could rely on tacit, if not open, support from local law enforcement officials. Second, in legal disputes, deprogrammers successfully employed "necessity" defenses--claiming they had violated a law to avoid a greater evil than the law was designed to prevent. However, as necessity defenses traditionally applied only where "forces of nature" compelled action, legal scholars have questioned its extension to cases involving pressure by other individuals [1699, 1704, 1710]. Other scholars noted that deprogrammers face serious risks under current interpretations of U.S. civil rights legislation which has been extended to protect religious as well as racial minorities. See Kimball

[1702] and Shepherd [1720] for discussions of cases won on this basis by UC members.

Legalized or state-sanctioned deprogramming became an option in the mid-seventies due to loopholes in certain state statutes which enabled relatives to gain custody of UC and other NRM adherents through temporary conservatorship orders. Frequently granted in ex-parte hearings, this practice flourished until in *Katz v. Superior Court* [1778] a California appellate court overturned a lower court's ruling that granted temporary conservatorships to parents of five UC members. Based on this decision and subsequent tightening of language in state laws, temporary conservatorships were no longer viable as a deprogramming option by the end of the seventies. The strategy, itself, came under fire from legal scholars on two counts. First, as conservatorship statutes have been designed to protect the property of individuals under a disability, scholars objected to their use in religious deprogrammings as clearly outside the intent of these laws. Second, some scholars opposed the strategy as an unwarranted extension of the "theraputic state." Shepherd [1720], for example, objected to "involuntary civil commitment" as a practice bypassing due process constraints and legal safeguards "even the most hardened criminal may expect as a matter of course" (198).

1690. Anthony, Dick. "The Fact Pattern behind the Deprogramming Controversy: An Analysis and an Alternative." *New York University Review of Law and Social Change* 9 (Fall 1980): 73-89.

1691. Aronin, Douglas. "Cults, Deprogramming and Guardianship: A Model Legislative Proposal." *Columbia Journal of Law and Social Problems* 17 (1982): 163-286.

1692. Ashman, Allan. "Civil Rights ... 'Deprogramming.'" *American Bar Association Journal* 87 (November 1981): 1546.

1693. Babbitt, Ellen M. "Deprogramming of Religious Sect Members: A Private Right of Action under Section 1985 (3)." *Northwestern University Law Review* 74 (April 1979): 229-54.

1694. Brandon, Thomas S., Jr. *New Religions, Conversions and Deprogramming: New Frontiers of Religious Liberty.* Oak Park, Ill.: Center for Law and Religious Freedom, 1982. 60 pp.

* Commission on Law, Social Action, and Urban Affairs [American Jewish Congress]. The Cults and the Law. Cited above as item 1066.

1695. Delgado, Richard. "Cults and Conversion: The Case for Informed Consent." *Georgia Law Review* 16 (1982): 533-74.

* ———. "Limits to Proselytizing." Cited above as item 1179.

1696. ———. "Religious Totalism as Slavery." *New York University Review of Law and Social Change* 9 (1979-80): 51-68.

1697. ———. "Religious Totalism: Gentle and Ungentle Persuasion under the First Amendment." *Southern California Law Review* 51 (November 1977): 1-98.

* Eidsmoe, John. "The Christian and the Cults." Cited above as item 809.

1698. Fox, Martin. "Cults & the First Amendment: Constitutional Concerns against Block Efforts to Let Courts Appoint Conservators for Youth." *New York Law Journal* 184 (October 14, 1980): 1.

* Gillis, John W. "Rev. Sun Myung Moon: 'Heavenly Deception.' " Cited above as item 1204.

1699. Greene, Robert H. "People v. Religious Cults: Legal Guidelines for Criminal Activities, Tort Liability, and Parental Remedies." *Suffolk University Law Review* 11 (Spring 1977): 1025-56.

1700. Herbert, Carol S. "Constitutional Law-State Regulation of Public Solicitation for Religious Purposes." *Wake Forest Law Review* 16 (December 1980): 996-1030.

1701. Judah, J. Stillson. "New Religions and Religious Liberty." In *Understanding the New Religions* (item 1590), pp. 201-8.

1702. Kimball, Matthew L. "Protection of Religious Groups under 42 U.S.C. 1985 (c) (Fourth Circuit Court) (case note) Ward v. Conner 657 F.2d 45 (4th Cir. 1981)." *Washington and Lee Review* 39 (Spring 1982): 555-66.

1703. Lavine, Doug. "Cults and Deprogramming: The Legal Dilemmas." *Church & State* 32 (January 1979): 23-25.

1704. Lemoult, John. "Deprogramming Members of Religious Sects." *Fordham Law Review* 46 (March 1978): 599-640.

* Lifton, Robert J. "Cult Processes, Religious Totalism, and Civil Liberties." Cited above as item 1671.

1705. Moore, Joey Peter. "Piercing the Religious Veil of the So-called Cults." *Pepperdine Law Review* 7 (Spring 1980): 655-710.

1706. Murry, Leslye M. "Parent-child." *Journal of Family Law* 19 (August 1981): 778-82.

1707. Note. "Conservatorships and Religious Cults: Divining a Theory of Free Exercise." *New York University Law Review* 53 (December 1978): 1247-89.

1708. Notes. "Cults, Deprogrammers, and the Necessity Defense." *Michigan Law Review* 80 (December 1981): 271-311.

1709. "On the Civil Liberties of Sect Members (Parts 1 and 2)." In *Science, Sin, and Sponsorship: The Politics of Reverend Moon and the Unification Church* (item 1567), pp. 192-207.

1710. Pierson, Kit. "Cults, Deprogrammers, and the Necessity Defense." *Michigan Law Review* 80 (December 1981): 271-311.

*   Richardson, Herbert. "Mental Health, Conversion, and the Law." Cited above as item 1677.

*   Robbins, Thomas. "Government Regulatory Powers and Church Autonomy: Deviant Groups as Test Cases." Cited above as item 1600.

1711. _____. "New Religious Movements, Brainwashing, and Deprogramming--The View from the Law Journals: A Review Essay and Survey." *Religious Studies Review* 11 (October 1985): 361-70.

*   _____. "New Religious Movements on the Frontier of Church and State." Cited above as item 1601.

1712. _____. "Religious Movements, the State, and the Law: Reconceptualizing 'The Cult Problem.' " *New York University Review of Law and Social Change* 9 (Fall 1980): 33-49.

*   Robbins, Thomas, William C. Shepherd, and James McBride. *Cults, Culture and the Law.* Cited above as item 1612.

1713. Rosenzweig, Charles. "High Demand Sects: Disclosure Legislation and the Free Exercise Clause." *New England Law Review* 15 (1979): 128-59.

1714. Rudin, Marcia. "The Cult Phenomenon: Fad or Fact?" New York University Review of Law and Social Change 9 (1979-1980): 17-32.

*   Schwartz, Lita Linzer, and Jacqueline L. Zemel. "Religious Cults: Family Concerns and the Law." Cited above as item 1680.

1715. Sciarrino, Alfred J. "United States v. Sun Myung Moon: Precedent for Tax Fraud Prosecution of Local Pastors?" *Southern Illinois University Law Journal* 2 (1984): 237-81.

1716. Shapiro, Robert N. "'Mind Control' or Intensity of Faith: The Constitutional Protection of Religious Beliefs." *Harvard Civil Rights-Civil Liberties Law Review* 13 (1978): 751-97.

1717. _____. "Of Robots, Persons, and the Protection of Religious Beliefs." *Southern California Law Review* 56 (September 1983): 1277-1318.

1718. Shepherd, William C. "Constitutional Law and Marginal Religions." In *The Brainwashing/ Deprogramming Controversy: Sociological, Psychological, Legal and Historical Perspectives* (item 1536), pp. 258-66.

1719. _____. "The Prosecutor's Reach: Legal Issues Stemming from the New Religious Movements." *Journal of the American Academy of Religion* 50 (June 1982): 187-214.

1720. _____. *To Secure the Blessings of Liberty: American Constitutional Law and the New Religious Movements.* New York and Chico, Calif.: Crossroads and Scholars Press, 1985. 155 pp.

1721. Siegel, Terri I. "Deprogramming Religious Cultists." *Loyola University Law Review* 11 (September 1978): 807-28.

*   Slade, Margot. "New Religious Groups: Membership and Legal Battles." Cited above as item 1683.

1722. Spendlove, Greta. "Legal Issues in the Use of Guardianship Procedures to Remove Members of Cults." *Arizona Law Review* 18 (1976): 1095-1139.

*   "Sun Myung Moon and the Law." Cited above as item 1368.

E. DISSERTATIONS, THESES

In addition to published scholarly treatments, there have been a number of dissertations and master theses written on the Church. These are important for at least two reasons. Some have been published in revised form or cited in academic literature. Others too restricted in scope for a wider readership are, nonetheless, useful for specialists on the UC. Doctoral dissertations, primarily analytical in orientation, recaptitulate emphases of particular disciplines, especially in the fields of sociology and psychology. M.A. theses are descriptive and frequently cross-disciplinary, examining the Church from several different perspectives.

As stated, dissertations on the UC, most of which have been written from the perspective of sociology or psychology, recapitulate emphases of these disciplines. This is particularly the case for dissertations which have been published in abridged or revised form such as James H. Grace's "Sexuality and Marriage in the Unification Movement" [1725] and John Lofland's "The World-Savers: A Field Study of Cult Processes" [1730]. Other dissertations by Dean [1724], Kilbourne [1727], Skonovd [1735], Solomon [1736] and Wright [1737] contain empirical data and findings utilized by these authors in published articles. For comparative analyses, examining the UC in relation to *est*, contemporary evangelism and Jewish orthodoxy, see Miller [1732], O'Byrne [1733] and Selengut [1734]. Although not a dissertation, David Taylor's "The Social Organization of Recruitment in the Unification Church" [1745] has been cited as an authoritative account of UC recruitment practices in Northern California during the mid-seventies. D. Minn. dissertations differ from the above-listed treatments in that they reflect confessional orientations. Examples are Randall Bayles Bosch's "A Local Church's Study of Its Relationship to the Seminary of the Unification Church" [1723] and Sang Koo Kim's "A Critical Study of the Reverend Sun Myung Moon's Movement" [1728].

Rather than filtering analyses of the UC through the lenses of particular disciplines, M.A. theses tend to be cross-disciplinary, examining the Church from a variety of perspectives. Examples are Young Choon Chang's "The Tongil Kyo: A New Cult in Korea" [1740], Michael L. Mickler's "A History of the Unification Church in the Bay Area: 1960-74" [1742], Carl Rapkins' note on "Contemporary Religious Intensity" [1743], and Mark Savad's "Study of a Modern Religious Movement: The Unification Church" [1744]. See also David Carlson [1739] for a commentary on the "Pledge Service," a worship tradition observed by the UC.

Dissertations

1723. Bosch, Randall Bayles. "A Local Church's Study of Its Relationship to the Seminary of the Unification Church." D.Minn. diss., Princeton Theological Seminary, 1980.

1724. Dean, Roger Allan. "Moonies: A Psychological Analysis of the Unification Church." Ph.D. diss., The University of Michigan, 1981. 248 pp.

1725. Grace, James H. "Sexuality and Marriage in the Unification Movement." Ph.D. diss., Temple University, 1982. 341 pp.

1726. Harrigan, John Edward. "Becoming a Moonie: An Interview Study of Religious Conversion." Ed.D. diss., University of Maine, 1980. 160 pp.

1727. Kilbourne, Brock K. "An Activist Conception of Conversion and Attribution." Ph.D. diss., University of Nevada, Reno, 1983.

1728. Kim, Sang Soo. "A Critical Study of the Rev. Sun Myung Moon's Movement." D.Minn. diss., San Francisco Theological Seminary, 1981.

1729. King, Karen Mae. "The Rhetoric of the New Religious Cults: A Fantasy Theme Analysis of the Rhetoric of the Unification Church." Ph.D. diss., The University of Iowa, 1980. 249 pp.

1730. Lofland, John. "The World-Savers: A Field Study of Cult Processes." Ph.D. diss., The University of California at Berkeley, 1964. 588 pp.

1731. Lukas, Brian N. "Identity Status, Parent-Adolescent Relationships, and Participation in Marginal Religious Groups." Ph.D. diss., The California School of Professional Psychology, 1982. 199 pp.

1732. Miller, Edward V.B. "Authoritarianism: The American Cults and Their Intellectual Antecedents." Ph.D. diss., University of Hawaii, 1981.

1733. O'Byrne, William L. "A Comparative Study of the Hermeneutics of Sun Myung Moon and Contemporary Evangelism as Represented by James Oliver Boswell, Jr." Ph.D. diss., New York University, 1978. 302 pp.

1734. Selengut, Charles. "The Unification Church and Jewish Orthodoxy in America: A Sociological Study of Belief, Lifestyle and Reality-Maintenance in the Cognitive Minority Communities." Ph.D. diss., Drew University, 1983. 251 pp.

1735. Skonovd, Norman. "Apostasy: The Process of Defection from Religious Totalism." Ph.D. diss., The University of California at Davis, 1981. 201 pp.

1736. Solomon, Trudy. "Deprogramming: Nemesis or Necessity?" Ph.D. diss., The University of California at Berkeley, 1978. 79 pp.

1737. Wright, Stuart. "A Sociological Study of Defection from Controversial New Religious Movements." Ph.D. diss., The University of Connecticut, 1983.

1738. Zerin, Margory Fischer. "The Pied Piper Phenomenon: Family Systems and Vulnerability to Cults." Ph.D. diss., The Fielding Institute, Santa Barbara, Calif., 1982.

Master Theses

1739. Carlson, David A. "A Commentary on the Pledge Service Focusing on the Children's Pledge: One Tradition Observed by the Unification Church Movement." Master's thesis, Pacific School of Religion, 1981. 131 pp.

1740. Chang, Young Choon. "The Tongil Kyo, A New Cult in Korea." Master's thesis, Central Baptist Seminary, 1970. 181 pp.

1741. Eden, Eve. "The Unification Church: A Study of Structure and Conversion." Master's thesis, University of Michigan, 1979.

1742. Mickler, Michael L. "A History of the Unification Church in the Bay Area: 1960-74." Master's thesis, Graduate Theological Union, 1980. 286 pp.

1743. Rapkins, Carl. "Contemporary Religious Intensity: Deprivation, Felt Perceptions of the Sacred and Conversion in the pre-1972 Unification Church." Appendix in "Religious Intensity: A Study of Conversion and Deviance in Pascal and Tolstoy." Master's thesis, San Francisco Theological Seminary, 1978.

1744. Savad, Mark Harry. "Study of a Modern Religious Movement: The Unification Church." Master's thesis, Georgetown University, 1976. 164 pp.

1745. Taylor, David. "The Social Organization of Recruitment in the Unification Church." Master's thesis, University of Montana, 1978. 162 pp.

VI.

GOVERNMENT DOCUMENTS

A. LEGAL RECORDS

The UC has been embroiled in near constant litigation since 1975. Though costly and time-consuming, several decisions, won on appeal, have gained the Church gradual recognition as a *bona fide* religion with tax exemption privileges, public solicitation rights and access to missionary visas. In addition, the UC has been able to extend constitutional protections to its members, successfully press for action against deprogrammers and combat inappropriately applied conservatorship statutes. To a certain degree, these organizational gains have been overshadowed by Rev. Moon's conviction on tax evasion charges in 1982. Nonetheless, it is important to examine that case in light of unambiguous court affirmations of the UC's legal and religious status.

United States v. Sun Myung Moon [1800] involved 1.7 million dollars deposited in two accounts with Chase Manhattan Bank between 1973-76 and fifty-thousand dollars worth of stock held in a UC-related import firm. Although Rev. Moon's personal tax liability (using government figures) amounted to only $7,300 plus interest, prosecutors sucessfully pressed criminal conspiracy charges based on back-dated documents submitted by the Church to account for those funds. Defense lawyers contended that Rev. Moon held these assets benefically as a trustee for the Church and had no tax liability. They further cited selective prosecution, refusal of Rev. Moon's request for a bench trial and improper jury instruction as sufficient cause to overturn the decision. Despite broad support from the American religious community [1790], these objections were denied on appeal.

As stated, it is important to view Reverend Moon's 1982 case in the context of other court rulings. For example, in that same year, rights of the UC and its members were upheld by federal and state courts in six separate decisions. In *Ward v. Conner* [1802], the U.S. Supreme Court upheld on appeal a lower court decision allowing a Church member to bring suit against deprogrammers, arguing that UC adherents are entitled to the same civil rights protection which the law grants to racial minorities. In *Larson v. Valente* [1779], the U.S. Supreme Court struck down a Minnesota law which discriminated against UC solicitation practices while not affecting established denominations. Similarly, by unanimously overturning lower court decisions which had refused to recognize the UC's religious purposes, the New York Court of Appeals in *HSA-UWC v. Tax Commission of New York City* [1772] held as a matter of law that the UC was a *bona fide* religion. In *In Re:*

HSA-UWC, Reverend Sun Myung Moon and Anthony Colombrito [1776] and *Eden v. Reverend Sun Myung Moon, HSA-UWC et al.* [1756], the UC won rulings against subpoenaed testimony on religious beliefs and against a damage suit brought by a former member on the grounds of alleged "mind control." Finally, after several years of struggle, *Unification Church, Nikkuni, et al v. INS* [1799] recognized the right of foreign members of the UC to enter the country as missionaries on the same basis as members of other churches. Reference earlier was made to *Katz v. Superior Court* [1778] which, in effect, outlawed conservatorship proceedings as a method for extricating adherents from the UC and other groups.

1746. *Alexander v. Unification Church of America,* 634 F.2d 673 (2d Cir. 1980).

1747. *Aman v. Handler,* 653 F.2d 41 (1st Cir. 1981).

1748. *Augenti v. Cappellini,* 84 F.R.D. 73 (M.D. Pa. 1979).

1749. *Baer v. Baer,* 450 F. Supp. 481 (N.D. Cal. 1978).

1750. *Cherris v. Amundson,* 460 F. Supp 326 (E.D. La. 1978).

1751. *Chestnut v. St. Louis County,* 656 F.2d 343 (8th Cir. 1981), *aff'g in part and rev'g in part* 495 F. Supp. 120 (E.D. Mo. 1980).

1752. *Colombrito v. Kelly,* 764 F.2d 122 (2d. Cir. 1985).

1753. *Conlon v. City of North Kansas City,* 530 F. Supp. 985 (W.D. Mo. 1981).

1754. *Cooper v. Molko,* 512 F. Supp. 563 (N.D. Cal. 1981).

1755. *Dixon v. Mack,* 507 F. Supp. 345 (S.D.N.Y. 1980).

1756. *Eden v. Reverend Sun Myung Moon, HSA-UWC et al,* Michigan, Wayne County Circuit Court, No. 77-736-880 NO, Dec. 3, 1982.

1757. *Erskine v. West Palm Beach,* 473 F. Supp. 48 (S.D. Fla. 1979).

1758. *Evans v. Fullard,* 444 F. Supp. 1334 (E.D. Tenn. 1978).

1759. *Greene v. Sinclair,* 491 F. Supp. 19 (W.D. Mich 1980).

1760. *Hall v. McNamara,* 456 F. Supp. 245 (N.D. Cal. 1978).

1761. *Harnett v. Schmidt,* 501 F. Supp. 1024 (N.D. Ill. 1980).

1762. *Hayashi v. INS,* U.S. District Court (C.D. Cal.) No CV 83-0299-WJR (G) Sept. 28, 1984.

1763. *Heritage Village Church and Missionary Fellowship v. State of North Carolina,* 299 N.C. 399, 263 S.E. 2d 726 (1980), *aff'g* 40 N.C. App. 429, 253 S.E.2d 473 (1979).

1764. *HSA-UWC v. Alley,* 460 F. Supp. 346 (N.D. Tex. 1978), *vac'd mem.,* 604 F.2d 669 (5th Cir. 1979).

1765. *HSA-UWC v. CIA,* 636 F.2d 838 (D.C. Cir. 1980), *vac'd as moot,* 50 U.S.L.W. 3715 (U.S. March 9, 1982) (No 81-1098).

1766. *HSA-UWC v. Caughley,* 455 F. Supp. 1154 (M.D. Pa. 1978).

1767. *HSA-UWC v. Harper & Row, Publishers,* 101 Misc. 2d 30, 420 N.Y.S.2d. 56 (Sup. Ct. 1979).

1768. *HSA-UWC v. Hodge,* 582 F. Supp. 592 (N.D. Tex. 1984).

1769. *HSA-UWC v. Michigan Department of Treasury,* 131 Mich App 743 (1984).

1770. *HSA-UWC v. Peterson,* 489 F. Supp. 428 (N.D. Ill. 1979).

1771. *HSA-UWC v. Sequoia Elseveier Publishing Co.,* 4 Media L. Rep. 1744 (Sup. Ct. 1978), *adhered to on motion for reargument,* 4 Media L.Rep.2311 (Sup. Ct. 1979).

1772. *HSA-UWC v. Tax Commission of New York City,* 59 N.Y.2d 512, 435 N.E.2d 662, 450 N.Y.S.2d 292 (1982), rev'g 81 A.D.2d 64, 438 N.Y.S. 2d 521 (1981), *prior opinion remaining for plenary hearing,* 62 A.D.2d. 188, 404 N.Y.S.2d 93, *leave to appeal denied,* 45 N.Y.2d 706, N.E.2d, 408 N.Y.S.2d 1025 (1978).

1773. *HSA-UWC v. Town of New Castle,* 480 F. Supp. 1212 (S.D.N.Y. 1979).

1774. *HSA-UWC v. United States Department of State,* 525 F. Supp. 1022 (S.D.N.Y. 1981).

1775. In *Re Helander v. Patrick,* Superior Court, Fairfield County (Conn.) No. 195062, Sept. 8, 1976.

1776. In *Re HSA-UWC, Reverend Sun Myung Moon and Anthony Colombrito,* United States Court of Appeals for the Second Circuit, Docket No. 82-3035, M16 28, 1982.

1777. *International Oceanic Enterprises v. Menton,* 614 F.2d 502 (5th Cir. 1980).

1778. *Katz v. Superior Court* (people). 73 Cal. App. 3d 952, 141 Cal. Rptr. 234 (1977).

1779. *Larson v. Valente,* 102 S. Ct. 1673 (1982), *aff'g* 637 F.2d 562 (8th Cir. 1981).

1780. *Levers v. City of Tullahoma,* 446 F. Supp. 884 (E.D. Tenn. 1978).

1781. *Lewis v. Holy Spirit Association for the Unification of World Christianity,* 589 F. Supp. 10 (D. Mass. 1983).

1782. *Love v. Mayor, City of Cheyenne,* 620 F.2d 235 (10th Cir. 1980); id., 448 F. Supp. 128 (D. Wyo. 1978).

1783. *McMurdie v. Doutt,* 468 F. Supp. 766 (N.D. Ohio 1979).

1784. *New Education Development Systems, Inc. v. Boitano,* 573 F. Supp. 594 (N.D. Cal. 1983).

1785. *New York ex rel Larson v. HSA-UWC,* 464 F. Supp. 196 (S.D.N.Y. 1979).

1786. *Pearson v. U.S. Postal Service,* U.S. District Court, (C.D. Cal.) No. CV 82-6510-ER (BX) Oct. 24, 1983.

1787. *Poe v. City of Humble,* 554 F. Supp. 233 (S.D. Tex. 1983).

1788. *People v. Wood,* 93n Misc. 2d 726, 402 N.Y.S.2d 726 (Justice Ct. 1978).

1789. *Rankin v. Howard ,* 633 F.2d 844 (9th Cir. 1980), *rev'g in part* 457 F. Supp. 70 (D. Ariz. 1978), *cert. denied sub nom. Zeller v. Rankin,* 101 S. Ct 2020 (1981); id., 527 F. Supp. 976 (D. Ariz. 1981).

1790. Richardson, Herbert, ed. *Constitutional Issues in the Case of Rev. Moon: Amicus Briefs Submitted to the United States Supreme Court.* New York: Edwin Mellen, 1984. 699 pp.

1791. *Risedorf v. Commanding Officer,* 508 F. Supp. 145 (E.D. Pa. 1981).

1792. *Schuppin v. Unification Church,* 435 F. Supp. 603 (D. Vt. 1977).

1793. *Smith v. City of Manchester,* 460 F. Supp. 30 (E.D. Tenn. 1978).

1794. *Swearson v. Meyers,* 455 F. Supp. 88 (D. Kan. 1978).

1795. *Stlte v. Metropolitan Government,* 493 F. Supp. 313 (M.D. Tenn. 1980).

1796. *Troyer v. Town of Babylon,* 483 F. Supp. 1135 (E.D.N.Y.), *aff'd mem. sub nom. Troyer v. Town of Southampton,* 628 F.2d 1346 (2d Cir.), *aff'd mem.,* 449 U.S. 988, 101 S. ct. 522 (1980).

1797. *Turner v. Unification Church,* 602 F.2d 458 (1st Cir. 1979), *aff'g per curiam* 473 F. Supp. 367 (D.R.I. 1978).

1798. *Unification Church v. Attorney General of the United States,* 581 F.2d 870 (D.C. Cir.), *Cert. denied sub nom. Unification Church v. Bell,* 439 U.S. 828, 99 S. Ct. 102 (1978).

1799. *Unification Church, Nikkuni, et al v. INS,* 547 F. Supp. 623 (D.D.C. 1982).

1800. *United States v. Sun Myung Moon,* 93 F.R.D. 558 (S.D.N.Y. 1982); id., 532 F. Supp 1360 (S.D.N.Y. 1982).

1801. *Walker v. Wegner,* 624 F.2d 60 (8th Cir. 1980), *aff'g* 477 F. Supp. 648 (D.S.D. 1979), *attorney's fees awarded,* 535 F. Supp. 415 (D.S.D. 1982).

1802. *Ward v. Connor,* 657 F.2d 45 (4th Cir. 1981), *Rev'g in part* 495 F. Supp. 434 (E.D.Va. 1980), *cert. denied sub nom. Mandelkorn v. Ward,* 102 S. Ct. 1253 (1983).

1803. *Weiss v. Patrick,* 453 F. Supp. 717 (D.R.I.), *aff'd mem.,* 588 F.2d 818 (1st Cir. 1978), *cert. denied,* 442 U.S. 929, 99 S. Ct. 2858 (1979).

1804. *Weissman v. City of Alamogordo,* 472 F. Supp. 425 (D.N.M. 1979).

1805. *Westfall v. Board of Commissioners,* 477 F. Supp. 862 (N.D. Ga. 179).

B. HEARINGS, LEGISLATION, REPORTS

Unlike legal rulings which, on the whole, have vindicated UC claims, legislative hearings, proposed legislation and investigative reports have linked the Church to alleged abuses in the areas of recruitment, fundraising, child care and political lobbying. These hearings, proposed laws and reports, however, have been non-substantive. That is, they have led neither to actual laws nor to further investigations. In this respect, legislative hearings and investigative reports shed no more light on the UC *per se* than on the social milieu within which it operated. This is true even of the U.S government's *Investigation of Korean-American Relations* [1825] which, while more thorough its treatment of the UC, nonetheless reflected an effort to protect government interests during the so-called "Koreagate" scandal of 1976-78.

The most important legislative hearings related to the UC were two *ad hoc* meetings convened by Senator Robert Dole (R-Kansas) in 1976 and 1979; five days of testimony heard by the Vermont Senate Committee for the Investigation of Alleged Deceptive, Fraudulent and Criminal Practices of Various Organizations in the State in 1976; and a legislative inquiry conducted by the New York State Assembly Committee on Child Care in 1979 [1807, 1826, 1819]. None of these hearings led to subsequent legislation. They did, however, highlight significant levels of strain between the UC and major sectors of the American public. Robert Dole's initial hearing, for example, was said to have been prompted by a petition signed by 14,000 Kansas residents. His second hearing and that of the New York Assembly Child Care Committee resulted from pressures to link the UC and other groups to the People's Temple. During the late seventies and early eighties, several states proposed legislation designed to hinder UC recruitment and to facilitate removal of members by guardianship statutes. Only one such law passed--in New York, and this legislation was vetoed by then Governor Hugh Carey [1806].

More substantive than any of the above-listed hearings or legislation was the United States House of Representatives Subcommittee on International Organizations' *Investigation of Korean-American Relations* [1825]. Funded, in part, to uncover details of alleged Korean influence-buying during the early seventies, the committee took pains to investigate and highlight possible connections between UC officials and "Koreagate." Though concluding that "the Moon organization was not an agent of influence for the ROK government so much as it was a volatile factor in Korean-American relations," the committee, chaired by Donald M. Fraser (D-Minnesota), alleged systematic UC improprieties and recommended "combining investigative activities related to the Moon Organization into an interagency task force" (389-390). This recommendation, however, was not acted upon. See *Our Response* [492] for the UC reaction.

1806. Carey, Hugh. "Return (Disapproval) Assembly Bill #11122-A, An Act to Amend the Mental Hygiene Law in Relation to Temporary Conservator." Albany, N.Y.: 1980. 8 pp.

1807. CEFM (National *Ad Hoc* Committee Engaged in Freeing Minds). *A Special Report. The Unification Church: Its Activities and Practices.* 2 vols. [transcript of informal hearings]. Arlington, Tx.: National Ad Hoc Committee, 1976. 121 pp.

1808. Connecticut, State of. "An Act Concerning Conservatorship (Temporary Guardians)." (Substitute Senate Bill 1429 File #649, Committee on Judiciary.) Hartford, Conn.: General Assembly, 1981. 6 pp.

1809. _____. "An Act Concerning Establishment of a Commission to Investigate Activities in Connecticut of the Rev. Sun Myung Moon and the Unification Church of America." (Proposed Bill No. 7337, Referred to the Committee on General Law.) Hartford, Conn.: Connecticut General Assembly, 1980. 1 p.

1810. Hill, Daniel G. *Study of Mind Development Groups, Sects and Cults in Ontario: A Report to the Ontario Government.* Toronto, Canada: Office of the Special Advisor, 1980. 773 pp.

1811. Illinois, State of. *Transcript of Hearings to Consider Cult Activities in the State of Illinois.* Conducted by State Representative Betty Hoxsey. Springfield, Ill.: Illinois House of Representatives, 1979. 135 pp.

1812. Lee, Jai Hyon. "The Activities of the Korean Central Intelligence Agency in the United States." In *Science, Sin, and Sponsorship: The Politics of Reverend Moon and the Unification Church* (item 1567), pp. 120-47. Reprinted from testimony before the Subcommittee on International Organizations of the Committee on International Relations, the United States House of Representatives, September, 1976.

1813. Maryland, State of. *A House Joint Resolution Concerning Cults in Maryland.* (House Joint Resolution No. 67) Annapolis, Md.: House, 1981. 2 pp.

1814. Massachusetts, State of. *Transcript of Commonwealth of Massachusetts Public Hearing.* Reprint. Lexington, Mass.: American Family Foundation, 1979. 83 pp.

1815. Minnesota, State of. "A Bill for an Act Relating to Civil Actions; Authorizing Converts to Organizations Promising Religious of Philosophical Self-Fulfillment to Maintain Actions for Damages: Authorizing Family Members of Converts to Organizations Promising Religious or Philosophical Self-fulfillment to Maintain

216

Actions for Damages, Proposing New Law Coded as Minnesota Statutes, Chapter 608. St. Paul, Minn.: Legislature of the State of Minnesota, 1981. 2 pp.

1816. _____. "Charitable Funds--Regulation of Solicitation." (Section 209-50, Subdivision 10 of Minnesota Statues 1976. Amendment of Chapter 601 [H.F. No. 1248]) St Paul, Minn.: 70 Minnesota Legislature, 1978. 12 pp.

1817. New York, State of. "An Act to Amend the Mental Hygiene Law, in Relation to the Appointment of Temporary Guardians." (Article 80) Albany, N.Y.: New York State Assembly, 1981. 13 pp.

1818. _____. "An Act to Amend the Mental Hygiene Law, in Relation to Temporary Conservator." (Proposed Article #11122-A.) Albany, N.Y.: New York State Assembly, 1980. 4 pp.

1819. _____. *Transcript of Public Hearing on Treatment of Children by Cults.* Albany, N.Y.: The State Assembly of New York, 1979. Reprinted by the American Family Foundation, Lexington, Mass., 1979. 678 pp.

1820. _____. *Recommendation of the New York State Regents' Committee to Review Application of Unification Theological Seminary for State Charter.* Albany, N.Y.: New York State Board of Regents, 1978. 6 pp.

1821. _____. "Promoting a Pseudo-Religious Cult." (Proposed Bill AB 9566-A, Section 240.46.) Albany, N.Y.: New York State Assembly, 1977. 1 p.

1822. Pennsylvania, State of. "Creating a Temporary Study Commission to Study Groups Which Seek to Unduly Exert Control over Children and Youth." (House Bill No. 406.) Harrisburg, Pa.: General Assembly of Pennsylvania, 1981. 4 pp.

1823. Texas, State of. *Senate Resolution No. 485.* Austin, Tx.: Senate Committee on State Affairs, 1979. 2 pp.

1824. _____. *House Resolution No. 35.* Austin, Tx.: House of Representatives' Committee on Criminal Jurisprudence, 1977. 3 pp.

1825. United States Government. *Investigation of Korean-American Relations.* Report of the Subcommittee on International Organizations of the Committee on International Relations, United States House of Representatives. Washington, D.C.: U.S. Government Printing Office, 1978.

1826. Vermont, State of. *Report of the Senate Committee for the Investigation of Alleged Deceptive, Fraudulent and Criminal Practices of Various Organizations in the State.* Montpelier, Vt.: Vermont Senate, 1977.

Author Index